More praise for
TOP SECRETS: Screenw

"An excellent source of insider insights and know-how, this volume will interest movie fanatics and screenwriter wannabes." —**ALA Booklist**

"I do not believe that I have seen such a unique and illuminating combination of screenwriters' work and thoughts in one book. Rather than a technical lecture, 'for writers only', I found **TOP SECRETS: Screenwriting** informative (perhaps necessary!) for anyone in or out of this business who is interested in really seeing where movies come from. I think that it deepened my appreciation of the craft of the screenwriter. I intend to apply what I have learned both behind my desk and at the movies!" —**Rick Nicita, Creative Artists Agency**

"A much-needed, much appreciated glimpse of 'the process'. **TOP SECRETS: Screenwriting** provides that unique oppportunity to climb into the creative mind and observe screenwriting from the inside out. Recommended!"
—**Paula DiSante, Story Analyst**

"**TOP SECRETS: Screenwriting** is an invaluable addition to the literature of screenwriting, full of insights and good advice for anyone interested in making movies. Highly recommended." —**Paul Lucey, USC School of Cinema/Television** and author of *Story Sense: A Guide To Writing Film and Television.*

"I highly recommend this book to anyone who has an ambition to write professionally for motion pictures. By reading excerpts of scripts by masters of the genre, as well as seeing the writers' own commentaries of their work, the aspiring screenwriter will gain an invaluable understanding and insight into the craft of screenwriting." —**Lee Dinstman, Vice President, Agency for the Performing Arts, Inc.**

About The Authors

Jurgen Wolff writes for television, films and the stage. His television credits include *Benson, Family Ties, The Ted Knight Show* and *Gloria*. He is currently writing a pilot for Anglia Television Films in London. His play, *Living Skills*, has been produced in London and New York. He has been commissioned to write a total of six television films, for all three U.S. networks. He is currently doing a rewrite of a feature for Universal Studios and has served as script doctor on several major film projects. He has also taught screenwriting at the University of Southern California and in private workshops around the world. He is the author of *Successful Sitcom Writing* [St. Martins Press] and co-author of *Successful Scriptwriting* [Writers Digest Press].

Kerry Cox has written over two dozen television scripts for The Disney Channel, Aaron Spelling Productions and others. He is co-author of *Successful Scriptwriting* [Writers Digest Press] and editor publisher of the *Hollywood Scriptwriter*, and international newsletter for screenwriters. He currently writes a weekly newspaper column, and is one of the premiere writers in the Southern California corporate/industrial and infomercial market.

Top Secrets:
SCREENWRITING

by
Jurgen Wolff
and
Kerry Cox

LONE EAGLE PUBLISHING CO
LOS ANGELES, CALIFORNIA

LONE EAGLE PUBLISHING COMPANY
2337 Roscomare Road, Suite Nine
Los Angeles, CA 90077-1851
310/471-8066 • FAX 310/471-4969

Printed in the United States of America

Cover design by Heidi Frieder

Library of Congress Cataloging in Publication Data
Top Secrets: Screenwriting / [compiled] by Jurgen Wolff and Kerry Cox.
    p.   cm.
ISBN 0-943728-50-9
1. Motion picture authorship. 2. Screenwriters—interviews.
        I. Wolff, Jurgen, 1956-   II. Cox, Kerry, 1956-
PN1996.T64   1993
808.2'3—dc20   92-41130
                                                    CIP

942407

TABLE OF CONTENTS

To my mother, and the memory of my father.

—J.W.

To Mackenzie, who missed out on the last one.

—K.C.

ACKNOWLEDGMENTS

WE WOULD LIKE TO ACKNOWLEDGE the following writers for their contributions to this book. Without their fine work, these TOP SECRETS would never have been revealed.

Jack Schaberg, for the Jim Cash interview; A.B. Cooper, for the William Kelley interview; and Chuck Scott, for the Nicholas Kazan interview.

For the research, and the hours spent in front of one screen or another, thanks to Scott Newton, Mark Tondow and David Howard.

Jurgen Wolff and Kerry Cox

INTRODUCTION

IN THE LAST FEW YEARS the amazing increase in the prices paid for original screenplays has been matched only by the amazing increase in the number of books on screenwriting. More and more authors, some of whom have never sold a script, are offering to tell you exactly how it's done.

In compiling this book, our theory was that if you really want to know how something is done, you should ask a person who's done it.

The writers interviewed in this book have not only done it, they've done it extraordinarily well. They are the people responsible for the scripts of the films that have entertained America and the rest of the world in the last decade. Their films have triumphed both in the review columns and at the box office. These are the people who wrote, among others, GHOST, DEAD POETS SOCIETY, TOP GUN, AIRPLANE!, 48 HOURS, WITNESS, and DANCES WITH WOLVES.

These screenwriters have been extremely generous with their knowledge. They discuss their techniques of characterization, plotting and dialogue construction. However, craft alone does not make a script great. Therefore, we also asked these writers what ignites their passion for writing, what drives them to tell their stories. We believe you will learn as much by looking

In order to make the interviews more helpful, we preface each one with a brief essay that discusses the writer's background, the way the selected film was received at the time it was released, and the place that the film has earned in modern film history.

When master screenwriter William Goldman was asked what are the three most important aspects of screenplay writing, he said, "Structure, structure, structure." Most screenwriters agree. Therefore, we also provide you with a three-act breakdown of each featured film. You'll see, scene by scene, how the characters develop, how the conflict builds, and how all the story strands are brought together and resolved at the end.

Finally, we asked each writer to choose one or two scenes from his or her film. We have reproduced those key scenes here; some are long, some quite short. It's our goal here to find out what goes into the *writing*; after the script is finished, the writer rarely has much to say about the finished film. By the way, all the films we've selected are available on videotape. It's interesting and educational to compare the writer's draft of these scenes to the corresponding scenes in the finished films.

When you have read all the interviews, observed the structure of all the films, and read the sample scenes, you'll see what elements the most successful films have in common. Ideally, you'll be able to see how to apply these insights to your own work.

In the old studio days, new writers were teamed with the award-winning old hands — in effect, it was an apprenticeship system. It left a lot to be desired in terms of working conditions and payment, but it was a wonderful way for novices to learn on the job. That system is no more, but we feel this book offers the next best thing — a chance to study with the experts, to learn their "Top Secrets" — and then to apply their wisdom to the exciting and wonderful stories you wish to tell.

Top Secrets:
MICHAEL BLAKE

Michael Blake

DANCES WITH WOLVES

A THREE-HOUR LONG WESTERN? In which the Native Americans speak their own language and we have to read subtitles for almost a third of the movie? At the beginning of the 90s, by which time the Western had been declared dead for twenty or thirty years? You've got to be kidding.

The author of DANCES WITH WOLVES heard that reaction more than once. Fortunately, he refused to take "No" for an answer.

Some of the publicity surrounding the author of the film that defied all these conventions, Michael Blake, hailed him as an overnight success—"Yesterday he was working in a Chinese restaurant, now he's collecting awards." True, but there's nothing overnight about it. His journey was one of single-minded perseverance and dedication, of a discipline and dedication strong enough to keep him writing after his friends and family, and even he had begun to doubt that success would ever become a reality.

Small wonder that Blake and those around him had doubts: five years before he was sitting in a prime seat at the Academy Award presentations he was living in his car and crashing on friends' floors for the night while working on his novel. It took nine months. As a form, the Western novel was considered almost as dead as the Western film, except for those geared to the shoot-em-up, "There's an Injun behind that rock!" kind of pot-boiler that still has a hard-core following. Blake's book went directly into paperback and didn't become a best-seller until the film was a smash hit. His advance was the magnificent sum of $6,500.

Fortunately, Blake did have friends who believed in him and his project, most notably Kevin Costner and the film's co-producer, Jim Wilson. Blake met Wilson in 1977 at film school (at the University of California at Berkeley). He got to know Costner in 1981, while writing a script called STACY'S KNIGHTS, which was directed by Wilson and gave Costner his first starring role. Conventional wisdom states that once a writer has had a film made, he or she is on Easy Street thereafter. Wrong. It's true that Blake moved to Los Angeles and kept on writing, doing a series of low-budget feature scripts. But they were not produced, and he was working for sums that fell short of allowing him to pay his rent and bills.

He had long been interested in American Indians, and came up with the central idea for DANCES. He told Costner about the idea. In an interview with Mervyn Rothstein in the *New York Times*, Blake describes Costner's reaction: "[He] said, 'Don't you dare write another movie.' Because I'd written probably fifteen screenplays by that time. He said, 'Write a book. You have a much better chance of reaching somebody with a book.' He was adamant."

Blake did, and the interview that follows tells in detail how, at the age of 45, he finally gained the recognition and satisfaction he'd long dreamed of.

What was it about this film, such an unlikely candidate for hit status, that made it such a smash? One factor is that, as William Goldman said, "Nobody knows anything." Film history is full of likely successes that flopped and likely failures that soared. Furthermore, when a genre has been out of favor long enough, a good film in that genre will seem fresh again. It had been a long time since there had been an excellent Western. Also, the film reflected several topics with which the American public has become concerned: how we treat other people, how we live now, and how it may be possible to get back in tune with nature.

Blake addressed the first of these when he told *The New York Times* that one reason for the film's success is guilt: "It is a guilt about the way we've treated our country: the people who used to live here, the land itself, and the animals that live here yet. And in a certain way, DANCES WITH WOLVES is a very contemporary movie. Because we are still treating certain people as if they're just in the way."

The film resonates with the awareness being felt in America, as reflected by the success of books like Robert Bly's *Iron John*. Writing in the *Los Angeles Times*, psychologist Thomas Hersh says, "The Indian within us has come alive and is hungry to look around and experience the world...Every time the American in us is captivated by the purring of the motor of our well-tuned car, the Indian in us cries for the once-clean sky."

The stunning cinematography had a psychological impact as well (even though a joke in the industry was that the film should have been called "Plays With Camera.") It was the first film in a long time to remind us of the grand sweep of the Western landscape. Many took delight in the fact that it's still possible to find such wide open spaces. The frontier has disappeared, but comforting echoes of it remain.

The film is also educational in a painless way. We see how the Indians lived, we hear their language, we get some insight into the way they looked at the world. We are drawn into their culture along with John Dunbar, Costner's character, and suddenly, like Dunbar, we find ourselves in a different reality; the movie helps us to walk a mile in another man's moccasins.

The heart of the matter, though, isn't camera work or political issues, or redemptive psychology or anthropology. It's that the movie tells a good story. Writing in *New York Magazine*, critic David Denby says, "It's as close as white Americans are likely to come to a central ethical myth—and perhaps it needs to be told in every generation." The moviemakers tried to be as accurate as possible, but some liberties were taken in the interests of the story. Costner told reporters, "I'm not in the message business. I'm in the entertainment business."

David Denby rightly points out that the movie could have used more conflict, and there are a few narrative holes. But we have a likable hero, someone who is heroic only out of desperation and who approaches an unknown civilization the way we perhaps like to think we would: with curiosity, openness, respect, and more than a little apprehension. The main conflict turns out not to be with the Indians, but with his own people. As Pogo was fond of saying, "We have met the enemy, and he is Us."

Some consider the film's outlook to be idealistic, simplistic and sentimental. In countering the "only good Indian is a dead Indian" philosophy that dominated the big and small screen (as well as actual frontier thinking), did Blake and Costner go too far in the other direction? That's a judgment call. What is indisputably true is that the film has a consistent vision. From the start, the filmmakers wanted creative control over their project. If they had done it through a major studio—assuming that a major studio would have wanted it—there would have been the danger of a studio exec at some point saying, "Kill the subtitles," or "Trim it to two hours." Wilson says, in a *Daily Variety* interview, "I have nothing against the studios, but this was very much an in-house project among three friends."

It's ironic and perhaps instructive and inspirational to realize that the script that finally made Blake successful wasn't one of the low-budget pieces he wrote purely for the money, it wasn't a script that tried to follow trends or out-guess the marketplace. Instead, it was a story he was eager to tell because it meant something to him, and in the end it aroused great passion in several people who fought for the film to have the same kind of integrity the script did. Whether or not you consider DANCES WITH WOLVES a masterpiece, its making was a victory for thoughtful and dedicated writers and filmmakers.

Interview with Michael Blake

DANCES WITH WOLVES

The overwhelming reception by the public for DANCES WITH WOLVES has no doubt changed your life. As an inspiration to all struggling writers out there, can you give us an idea of where you were in your career when all this happened?

It has changed my life. Forever. In a wonderful way, but also in ways where you have to make adjustments as a person. It's a strange and unique time for me—but it was a very, very short period ago that I was walking these streets of Hollywood, with no hope, in a constant state of despair of one sort or another. Pursuing a dream that no one believed any more. My family had finally given up on the idea that I was ever going to amount to anything, or have any kind of real life. (Laughter) And my peers had given up on me, too, not in the sense that they disapproved of what I was doing, but that they wished I could be more comfortable. That I could have, say, a relationship with somebody, a job, a home, you know, things like that.

I struggled a long time to get to this point. I would say that my success had to do with two things: talent, and perseverance. Those two ingredients are the key ingredients that can't be substituted for. And you might throw in a large dose of passion and heart. There were so many times that I wrote screenplays, or stories, or poetry, that came straight from my heart, but never went anywhere, never found support financially. Never encouraged by the industry, or society as a whole. But I kept writing from my heart, even when I wasn't supposed to be writing from my heart.

What do you mean, you weren't supposed to?

I have an anecdote to illustrate that. There is a producer, a man I have a lot of affection for, who produces, shall we say, low-end films. But the man, to his great credit in my eyes, hired me when I was just barely making a living as a writer.

He came to me when I was in a down period, in-between some scripts I had been working on for him, and I said to him, "Look, I need some money. I'm going to have to get a job or something." And he said, "All right, we'll get you a thousand dollars. Write three treatments for us."

So I had an assignment. I didn't want to be disturbed too much while writing these treatments, so I took the thousand dollars and went down to Mexico, and holed up in Ensenada. Now, the first story they wanted was a love story, so I wrote about these two unlikely people who fall in love and end up on an island together. It sounds dopey, but it's really a pretty good story.

The second story they wanted was a story about gangs. So I wrote one called, "Meet the Enemy," which I think may yet be a movie one day. And about halfway through this second story I came back to the States and submitted what I had so far.

Well, they read the first one, and the producer said to me, "Well, it's okay, it's not exactly what we had in mind, I thought, you know, you were going to write about four pages and there's twenty-five pages here. You're confusing me." I said, "Don't worry. If you didn't go crazy for that one, you're going to love this next one, `Meet the Enemy.'"

I finished it, and after they read it I showed up for a meeting with my friend and his cronies. They were all just sitting there, shaking their heads. "Look, Michael," they said to me, "you have to stop. You have to stop. We want garbage. You don't understand." [Laughter]

Well, I got kind of mad, and said, "All right, I'll write garbage for you, but you've got to give me back those two stories." They had no problem with that, and I went off to write garbage.

That was the hardest writing I've ever had to do in my life. I tried to do it with my eyes closed so I wouldn't have to see what I was writing. It was really difficult. But I wrote the garbage, because that's what I had to do. And the garbage never went anywhere, but the stories are still here, and they're still good, and I've got them—so you see, sometimes the writer has a victory.

There have been a number of different stories as to the genesis of DANCES WITH WOLVES. Can you give us the official version, for the record?

The press almost always gets things mixed up. It's not too disconcerting, because it's a blanket thing. Whether it's *Time* magazine or a mimeographed sheet, things get mixed up.

So now, the real story...

I wrote a book because I had written so many screenplays, and only one had been made, for which I had been paid a small amount of money. So, Kevin, [Ed. note: Costner is a personal friend of Blake's] because he knew I was suffering in Hollywood, and because he felt I was a good enough writer to deserve an audience, suggested that I write a book. In fact, he was quite adamant that I write a book about my vision of a cavalry officer arriving at a deserted fort, staying, and becoming involved with Native Americans. At that time, that was the only vision I had. And Kevin said, right away, "Write a book, man, write a book."

Of course, that was probably the best advice anyone has ever given me. I wrote the book. Technically, I was a homeless person when I wrote the book. I'm lucky I am so rich in friends, because I had plenty of people to stay with here in Los Angeles. But I had no home, I paid no rent, I had essentially no income for the entire time I worked on the novel.

When I finished, I was proud of the work I had done. But I didn't have an agent. I didn't know a publisher, anywhere. I had some influential friends, but just because you know a Kevin Costner or someone of his stature, doesn't mean you're going to get a book published.

At any rate, I felt bad. I felt that I was a failure as a writer, even though I felt good about my work. So, I borrowed a thousand dollars from Laura Zisken, a famous producer now who was doing pretty well then—she certainly had a lot more money than I did—filled my car, and headed east.

I ended up in a little town in southeastern Arizona, feeling pretty much washed up. I knew I would always write, but all I could think about was, "Gee, what could have been, what might have been great. But I'm forty-two years old, I can't afford any longer to entertain ideas of making it, whatever making it is."

So I exiled myself to Arizona. Of course, to some degree, my attempt to drop out was like all the other attempts to stop writing I'd made through the years. It failed. I was in Arizona, scraping paint off windows at apartment houses and doing other odd jobs, just to try to get money. I had a little room with another guy in a miner's cabin—not a bad miner's cabin, it was kind of a nice one [Laughter]—but it wasn't much. I still stayed in touch with Hollywood to some degree.

The person who eventually produced the film was very excited about what I had done with the book, and thought it would make a great movie. I knew that he was bugging Kevin, and bugging William Morris, and bugging a few other people, but my reality was so different at that time that I just didn't put much stock in any of it.

What eventually happened was that Kevin read the book. And liked it. He and the producer decided maybe they could do something with the book.

Meanwhile, I was washing dishes at a Chinese restaurant. I had just been fired. It was the first job I'd ever been fired from. I'd been fired for two or three days when Kevin calls up and says, "Hey, we think we've got a deal, why don't you come back to L.A.?" It didn't take me very long to say yes to that.

And, about three years later, DANCES WITH WOLVES opened.

DANCES WITH WOLVES is a story that obviously required a certain amount of research. At what point did you undertake that aspect of the work?

The book came out of research. But the research wasn't done because I had it in mind to write a book. I was curious about the history of my country. And when I began to read about what happened to Native Americans, it touched me in a way—well, I couldn't stop reading about it. I just kept reading these books, and they just kept busting my heart wide open, but I couldn't stop. And at

11

some point I became so full with all this history that something had to come back out. And what came out was a novel.

The novel took about nine months to write. It's probably the most fun I've ever had writing. DANCES WITH WOLVES had a life of its own. There were difficult periods in the writing—one of those times, for instance, was figuring out the Stands With A Fist character.

Did you create her because you felt the story needed a romantic interest?

Not necessarily a romantic interest, but some kind of strong feminine presence. With the exception of some specialized stories, to do stories that don't have a feminine presence doesn't make any sense. Half the world is female. Eventually, the character of Stands With A Fist just came to me.

A lot of my writing just comes to me. There's a great cartoon called, "Shoe," in which the little bird is in a room with the big bird, who is staring out the window. There's a typewriter in the room, and the little bird looks at it and says, "You're a writer, shouldn't you be typing?" And the big bird says, "Typists type. Writers stare out windows." And I do a lot of that.

Was any of the story based on true-life events?

There are bits and pieces that are real. For instance, Timmons and his wagon coming up to the fort, and there being no one there. That really happened, probably about that time, 1863. It happened down in Oklahoma, or Kansas, that area, where a guy drove out to a fort and there was nothing there. There was no Lieutenant Dunbar with him, but there was nothing at the fort except a piece of canvas floating in the breeze in the doorway. And when I read that in a history book—that's what started this whole thing. I just started to wonder, well, suppose there was a guy there. I would have liked to have been there. What if it was me? I'll call me Lieutenant Dunbar. And I'll get to have this great adventure.

You said that the book found its beginnings in research. In adapting the book to screenplay form, was factual authenticity a problem?

Authenticity wasn't too difficult. There were a lot of people around who could tell us the way things needed to be. We had a tremendous production designer, with a staff that really got into their work; no shortcuts with costuming, no shortcuts, for instance, with how you scrape a hide. Everyone had to learn how to do that.

Let's address some of the other problems you may have encountered in adapting your book to a screenplay.

The first draft that I did, I never looked at my book. I didn't want the movie to be the book—I wanted the movie to be the movie. Or something like that. Anyway, Kevin came back to me and said, "Well, gee, there was this part (in the book) here that was so good, and this other part too, we need to get all this in there." And so the story went through a lot of changes with the passage of time. I did six drafts of the screenplay. Looking back, the first and the sixth drafts look a lot more alike than any of the other drafts.

Let me comment on what it's like for writers to work in Hollywood, particularly when you're working with people that have achieved genuine stature. You are going to have to cooperate. It's difficult for the writer, who works alone, to then come in and present the work and have people say, "No, that's not what we want." And the writer says, "Yeah, but don't you see, this is how...? Forget that. Instead, throw the ball back to them. "Well, why do you want it that way?" "What's so special about having it that way?" "How do you envision that?" It's such a cooperative medium, you can't get out of working with people, so the trick is to try and pick really good people to work with. People who have intelligence, which most people in Hollywood have. People who have some sensitivity, which is something I think is growing in our culture. People who understand movies real well. Kevin, for instance, understands movies. He understands what turns people on and off, but not in a horribly manipulative way. Only in a mildly manipulative way. [Laughter]

When was the book published, and how widely read was it prior to the success of the movie?

It was published in 1988. All the big hardcover houses rejected the book, for millions of different reasons, I suppose, most of which I never knew about. We finally got a deal with two paperback companies in one day, they both made offers on the book. One was Fawcett, and they gave us a thousand dollars more, and said they had a big distribution system to get the book out there, and that sounded good to me.

The big paperback companies are not the place to go to get a book launched creatively. I learned this from my experience. Books, to them, are like ladies' pumps: shove 'em into the store, sell as many as you can, and go on to the next style. And that's what they did with my book. I didn't bring the "Conan" edition here tonight, I should have...

I assume you're referring to the cover art on one of the editions. You had some misgivings over the marketing of the book, right?

The publisher said to me, "First of all, we have a

problem with the title of your book." And I said, "What? What do you mean?" And they said, "Well, we had a staff meeting, and a couple of the people thought the public might be confused, you know, they might think it is an instructional book." [Laughter] I said, "No, we can't change the title, it's so important to the book." And so the lady who was my editor vowed to go in there and fight for me, and I guess she did because I got to keep the title.

Then, halfway through the publishing process, my editor left to take a job at a yachting magazine. Another person came in, a voice on the phone I'd never met, and I kept asking about the cover. A cover is so important, and I wondered what they had in mind. And this editor kept telling me, "We're working on a beauty. It's a humdinger. We're all running around here excited as hell about this cover."

They never sent me a photocopy of what they were working on. They sent me the book. Fifty books. And I open the box, and here is all this work, my life, and on the cover is a picture of this white man with muscles. It looked like Conan the Barbarian goes to an Indian village. He's got his woman behind him and a couple of tents back there and a horse with a circle on his eye—looked like Spot in an "Our Gang" comedy. And I thought to myself, here I've achieved something, I've got a book in print, which most people can only dream about, and I'm not going to be able to face my friends.

But I do think that my story is, in a little way, testament to the idea that, if you really work on trying to be a better person, somehow things do work out in your life. Things always have a way of working out. I went through so many periods of consternation and frustration over all of this. Now, using hindsight from this lofty crag I'm perched on at the moment, I can see that I could have made it a lot easier on myself if I had worked on myself as a person a little bit more. These things wouldn't have been so hard for me to deal with, and so hard for me to recover from. I recommend that to anybody who is a writer, an artist, a musician, or whatever. If you're not going to be able to live on your achievements, you are going to have to live with your achievements as a person in this life.

Writers of adaptations have told us that there are always scenes from the book that have to be sacrificed when writing a screenplay, and often that process is painful. Were there any scenes you had to reluctantly eliminate, and why were they eliminated?

There are lots of scenes (from the book) that I wish had made it into the movie, but didn't. I don't think there is any one scene that stands out. There are two scenes that, by the way, were both shot: One provided some background information on who was there (at the abandoned camp) and why they left; and one where Dunbar and Kicking Bird take a ride together to a sacred place. Both are missing. But when you have a three-hour picture, you're pushing things anyway, and something had to go. There's probably a good hour of footage that I think is real watchable and adds to the story, that has been excised.

Let's talk for a minute about the length of the picture. Was it difficult convincing the studios that this story needed to run longer than the more conventional ninety minutes to two hours?

The people at Orion were very good. They understood immediately that this was going to be a very special story. And we wanted to tell a full, complete story. We didn't want to cheat the audience, and not give them the full benefit of the story we wanted to tell.

In looking at the script, it's interesting to note that the page count would indicate a movie only about two hours long, if one were to go by the page-a-minute standard.

The page-a-minute rule is one that I've always followed, and I used to be nervous about keeping my work under a hundred and twenty pages all the time when I wanted someone to like my work. I was worried they might say, "Oh, this is a great script, but it's no good because it's 122 pages, and you know we can't do that!" But now, what I try to do is keep a sense that there is a movie going on, and an audience sitting there.

It's been pointed out that my script is a little spare, too. You come to the buffalo hunt, and it's an eighth of a page: "Guys chase buffaloes." What that requires (in terms of shooting) is a whole other thing—how that translates is a whole other thing.

The movie is big. It's big. So, there are lots of places for it to be expanded from the screenplay.

Another consideration in writing adaptations must be the retention of factual information; what to include, what to change, what to leave out completely. For example, in the book, the Indians were Comanches, while the Indians in the movie were Sioux. Why?

The main reason is because we needed buffalo, and the biggest herd in the world is in South Dakota. And there are at least sixty thousand Indians in South Dakota. So you had a large pool of people to choose from as well. And I think it worked out well, because in the popular mind, Sioux is a more exotic Indian group, and one we seem to know more about. The sad part is that the Comanche people are a small group of people whose language is dying; very few people speak Comanche any longer.

I've heard you speak of your strong feelings for the Native Americans, and the way they have been historically treated by Hollywood.

These people, who know so much about so many things—natural medicines, herbs, and a lot of things that run much deeper—have been devalued to the point where we consider them worthless people. I'm saddened that this condition exists today, and I think one of the great promises of this film is that perhaps it can start us looking at what some of our spiritual resources are. Resources that include not only the Indians, but our black, brown and yellow people, all kinds of different people that live in this country who have traditionally not been allowed to participate fully in our culture. Hopefully, DANCES WITH WOLVES is building a little bridge. It's a step.

Any final words of encouragement or advice? How do other writers find the path to success?

Everyone has their own story. Everyone finds success in their own way. There is no magic key, no yellow brick road that you can suddenly discover, get on, and go. Each individual is responsible for his or her destiny, when it comes to how your work is viewed by the rest of society.

Story Outline
DANCES WITH WOLVES

ACT I

LT. JOHN DUNBAR, rather than lose his severely wounded leg to amputation, slips away from a Union Army field hospital. He rides back to his unit, which is holding its position in a cornfield away from a Confederate army.

The delirious lieutenant grabs a horse and tries to commit suicide by riding unarmed into the Confederate troop positions. But his unit backs him up, and routs the rebels.

The general thinks Dunbar is a hero and orders his personal physician to look after the lieutenant's mangled leg.

Dunbar is rewarded with the horse he rode on his daring "assault", and with an assignment to anywhere he wants? He chooses a post out in the Great Plains, the vanishing American frontier.

Dunbar receives his formal orders to the outpost at Fort Sedgewick. The officer who gives those orders is obviously mentally disturbed.

Dunbar meets his guide, a crusty coot by the name of TIMMONS. As the two of them leave Fort Hayes, the commander shoots himself in the head.

The two wayfarers spend the night at the scene of an old Indian massacre. Dunbar makes the best of his humorous, but vulgar, companion.

The next morning, they get off to an early start. As they cross the prairies and badlands, Dunbar searches in vain for Indians and buffalo.

When they finally arrive at Fort Sedgewick, they find the place in a shambles and deserted. It doesn't look like anybody's been there for quite a while.

Dunbar insists on staying at his assigned post, and has to pull a gun on Timmons to get his help with unloading the provisions. That task done, Timmons gladly leaves.

That night, Dunbar writes in his diary that he has assigned himself cleanup duty. The next morning, the jumpy lieutenant is startled by his horse, Sisko.

While cleaning and rebuilding, Dunbar discovers that his missing comrades had lost all their provisions and had been living in caves just over the hill from the fort.

Out on the prairie, marauding Indians kill Timmons, the only person who knows exactly where Dunbar is and what he's doing.

Back at Fort Sedgewick, Dunbar waits for his relief and tries to figure out why the previous soldiers had been living in caves. He spots a wolf across the lake and draws a bead on it with his rifle, but reconsiders.

It's been 30 days now, and still no relief from Fort Hayes. Dunbar's been making friends with the stray wolf, which he named Two Socks.

While Dunbar is bathing and doing his laundry one day, Two Socks alerts him to a curious Indian [KICK-ING BIRD] who is poking around the fort. The startled Indian beats a hasty retreat when Dunbar, unarmed and naked, confronts him.

Dunbar buries his weapons so they can't be stolen by Indians, then prepares the fort for a possible attack.

Act II

At Kicking Bird's village, the tribal council discusses the strange ways of white men and the threat they pose. Kicking Bird thinks Dunbar might be a good man to try and make treaties with.

Three Indian boys who were spying on the meeting raid Fort Sedgewick. Dunbar knocks himself out trying to defend his post, and the boys take off with the horse Sisko, who later breaks free from his captors.

Sisko returns to Dunbar, but only for a short time. Two Socks the wolf again alerts Dunbar to the presence of Indians, this time led by WIND IN HIS HAIR, an aggressive young man from Kicking Bird's tribe. Wind In His Hair lets Dunbar know that he is not afraid of him, and rides off to join the other Indians, who have stolen Sisko.

But once again Sisko has broken free, and the horse returns to Dunbar, who has fainted after his close call with the angry Indian.

Dunbar realizes he has become a target for the Indians and decides to ride out to meet them as a representative of the United States.

On the way to the village he finds a white woman in Indian clothing who has tried to commit suicide. He rescues her against her will and carries her back to her village.

Wind In His Hair drags the woman away from the lieutenant, then yells for him to go away. Dunbar, dejected, does as he is told.

In a council meeting that night, CHIEF TEN BEARS orders Wind In His Hair and Kicking Bird to go have a talk with the white man at his soldier fort.

Dunbar welcomes the guests to his home and they all do their best to communicate. The lieutenant respects both of the emissaries, and though he likes Kicking Bird, he's a little scared by Wind In His Hair.

On the Indians' next visit, Dunbar entertains his guests over coffee. They are all getting along well.

Kicking Bird tries to convince the woman Dunbar saved, STANDS WITH A FIST, to interpret the white man's words. But she is scared of the soldier and declines.

Stands With A Fist flashes back to when she was a child, and a tribe of hostile Indians killed her family.

At Fort Sedgewick, Dunbar encourages the wolf's friendship with food. Kicking Bird and Wind In His Hair arrive with a gift of buffalo hide. Dunbar writes in his diary that the Indian stereotypes are wrong, and that he is growing to care greatly for these people.

Dunbar receives an invitation to join Kicking Bird, Wind In His Hair and Chief Ten Bears at the Sioux village, to share a peace pipe. Stands With A Fist shows up to interpret, and after introductions, the Indians politely ask Dunbar about the white man's intentions in Sioux territory.

At his own camp, Dunbar writes in his diary that he's afraid to tell the Indians too much about the white man's designs on the prairies. He is shaken out of bed early the next morning by thundering herds of buffalo.

Dunbar rides to tell the Indians the good news— that the buffalo are here—and the camp pulls up stakes to follow the herd. Dunbar joins the Sioux, to whom he has become a bit of a celebrity.

As they ride, Stands With A Fist and Dunbar exchange flirtatious glances.

The Indians find the carcasses of hundreds of buffalo, killed by white hunters for their hides and tongues, then left to rot in the sun. The Sioux are heartbroken, and Dunbar begins to think of white men as people quite different from himself.

That night, the lieutenant exiles himself to the edge of camp.

The next day, they find the rest of the herd—thousands upon thousands of buffalo, and the tribe, to include Dunbar, prepares for the hunt.

The hunt: In a flurry of horses, Indians, buffalo, and dust, the Sioux take only what they need to sustain themselves.

There's a tense moment when a large bull charges a boy who was thrown from his horse, but Dunbar saves the day with some skillful shooting.

Dunbar joins Wind In His Hair for a ritual mouthful of the dead animal's liver.

Saving the boy's life has made Dunbar a living legend. In camp that night, he has to tell the story of the rescue for the hundredth time. He and Wind In His Hair exchange gifts of clothing, and Wind In His Hair sticks up for Dunbar when one of the other Sioux decides that he now owns the soldier's hat.

The celebration goes on into the night, with Stands With A Fist admiring Dunbar.

Dunbar spends the night with Kicking Bird and his family, and the lieutenant and Stands With A Fist barely contain their mutual longing.

The next day the tribe moves out, and they drop Dunbar off at Fort Sedgewick. The soldier's respect and understanding of the Sioux has grown by leaps and bounds, and he misses his new friends almost instantly.

A couple of days later, Dunbar rides out to visit the Sioux village. Two Socks the wolf, who has been hanging around a lot lately, follows. Kicking Bird spots Dunbar and the wolf chasing each other around the field.

Autumn comes and the tribe has given Dunbar his own lodge. He talks his way around their questions concerning the white man's plans. He wants to join a war party going against the Pawnee, a tribe that has been harassing the Sioux, but Kicking Bird asks him to fulfill an even greater honor—to look after his family while the war party is away.

Dunbar learns that the tribe has christened him Dances With Wolves, after his romp in the field with Two Socks.

While the warriors are away, Dances With Wolves learns the Sioux language and gets to know Stands With A Fist better.

Dances With Wolves speaks the language fluently with one of the elders, and learns that Stands With A Fist is still mourning a dead husband, which is why she's not married. She will mourn until Kicking Bird, her adoptive father, says she is through.

Stands With A Fist learns that the whole camp knows how well she's been getting along with Dances With Wolves.

Dances With Wolves rides back to Fort Sedgewick and reminisces through his journal. On one page he writes, like a teenager with a crush, Dances With Wolves loves Stands With A Fist. He's distracted by Two Socks, who will now eat from his hand.

Back near the Sioux village, Dances With Wolves finds Stands With A Fist and they go for a romp in the bushes, then sneak back to camp. These two are in love.

That night she visits his lodge and they make love again. But they're interrupted by the news of an approaching Pawnee war party.

Dances With Wolves takes one of the boys to help dig up the rifles buried near Fort Sedgewick, then the battle begins. It's old men, women and children against the Pawnee warriors, but with the help of the rifles the Sioux prevail. Dances With Wolves realizes that he feels more like a Sioux than a white man.

The Sioux warriors return, and celebration follows. Dances With Wolves and Stands With A Fist sneak rather obviously off to bed. And Kicking Bird's wife convinces him to end their adopted daughter's mourning.

Dances With Wolves and Stands With A Fist get married.

Dances With Wolves is a full-fledged member of the tribe, in full costume now, and has a chat with his new father-in-law about having a baby with Stands With A Fist.

Dances With Wolves finally tells the full truth about the plans white men have for the prairies.

Chief Ten Bears tells Dances With Wolves the Sioux have driven away Spaniards, Mexicans, and Texans. But they fear they will not be able to hold off the white man.

The Sioux prepare to leave for their winter camp. Dances With Wolves realizes that his journal at Fort Sedgewick will tell all about his life with the Indians, and he rides back to retrieve the book.

But a large Union Army unit has already arrived at the abandoned fort. They kill Sisko and take Dances With Wolves prisoner.

ACT III

Wind In His Hair and Kicking Bird realize that something must have happened and send some men to check out the fort.

The soldiers interrogate Dances With Wolves, then club him senseless. He's chained and shackled, and when he regains consciousness he refuses to lead the army to the Indian camps.

At least the journal is less of a threat—two illiterate soldiers are using the pages for toilet paper.

Wind In His Hair's scouts observe Dances With Wolves being mistreated by the soldiers. The soldier-turned-Sioux is to be sent back to Fort Hayes and hanged as a traitor.

The army convoy pulls out for Fort Hayes. When the soldiers see Two Socks and start shooting at the wolf, Dances With Wolves tries to stop them, but gets clubbed again. When some of the soldiers walk up a hill to look for Two Socks' corpse, they nearly discover a group of Sioux warriors that have been trailing the group.

Wind In His Hair leads an ambush on the army convoy, and Dances With Wolves helps kill the soldiers. During the battle, Dunbar's journal falls free and floats down the river.

At the winter camp, Dances With Wolves comes home to a joyous reunion with the tribe, and of course, Stands With A Fist.

In order to keep the soldiers from finding the village, Dances With Wolves decides that he and Stands With A Fist must go away and try and negotiate peace with the white men. The Indians do not want their friends to leave. Chief Ten Bears tries to talk him into staying, but Dances With Wolves knows he must go.

Stands With A Fist tells Dances With Wolves she will go wherever he goes.

Dances With Wolves, Stands With A Fist and the rest of the Sioux say their good-byes, and exchange farewell gifts. Kicking Bird now speaks very serviceable English.

One of the boys had fetched Dunbar's diary from the river, and the youth returns the book to Dances With Wolves.

The soldiers were hot on the Indians' trail, but by the time they find the campsite the Sioux are gone, and Dances With Wolves and Stands With A Fist ride into the hills.

Michael Blake's Pick

DANCES WITH WOLVES

EXT. FEASTING FIRE-NIGHT
All over camp people are crowding around fires,
feasting on fresh meat. Children are playing
everywhere, the dogs are having a field day with
scraps and the voices of the people are happy.

At a little distance, we see LIEUTENANT DUNBAR and
WIND IN HIS HAIR excusing themselves from one of
the fires. They start toward us. Wind In His Hair
is sucking on a rib bone and seems to show no sign
of slowing down his celebrating. Dunbar, following
a couple paces behind, is a different story. He's
had it. He spreads his hands to indicate an over-
sized belly.

> DUNBAR
> Look I'm full... I can't tell
> the story again.

Wind In His Hair doesn't seem to hear. He points
at the epaulettes on Dunbar's tunic.

> DUNBAR
> Go ahead.

Wind In His Hair reaches out and fingers the gold

lieutenant's bars. He fingers a couple of the brass buttons as well. The tunic is something he obviously puts much store in.

> DUNBAR
> (signing)
> You want to try... put it on.

He unbuttons the tunic.

> DUNBAR
>
> Here.

He sloughs off the tunic and hands it over. Wind In His hair slips out of the magnificent bone-pipe breastplate he's wearing and gives it to Dunbar as he wriggles into the tunic. The fit is too tight, the material too scratchy, but those things are of little consequence to Wind In His Hair. He loves the tunic.

With urging signs he asks the lieutenant to put on the breastplate. Dunbar slips it over his head and Wind In His Hair helps him with the ties.

Now it's the lieutenant's turn to be amazed. The breastplate is craftsmanship at its finest. He runs his fingers over the ridges of bone now covering him from neck to waist. He looks up at Wind In His Hair.

The warrior nods approvingly, as though a good deal has been struck.

> DUNBAR
> This is too much... I can't
> take this...

But for Wind In His Hair it is already a trade. Wind In His Hair spots the next fireside and veers toward it. Dunbar holds him back.

                    DUNBAR
          I can't... No more...

Wind In His Hair grins. He holds up a single finger.

                WIND IN HIS HAIR
          One more... eat...

                    DUNBAR
          I can't, I'm full... very
          full...

Still holding up the finger, he guides Dunbar into
the firelight of the next party.

Immediately, men jump up to greet the celebrities.
Women begin to saw off more meat.

                    _____

Top Secrets:
Jim Cash

Jim Cash

TOP GUN

O NE QUESTION THAT ASPIRING SCRIPTWRITERS OFTEN ASK IS, "Is it possible to be a successful film writer without living in Los Angeles?" Perhaps the most resounding "Yes" comes in the form of the career of Jim Cash, who lives 2,513 miles from Hollywood. Of course, there is a catch: his partner, Jack Epps, Jr., works out of an office at Universal Studios.

Cash's lifestyle in East Lansing, Michigan, is far removed from the fast-lane Hollywood stereotype. He teaches writing, he plays ball with his kids, and enjoys the seasons [note to L.A. residents: "seasons" are when it's not 75 degrees and sunny every day including Christmas.] The only clue that he is one-half of Hollywood's hottest writing duo is the fact that, according to one of his neighbors, "Every time they have a hit movie, Jim adds on to his house" (the indoor pool is one example.)

Cash and Epps are most often associated with the pounding action of films like TOP GUN, which makes it all the more interesting that the big screen wasn't Jim Cash's original destination. "I was a novelist before," he says. "I wrote about six novels, all unpublished, all very artistic and introspective. Very self-indulgent, young American man stories."

At Michigan State University in the early and mid-

33

sixties, he was one of about twenty students who went on to become successful writers, including Thomas McGuane and Jim Harrison. Rather than being daunted by the plethora of talent around, Cash found it stimulating: "We were young, we were very competitive with each other, and at the same time, very respectful of each other."

His writing teachers added to the challenge, especially one named Clint Burhans, whom Cash credits with being his writing mentor for a while. "He would read one of my stories and he would challenge every single word. 'Why'd you use this word, why'd you use that word.'...And I said, 'All right, I can get into this...and I'd take it home and go back to work on it, and I'd bring it in and he'd say, 'Yeah, this is better, but what about this and what about that.' He just kept it up and kept it up. It was great experience, it was really tough." Cash couldn't have known it, but the competition and the challenge were perfect preparation for dealing with film producers.

Cash dropped out of college for two years and went to work in a factory, and in his spare time began to write those six novels. That experience taught him how to write well—and how to work hard. He says, "I worked the 4:00 p.m. to midnight shift. When I came home to my apartment about 12:30 a.m., I'd start writing. I wrote until about 6:30 in the morning, then I went to bed and got up about 10:00 and wrote until about 3:00. I did this literally every day for two years, except on weekends, when I wrote sixteen hours a day. And I found out that the longer I wrote, the better I got...At the end of that time, I said, 'Well, that's it. That's as good as I can learn to write, I think I've got it all, I don't think I'm going to lose it.' It's like swimming, you don't forget how to swim, you don't forget how to ride a bike, you don't forget how to do things that you master as a skill."

Eventually he began teaching at Michigan State, where Jack Epps, Jr., was one of his students. They decided to write a screenplay together, and the rest is cinematic (and banking) history—although not before they spent a number of years writing and selling scripts that weren't made.

Once they had TOP GUN, LEGAL EAGLES, and THE

SECRET OF MY SUCCESS all released within a relatively short period, all their old scripts suddenly sprang back to life, reaffirming the Hollywood maxim, "You're as hot as your last [produced] picture." Looking back on the days when he was writing novels, Cash says, "I think that I was the same writer then as I am now in terms of skill. It's just that now I get paid more money."

The origin of TOP GUN dates back to 1983, when Jerry Bruckheimer was leafing through *California* magazine and spotted some sexy photos of fighter jets, illustrating an article about the navy pilots' school at Miramar. He took the article to his partner, Don Simpson, who read it while on the phone. They immediately optioned the film rights to the article, took the notion to Paramount, and got the go-ahead right away. Simpson told a *Boxoffice* magazine reporter that they saw the elite trainee pilots as "a combination of Olympic athletes in the sky and rock and roll heroes...We wanted to make a movie about Yankee individualism, about a commitment to excellence and a world that few civilians will have an opportunity to see."

Cash and Epps were called to a meeting at Paramount and asked to develop the project into a script. Their take on the story was that the character played by Tom Cruise is a maverick (which ended up being his actual nickname...well, nobody said the film was subtle) who bucks the rigid system within which he has to operate.

Undoubtedly the film owes a great deal of its success to Tom Cruise's physique and pearly white smile, the visual sense of director Tony Scott and cinematographer Jeffrey Kimball, and a throbbing, non-stop rock sound track. Its popularity with young people (many of whom went back to the theater several times) was due to the fact that it was as much a fantastic visual arcade game as much as it was a film.

The plot of TOP GUN is simple and not unfamiliar to fans of classic Westerns and Word War II movies: there is a handsome, clean-cut hero, his faithful sidekick, an arrogant opponent, a beautiful love interest, and it all culminates in a showdown. *Daily Variety's* review complained that the script "failed to make the necessary emotional connections," that "buried in the background are some very disturbing political notions for anyone who wants to consider them," and that "life is given the texture of a three-minute pop song." But doubtless very few people did want to consider its political notions, and for a lot of the MTV generation the texture of a three-minute pop song is just fine, thank you.

Cash and Epps agree that in terms of the love interest, the picture failed to make the necessary emotional connections, but as you'll read in the interview that follows, they were replaced by another writer when they had a scheduling conflict. The love interest is one of the elements that was changed from their original conception. Saying that TOP GUN tells a simple story is not a negative criticism, for simple stories are not necessarily easy to write. In a picture like this, keeping the story simple is essential if the other elements, notably the fantastic visuals, are going to be given pride of place.

Perhaps if Cash and Epps had been allowed to do the final draft it would have been as gripping in story terms as it was in visual terms. That would have required a little—not a lot—more complexity in the characters and a greater variety of pacing in the story-telling. As it is, TOP GUN remains a driving, exciting action flick, and anyone interested in that genre will benefit from a close look.

Interview with Jim Cash

TOP GUN

In TOP GUN there were a lot of action sequences. How much of that was written, versus...

Very much. Almost all of it. In fact, TOP GUN is an extremely imagistic screenplay. We were very, very detailed in the fight sequences, because they were very important.

So you sort of blocked out what was going to happen and then sat down and wrote exactly...

Not truthfully, no. We talked in general terms about what was going to happen. In that scene, for example, we said, "All right, he's going to go up against his first Top Gun instructor, it's got to be a very tough fight. He's got to win, and at the same time lose. How can we have that happen?? And it was Jack [Epps] who came up with the answer. He said, "It's easy. He breaks the rules to win." And I said, "Well, yeah, but he can't be a cheater." And Jack said, "No, no, but he breaks the rules *just slightly*, and the instructor actually gets him on a technicality." And that's what he did. He came below the hard deck, which was 10,000 feet. In that particular hop, the pilots were not supposed to go below 10,000 feet. Anyway, in maneuvering to get away, Roman came below 10,000 feet and Maverick followed. So Maverick's thinking was, "Well, if he went below 10,000 feet because I was going to get him, then I'm going below 10,000 feet and *get* him." So that way, he won *and* lost.

So, the exact description of it was kind of easy in a sense, because a dog fight is a dog fight. The principle of a dog fight is to get on top of your opponent so you can get him in your sights. It's been that way ever since The Red Baron in WWI. They use the same techniques, but instead of going 30 MPH, they're going 600 MPH.

You said in another interview that some of your original dialogue was changed quite a bit on the set, in the heat of the moment so to speak. Do you feel that more was lost than was gained?

The dialogue was changed before it got to the set, and I think it lost certain things in the process. We had moved onto another project, LEGAL EAGLES, and so another writer came in to make some changes on TOP GUN. It was a major mistake, because it was our story. Nobody could write TOP GUN like we could write it. We feel that to be obvious from the final results.

Although it's a big box-office smash, although it's a good movie, it could have been a great movie. It could have been FROM HERE TO ETERNITY in the air. It could have been a *great* movie. But they never should have put another writer on it, they should have waited for us to finish LEGAL EAGLES, and they certainly should not have concocted the love story that they did.

You originally had the love interest as a gymnast, right?

She was an athlete who was as competitive as Maverick was. The problem with the girl in the movie was that she wasn't competitive, there was nothing to her. She had no conflict to her. She had *nothing* to her. She was not interesting in the least, especially to someone

38

like a fighter pilot. So, she might have been interesting for one night because she was pretty, but that's all, there was nothing there. So, all the conflict went out of the love story and when conflict goes out of a story, there is no story. Conflict is story. So that was the problem there.

As far as conflict goes, do you generally set up conflicts and then build the story, or start with a story and then find the conflicts inside? Or do you start with a character?

It's different every time. Every story has its own way of being born.

Is there any one way that seems to work best?

It's been different every single time. You just write. You start with something, though. You start with what you feel to be the heart of the story, one way or another. Sometimes the heart of a story is a character, sometimes it's a situation, sometimes it's a personal story of a character. When I say a situation, I mean it's something so unique that you can make a story out of it. It's just different every time.

This way, you can take whatever appealed to you about the story in the first place and always go back to that. When Paramount Studios said, "We want you to write TOP GUN," I said, "What's that, a western?? They said, "Here's what it is." And as soon as they told us what it was, Jack and I both said, "I see, I see. This is Montomery Clift. This is the rebel within the system. This is the Maverick. This is the character who's in the rigidly disciplined system who is not rigidly disciplined, but is extraordinarily gifted." And we said, "That's the story there, we can't wait to write this."

And so that's the hook that you can always go back to if you're straying and/or feel that you've lost something.

Yeah, then you say, "Wait a minute, where am I, where am I? Now *what was it that I liked about this story?*" And then you say, "Oh yeah, there it is. This is the Maverick in the system, etc., etc."

LEGAL EAGLES, I understand, was originally written for two male leads...

LEGAL EAGLES was originally written for Bill Murray and Dustin Hoffman [Interviewer's note: after the success of TOOTSIE.] It would have been a very good picture. It was much broader the first time through. It would have been a very funny movie. But then it was switched to male/female. Bob Redford came on—I have tremendous respect for Redford, he's an extraordinarily intelligent actor. Every comment he seems to make on a script is usually right on the money. Warren Beatty has that same gift. Most actors don't. At least most actors that I've been involved with in any way, but Redford does, and Beatty does. And Hoffman probably does, I don't know, I've never worked with him. And Debra Winger I've got a lot of respect for too, because I just think she's incredibly talented. I love to watch her on the screen. I just love to watch the way she does things, the way she moves, the way she talks. There's just something about her that's very magnetic.

So I thought, "This is great. We've got Redford and we've got Winger. Hot dog!" But I don't know. Something never quite caught fire with LEGAL EAGLES. Again, I think it was a good movie, entertaining, a lot of fun, with a lot of really wonderful moments, but nothing quite came together quite right, and I don't know exactly why. I guess it's probably the script. When you get down to it, the success or failure of every movie ultimately depends on the script, because that's what you're working from. But on the other hand, like I said, I'm not apologizing for it, because I watch it still and I enjoy it. It's fun. It lacked an element, it lacked another level—and if it had had that, it would have been a lot better picture.

As far as your computer collaboration and how you handle pitching—with Jack being out there and you here, how does it all come together?

I don't know. I don't work that machine (gestures toward computer on the desk), it intimidates me. I write long-hand. I've always written long-hand, and I'll always write long-hand, I think. I like it better. It looks prettier. I like the way written words look on a page. They are more personal, they're warmer. I can relate to them. Then I give them to my secretary. She types them into the computer, which is connected to Jack's computer at Universal Studios and he can read it two minutes later.

Then I get a copy back and say, "Wait a minute! Where did the warmth go? This is cold, type-written print." I always prefer the hand-written version.

When you get right down to writing scenes, do you literally go back and forth across the phone lines?

I do most of the writing, because I'm a natural stylist. Jack is a natural story teller in terms of structure. He's a great structurist. In fact, I think that he is *the* best structurist in Hollywood. He knows by instinct what comes next, where, why, how, etc. He's always got his finger on it, he's always two or three steps ahead of me, because he's working several scenes ahead of me. And then we talk the scenes and then I write the scenes and then sometimes he does some editing, and then I do some editing, and it goes back and forth like that.

But basically, we have our defined roles, and we understand them very clearly, and it works. So we don't tamper with it, we don't question it. We just leave it alone and we do it because it's fun and we like each other and we like our work.

As far as the pitching goes, I assume he handles all the meetings?

I do as little as possible. I don't enjoy that. I like to write. I like to spend the rest of my time with my kids and my beautiful wife. Playing basketball with my kids, coaching them, just enjoying everything. I want nothing to do with the business. And the less I have to do with it, the happier I am.

And so you've been to Los Angeles a grand total of...?

A couple of times. It's irrelevant to me. I'm a Mid-Westerner. This is where I live and I love it here. The people I've met in Hollywood I think are just terrific people, they've been really good to me. I don't have any enemies that I know of. Maybe that's because most of them haven't met me, except on the telephone or something, who knows? But I'm enormously happy to live in the mid-West. We've got seasons, there's a great beauty to it, we've got a lifestyle and attitude of people that's warm and open, and this is my kind of country.

When you start on one story, do you try to finish it, even if it might turn sour, or do you...

They all turn sour and none of them sour, and both. They turn sour all the time. I haven't talked to Jack for a week because I told him Friday, "Jack, you've got to walk away from this. You're killing this story (the one we're working on now) because you've lost it. Get away. I don't want you to think about it for a week." So, he will come back after a week filled with ideas. He'll know now what was bothering him about it. But this story died for him last week. It'll be reborn, but he's gotta walk away from it.

I do that sometimes, I say, "Jack, leave me alone for a week. I hate this story. This is the biggest mistake we've ever made." And that happens on every story. So you walk away and you forget it, and then there it is, it's back.

But do some of those die and *never* come back?

No.

You *always* complete them?

Yeah. Because there was *always a reason* we started it. *What was the original thing that appealed to us?* We go back to that.

Does working with a partner make it easier to keep ideas flowing?

It does for us. But don't look for formulas. There's only one rule in writing; if it works, do it; if it doesn't, stop.

What advice do you have for unproduced writers, both living in Hollywood and elsewhere?

Simple. Don't ask anybody how to write or succeed, and don't listen to anybody if they try to tell you. There's only one way to succeed; accept failure as a temporary state, however long that state might be, and simply outlast it. I put in hard time for seventeen years before we sold our first screenplay, and finally one day, failure gave up and decided to go bother somebody else. I was the same writer the day before we succeeded as I was the day after. Same person too. I've got to tell you the truth—I like that about me.

Any last thoughts to share?

I just want to enjoy life. I mean, what are you writing for if not to have freedom? What are you writing movies for? And what is freedom but time with people? And that's my top priority in life.

Story Outline

TOP GUN

ACT I

Opening titles over scenes of aircraft carrier flight operations.

Below deck, controllers notify a flight of U.S. aircraft that they are about to make contact with a bogey. The commander is less than pleased when he learns that MAVERICK and GOOSE are flying one of the intercept planes.

In the skies over the Indian Ocean, Maverick leads his wing, flown by COUGAR and MERLIN, into action.

The American fliers spot what they believe to be a lone bogey, but it turns out to be a pair of ultra-modern MIG 28's. Maverick and Cougar split up to play cat and mouse with the hostile jets. Maverick immediately gets a missile lock on his opponent, who hastily flies away.

The other MIG, however, gets a missile lock on Cougar. But Maverick blasts in and chases off the enemy plane with some hotshot, unorthodox maneuvering.

Maverick and his wing are both low on fuel and need to return to the ship, but Cougar has been badly shaken by the encounter and flies off in no particular direction.

Against orders and common sense, Maverick chooses not to land, but circles around and guides Cougar back to the ship.

In the commander's office, Cougar turns in his wings. He's lost the edge.

Maverick and Goose see the commander next, and they—especially Maverick—get their asses chewed. But the commander reluctantly announces that since Cougar quit flying, they are next in line to go to the Navy Fighter Weapons School—Top Gun.

Mirimar Naval Air Station, Fightertown USA: Maverick satisfies his need for speed on his motorcycle.

At the initial Top Gun briefing, a Navy officer briefs the pilots on the history and successes of the Top Gun program, then introduces the school's commander, Viper, who gives a pep talk and explains the schedule for the upcoming weeks. And Maverick has a chilly introduction to one of the other top pilots, ICEMAN.

At a bar that night, Maverick and Goose butt heads with Iceman and his co-pilot, SLIDER.

Then Maverick spots a pretty blonde, and along with Goose and a couple dozen other pilots, he serenades her. The stunt gets him an introduction, but as Maverick's ego shines through, the woman leaves to sit at a table with an older man.

Later, Maverick follows her into the ladies' room and hits on her with all the subtlety of a battleship in a bathtub. To say the least, she's not at all charmed.

In class the next day, Maverick and Goose discover that the woman, CHARLIE, has a Ph.D. in astrophysics and is one of their Top Gun instructors. And she knows her stuff. She locks horns with Maverick over the enemy plane that he (and Goose) had intercepted earlier.

After class she corners Maverick in a hallway. He thinks she's warming up to him, but she only wants to know more about the MIG. So he leaves her hanging.

Then he runs into Iceman, who accuses Maverick of lying, having an obnoxious attitude, and just generally being full of crap.

During the first aerial maneuvers, Maverick manages to shake JESTER, an experienced instructor pilot, and get on his tail. But Jester flies down low—out of bounds—so Maverick breaks the rules and follows him down for "the kill" Maverick is feeling cocky, and to prove it he disobeys orders and buzzes the air traffic control tower with his jet.

In the locker room, Maverick and Iceman go nose to nose. They do *not* like each other.

In VIPER's office, Maverick and Goose get another severe ass-chewing. If they disobey the rules one more time, they're history.

Act II

Jester and Viper don't know quite what to make of the young hotshot.

Goose has a heart-to-heart with Maverick, asks him to think of his partner for a change and take it easy. Maverick promises not to let his co-pilot down.

In class the next day, Charlie and Maverick talk about flying and Maverick's embarrassing show in the bar. By the time the conversation's over, he has her address and a dinner invitation.

The pilots gather outside for an intense volleyball game. They compete fiercely, even when they're supposed to be relaxing.

After the game, Maverick is running late for his date with Charlie. She's afraid he might not show, but when he finally does arrive she plays it cool.

Over dinner, she says the real reason she invited him over was to learn more about that MIG he intercepted.

After their meal they lounge around and listen to Otis Redding, and Maverick talks about his past. His father was in the Navy, and still has a bad reputation, even though he's been dead nearly twenty years. When Charlie makes a slight overture to Maverick, he brushes her off with a grin. Now it's his turn to play hard to get.

In an elevator on the base the next day, she admits that she likes him a little more than she's letting on. Again he grins, and stops just short of kissing her.

Goose's wife CAROL and their daughter arrive in California to be with their man.

During a debriefing for a previous mission, Charlie and Viper take turns bashing Maverick's outrageous flying. Iceman gets a kick out of the browbeating, but his co-pilot, Slider, compliments Maverick.

After class Maverick blows Charlie off completely and races through town, with her in hot pursuit. They argue in the street, and she admits that she's fallen for him. Then they retire to a bedroom for the evening.

During flight maneuvers, Iceman and Maverick take to the air. Halfway through training, the rivals are running neck and neck for the Top Gun trophy.

In the thick of a mock dogfight, Maverick breaks the rules again and leaves his wing man hanging to go after Viper.

As they thunder through the desert canyons in pursuit of Viper, Maverick and Goose are ambushed and "killed" by Jester.

On the ground Jester, then Iceman, tear into Maverick for his reckless attitude. Maverick admits to Goose that what he did was stupid, and promises it won't happen again. Goose doesn't seem convinced.

That night, alone in his room, Maverick wonders about what really happened to his dad.

Maverick and Goose yuk it up in a burger joint; Charlie hears that Maverick is head over heels in love with her.

Later that night, Charlie and Maverick race about town on his motorcycle, stopping occasionally to test fly each other's lips.

With only two weeks left until graduation, the Top Gun trophy is still up for grabs. During an intense, frenzied mock battle over the desert, Maverick and Iceman go for each other's throats as they maneuver their jets for a kill on a single adversary.

Maverick flies in too close to Iceman and his jet wash, and loses both engines to a flameout. Maverick and Goose fall into an extremely dangerous flat spin, losing altitude rapidly as they head out over the ocean. In a frantic ejection, Goose slams into the jettisoned canopy and is killed. Maverick survives the ejection unharmed.

On the ground, Viper tries to console Maverick. It doesn't work—the subdued hotshot blames himself for the death of his co-pilot and best friend.

Maverick gathers Goose's personal effects and brings them to his widow

A panel of inquiry clears Maverick of any blame in Goose's death, and restores him to flying status.

Maverick goes up in a jet for the first time since the accident, but passes up a perfect shot and breaks away. He's lost the edge.

When Maverick blows up at his new wing man, Viper and Jester decide that the best therapy is to keep sending him up.

Iceman does his best to offer condolences, but it doesn't help.

After Charlie learns that Maverick has quit flying, she finds him in an airport lounge, and tells him that she has a lucrative job offer in Washington, D.C. She also tries to convince him that he can't blame himself for Goose's death. But Maverick has gone off the deep end, and without a sound he lets her walk away.

Act III

Maverick visits Viper's house, and demands to know the true story of what happened to his father. They then discuss Maverick's options for the future.

Maverick rides over to Charlie's. Her house is for rent and she's already gone. He spends a lonely evening watching the jets come and go at the base.

At the Fighter Weapons School graduation, Maverick shows up just in time to congratulate Iceman and Slider for winning the Top Gun trophy. Viper breaks up the party by handing several pilots emergency orders. Two of those pilots are Maverick and Iceman.

Out at sea, it's a real-world situation. The stakes are high. So is the tension. Maverick is assigned to stand by on alert, ready to cover Iceman as he intercepts enemy aircraft approaching the fleet. Iceman doesn't trust Maverick.

On patrol, the bogeys are sighted and the intercept is on. Five MIG 28's swarm the American jets, and immediately shoot down Iceman's wing man. Maverick takes off with orders to assist his old rival.

In the middle of a harrowing dogfight, with Iceman outnumbered 5 to 1 and all alone, Maverick loses his cool and breaks away.

But he finds strength in the memory of Goose, and returns to engage the enemy. One MIG goes down straight away. Ice and Maverick work together now...Iceman gets a kill...but he's hit...and hit again...teamwork...another jet down... Maverick lures in the fourth MIG then destroys him; the last enemy pilot heads home with his tail between his afterburners.

Maverick, back to his old self, buzzes the tower on the aircraft carrier. But you can bet he gets away with it this time.

A hero's welcome for Maverick on the flight deck, and a big hug from Iceman.

Maverick tosses Goose's dog tags out to sea, sending with them the guilt he's carried since the accident.

Maverick is offered his pick of assignments to anywhere in the world—he chooses Mirimar Naval Air Station, and a job as Top Gun instructor.

Back in Fightertown USA, Maverick discovers that Charlie left her job in Washington to come back and be with him. If this assignment wasn't a sweet deal before, it is now.

TOP GUN

EXT. CLOUD COVER-DAY
We are above the clouds, above all reality with
earth. The silence and stillness are eerie.

Suddenly MAVERICK'S F-14 breaks through a cloud
bank like a hawk shooting out of the ground. The
plane reeks with energy as it searches the combat
zone like a terrible bird of prey.

INT. F-14
GOOSE watches his radar screen tensely. Maverick's
eyes search the horizon.

> GOOSE
> It's too quiet up here, Mav...

> MAVERICK
> Come on, you bastards, where
> are you?

Suddenly, Goose sees a blip appear on the radar
screen. His throat tightens up like a fist.

> GOOSE
> Bogey! Nine o'clock low! You
> see him?

                    MAVERICK
          Relax—relax.

                     GOOSE
          Nine o'clock low, heading two-
          four-zero.

                    MAVERICK
          Got him. You with me?

                     GOOSE
          I'm good. I'm fine. I'm scared
          shitless.

                    MAVERICK
          Let's see how good this
          hambone really is.

EXT. F-14
Maverick jerks the stick, and the F-14 takes a hard
left. The maneuverability is startling—it isn't a
plane, it's a futuristic space craft. And here comes
the bogey, our first view of the instructor plane.
The two aircraft head straight toward each other,
closing at the rate of a mile every four seconds
in a battle of nerve, a game of chicken.

The bogey is a speck in the distance—then it's
there, upon us, in our faces, large and menacing—
and then it's gone. The two planes flash past each
other with a thundering roar that shakes the sky.

The instructor in the bogey is VINCE CANDELA
("ROMAN"), who speaks with a bogus Italian accent.

                     ROMAN
          Eh, paisano. You the new dog
          meat from the Kitty Hawk?

                    MAVERICK
          Maverick and Goose—Ghost Rider
          Squadron, sir.

> ROMAN
> Don't "sir" me—'attsa
> bullshit. You can't "sir" me
> and fight me at the same time,
> capice? I am Roman, and it's
> an insult they send baby
> chickens like you to fight me.

> MAVERICK
> Judging from your first pass,
> Roman, you're probably used to
> insults.

> GOOSE
> (warning him)
> Maverick...

But Roman is laughing.

> ROMAN
> For that, you die, Yankee
> imperialistic pigs. Countdown:
> three... two... one... fight's
> on!

Roman jerks his plane into a hard left a moment
before he says "fight's on," and Maverick jerks hard
right a moment later.

> MAVERICK
> He jumped the gun!

> GOOSE
> Foul, you son-of-a-bitch...
> uh, sir.

> ROMAN
> I use Ivan's rules, bambini.
> Get used to it.

Roman's laugh taunts them as the two planes make
another pass toward each other. Again, Roman is upon

them with futuristic speed, like the flash of a sword, and gone.

There are dogfights all over the sky now, aircraft streaking in every direction as the instructors close in on the students. Maverick's eyes flash left and right—the movement around him almost takes his breath away.

We hear voices from all the planes: taunting, tense, steady, confused. Maverick and Goose exchange rapid-fire information.

>   MAVERICK
>   Airspeed?

>   GOOSE
>   Four-fifty! Steady!

>   MAVERICK
>   You got him?

>   GOOSE
>   No—yes! Ten o'clock! Three
>   miles!

>   MAVERICK
>   I got him, I got him.

At twenty-eight thousand feet, the two planes peel away from the others and circle each other in opposite directions. Jockeying for position, they snap past each other like ends of bullwhips.

The horizon ceases to exist as the earth spins, turns, appears and disappears. Gravity has no meaning—only G's—gravitational force. With each hard turn, Maverick and Goose grunt to keep blood in their brains, to keep from passing out.

The fight is hard, physical, exhausting. the extreme G-forces flatten them against their seats,

causing their heads to weigh over a hundred pounds.
Maverick strains to turn his head and track the
other jet as it streaks past at Mach One.

> GOOSE
> Watch your six! Watch your
> six!

> MAVERICK
> I've lost him! Where is he?

> GOOSE
> On your six—coming hard!

> MAVERICK
> Airspeed!

> GOOSE
> Four hundred! Losing airspeed!
> He's on your six and closing
> fast!

> MAVERICK
> Where's the goddamn energy!

> GOOSE
> Hard left! HARD LEFT!

Maverick jerks the stick left, and the F-14 takes
an astonishing turn. Roman skims past and sails into
a wide arc.

> GOOSE
> Good, good—<u>great!</u>

> MAVERICK
> Jerk should've had me.

> GOOSE
> Take it down. Let's bug-out.
> Call it a draw.

> MAVERICK
> Draw? I'll tear his ass up
> this time. Going vertical.

Maverick regains speed and takes the F-14 straight
up in an aggressive vertical move.

> MAVERICK
> Zone five—going ballistic.

The huge fighter plane explodes into afterburner—
soaring, rocketing, screaming toward space, and
streaks like an eagle toward the sun. Roman is left
in direct line with the sun, and his windshield is
sprayed with a blinding glare.

> GOOSE
> He's blind—you got him!

> ROMAN
> No joy! No joy! I've lost
> sight!

Goose is looking back over his shoulder.

> GOOSE
> He's out of energy! Dive!
> Dive!

The F-14 peels over the egg, like a backward swan
dive. It comes down nose first, a silver bullet,
as angry as a fist. We see Maverick's eyes for a
moment, and they're on fire.

The sound of speed dominates everything, the roar
of the jets, the slash of the wings. Goose is
shouting information, but it's muffled, a distant
voice in a typhoon. Through the cockpit window, we
see Roman's eyes are panicked as he glares into the
sun, searching for the F-14. No trick will save him
this time: he hangs in the air like a sparrow in
the path of a falcon.

On the windshield of the F-14, Maverick lines up the diamond with Roman's plane. We hear the high-pitched tone beeping very rapidly in Maverick's headset.

> ROMAN
> We're below hard deck! Fight's off!

> GOOSE
> Shit, he's right! We're at ten thousand.

> MAVERICK
> No way. I got you right in the diamond, sucker. You're going down!

Roman attempts to maneuver, but Maverick keeps him in the diamond on the windshield. The high-pitched tone goes crazy, beeping louder and more rapidly than before.

> MAVERICK
> Sidewinder one fire. Fox two missile shot. You're gone, Roman. Dead. Capice?

> GOOSE
> (stunned)
> We beat the bastard... hey! We beat him!

There is an edge of anger in Roman's voice.

> ROMAN
> Missile shot confirmed. Get your ass above the hard deck and return to base immediately.

Maverick's eyes are laughing, and Goose lets out a war whoop.

> MAVERICK
> Goose? I feel the need...

> GOOSE
> The need for speed!

The F-14 is a puppy in the sky: rolling happily, looping lazily, glad to be alive. The young men in the plane are laughing warriors, riding on top of the world.

Top Secrets:
STEPHEN E.
DE SOUZA

Stephen E. de Souza

DIE HARD

W ITH THE BLIND, UNRELENTING FAITH OF LEMMINGS, dreamers come to Hollywood. Many of them carry a
script. You know, the one that's going to sell for a
million bucks within a month, enabling them to send for the
family back in Montana and set up housekeeping in Malibu and
field phone calls from pleading producers and members of the
Academy.

But some of these dreamers have a realistic streak, too.
Many of them give themselves what they consider to be a
reasonable amount of time to "make it," and if they don't score
within that time frame, they figure it just isn't going to happen
and it's back to Montana for good.

Stephen E. de Souza was one of those. He gave himself
a time limit. A whole ninety days.

It took twelve.

Twelve days, that is, if you skip "Four or five years of
knocking around in Philadelphia, and being out of work, and
directing a talk show with Muhammed Ali as host, or a Sunday
sermon show with a blind host we used to cue with a string tied
around his leg. If you skip all that," says de Souza, "I'm an
overnight success."

A film major at Penn State, de Souza recalls a dearth of
classes focused on his passion: writing movies. "In those days,
to make a student film all you really had to do was shoot a bunch

of winos asleep in alleys, graffiti on a wall, some rich people riding around in Cadillacs, put some Simon and Garfunkel music behind it, and you had a film and an `A' in the class."

After school he became a television director for a UHF station in Philadelphia, working with such shows as "Bowling for Dollars," and making ends meet writing short stories and magazine articles. Then along came his twenty-seventh birthday, and a moment of truth. "I was feeling very frustrated. I'd been out of work for several months, and one day I happened to turn on the TV. There on the screen was without question the most abysmal movie I'd ever seen, and I thought, I can do better than that. I have to go to Hollywood!"

Before making the trip he churned out a couple of spec scripts—an action/detective yarn and a horror film. Armed with those scripts, his dreams, and his ninety-day deadline, he sought out the one friendly face he knew in Hollywood, a then-unemployed Barney Rosenzweig. When his friend offered to show his scripts to an agent he knew, the countdown began.

THURSDAY: de Souza drops his scripts off with the agent.

SUNDAY: de Souza responds to an ad in the newspaper looking for quiz show contestants. That evening he's called, and told to report for taping on Monday.

MONDAY: He wins a car, a color TV, and a stereo.

TUESDAY: A package arrives from the agency. Inside are the scripts, coffee-stained, wrinkled and torn. There's a note attached: "Sorry, too busy to read these right now. Dictated but not read." de Souza phones Rosenzweig, who says he knows one other guy who was a lawyer, but was just embarking on an agenting career. The man's name is Jim Berkus, and he'll read de Souza's material.

WEDNESDAY: The scripts go to Berkus.

THURSDAY: Berkus phones, raves about the scripts, wants to represent them, and offers to send them immediately to Universal's *Six Million Dollar Man*, where he feels they will serve as an excellent sample of de Souza's abilities.

FRIDAY: The scripts are delivered to Universal.

MONDAY: Berkus gets a call from Universal. They would like to buy one of the scripts, and want to know if de Souza would be interested in expanding it into a two-part episode for *Six Million Dollar Man*.

And that was it. Who says it's hard to break in to Hollywood?

Since then, Stephen E. de Souza has pumped up the adrenaline of audiences worldwide with crisp, crackling action/adventure tales that go beyond the standard cops-and-car-chase humdrum. Each tale is woven from a skillful pattern of strong story, unique characters, humor, and surprise. At no time does the juggernaut pace of such films as RUNNING MAN, 48 HOURS, and DIE HARD overshadow those basic elements of storytelling de Souza finds so important to his screenwriting success.

When DIE HARD exploded on the screen in the summer of 1988, the trade papers engaged in a battle of hyphenated superlatives in describing the action. *Daily Variety* termed it "as high-tech, rock-hard and souped-up as an action film can be." The *Hollywood Reporter* joined in, calling it "a shattering, knock-your-socks-off movie that should keep audience members bolt-upright throughout." Not everyone was as enthusiastic, though. The *New Yorker* said, "DIE HARD is a B-movie of gigantic proportions: a formula action picture, but with the extra-potency formula...it has the sweatiest hero, the most sinister bad guys (with the thickest foreign accents), the silliest plot twists, the loudest explosions, the most advanced weaponry, the stupidest law-enforcement officials, the most shameless human-interest subplot, the fattest, most Teddy-bearish black cop congratulating the white protagonist on his guts and independence. All in 70mm and bowel-rumbling Dolby sound." But whatever the critics had to say, not a single one ever used the word, "Boring."

DIE HARD was based on a novel by Roderick Thorp, and de Souza shares screenwriting credit with Jeb Stuart, another accomplished action scribe. It was de Souza, though, who was on the set when Alan Rickman, the ultra-cool sociopathic supervillian, was joking around between takes, showing off his startlingly authentic American accent. That triggered de Souza's imagination, and led to the scene he now points to as his favorite in the film.

"I instantly realized that—since McClane only knew Hans as a disembodied German voice over the walkie-talkie—there was a possibility here for some real suspense that would drive the audience crazy. On the spot I discussed this with the producer and the director, and they loved it. I wrote the scene that afternoon and it was shot the next day: a good lesson that there's always room for improvement, even *after* the eleventh hour!" That scene is presented in its original form at the end of this chapter.

It is exactly this kind of twist—this unexpected, wholly surprising turn of events that sinks the hero even deeper into the mire, while still showcasing his quick-witted talent for survival—that makes DIE HARD tower above the run-of-the-mill action picture. The basic structure of the story is not unique, pitting a violent, renegade loner against coldly-efficient, frosty-veined forces of evil. John McClane is the fly in the ointment, the unexpected wrench in the works of a perfectly oiled machine, and, of course, the underdog. This kind of formula has been used successfully time and time again, in movies like 3 DAYS OF THE CONDOR, BEVERLY HILLS COP, and even movies that are not action films, such as ONE FLEW OVER THE CUCKOO'S NEST or COOL HAND LUKE. Is the formula, then, the reason the movie works so well?

No. Audiences know a formula when they see one, and they're only willing to buy into that formula, and go beyond it into a relationship with the main character, if they are constantly surprised, delighted, scared, shocked, angered, or even confused. Emotions must be evoked, which the writer can do through the use of such tools as sharp, intelligent humor, exceptional characterization, superb plotting, subtle exposition, dynamic pacing and clever foreshadowing. One cannot depend on terrific special effects or extraordinary stuntwork to save a mediocre script. Today's viewer has pretty much seen it all, and while the actual execution of the script is of utmost importance, the time has long passed when an audience could be convinced that a weak story is good simply by adding a few spectacular explosions and screeching car chases.

The key? The character. Do we care whether he or she makes it through this mess, and overcomes seemingly insurmountable odds? Do we see a change in the character? In other words, has the character grown, thanks to this harrowing experience? And even if he or she doesn't physically survive, is there a heroic triumph of some sort? In DIE HARD, McClane rediscovers his deep love for his estranged wife, and understands more fully her desire to be a complete person with a life of her own. So, he changes, and in the process he survives—and certainly his triumph is heroic. It should be noted that physical survival is not a requisite to triumph—witness such films as THE GREAT ESCAPE—but the death of the hero must be heroic. There must at least be a spiritual triumph, although in action films at least one of the major characters usually makes it out alive. If nothing else, you have to give the audience someone to applaud—and after all, somebody has to get the girl, or boy. Especially since that's usually what they've just spent an hour-and-a-half fighting for.

Interview with Stephen E. de Souza

DIE HARD

In action films, is the action considered the most vital element, taking precedence even over characterization and story?

I don't shortchange the other elements, but I think on a certain level that may happen among the studio executives. Their main concern is often the sheer amount of action in the film. I've done a lot of work with Larry Gordon, who started as a writer and is now a producer. He has a scale, one he borrowed from A.I.P., where he used to work. It's known as the "Whammo Chart," and what it basically says is that every ten pages or so there has to be a real whammo, a real shot of action. And I think that's something they still look for, that in every ten pages, every reel or so, there should be a big action sequence.

And that's something you keep in mind during the writing phase?

Yes, I think I do. But what I try to do every time is avoid the trap so many action films fall into. There is certainly no shortage of action films that work only on the level of action every ten pages and nothing else matters. I try to include something more, something that will make the film work on a couple of levels. I try never to write "down." I want the film to work for adults and by that I mean intelligent adults. If you look at the really successful action films, ones that were not only box office successes but critically acclaimed as well, such as RAIDERS OF THE LOST ARK, TERMINATOR, even STAR WARS, you'll find they are not simple-minded. There are plenty of simple-minded actions films around that we don't have to name and they make a lot of money, but they get trashed by the critics. The "smart" action films, like 48 HOURS or LETHAL WEAPON, are not only action-packed, but contain believable, real characters we care about as well.

Another thing these films have, and something I feel is very important, is a villain who is also smart. A good villain is the key to a successful picture. People have been saying that for years in Hollywood, and yet in a lot of action pictures the villains are just legions of cardboard characters to be mowed down with Uzis.

How do you go about creating a worthy antagonist?

Since most of the traditional Hollywood heroes going back to Gary Cooper are kind of taciturn, I think you want a kind of garrulous villain. He can be kind of snide, very talkative—the classic example is the Alfred Hitchcock villain who would say, "Yes, you're going to talk about democracy and the rights of the little man, but you don't see the big picture, my friend..." I don't know whether I'd go quite that far, but the point is that you want someone who has a definite plan. And he can tell this plan to his confeder-ates, thereby letting the audience in on what's in store for the hero before the hero finds out. Along these lines, it obviously helps if you are able to cast a terrific actor as the villain. I've been lucky. In COMMANDO we had Dan O'Day, in RUNNING MAN we had Richard Dawson doing a dark, twisted version of himself, and Alan Rickman, the villain in DIE HARD is a British stage actor, and he is just phenomenal.

So you consider the antagonist to be every bit as important as the protagonist?

Absolutely. If you have a pushover for a villain, what kind of triumph is that for the hero?

So in creating your hero, do you aim for a sort of comic book invulnerability?

No, I don't think you have to have a comic book hero. Now, certainly in a film like COMMANDO the hero is larger than life...

But the little witticisms that are delivered prior to each punch or shot, the clever repartee that goes on even in the heat of action, are all very reminiscent of comic book heroes.

But that's been going on forever in film. James Bond is a prime example. Go back even further, to a picture like THE BIG SLEEP. Look at the wisecracks he makes throughout that movie. It's a long-standing American film tradition, even some of the cowboys like Errol Flynn could be fairly glib, so I don't think that necessarily makes the heroes comic book characters. COMMANDO I would definitely say *is* comic book inspired, it's Nick Fury and the Howlin' Commandos. But 48 HOURS wasn't, and DIE HARD is not. Yes, they're all the same in terms of the fact that they are heroes in action films. But comic book heroes such as the one in COMMANDO are usually unstoppable machines, while the heroes in the other two films mentioned are much more real, and more vulnerable. In those movies you have a hero who is imperfect. In the long run, I feel that's a much more interesting way to go, and pictures with that kind of hero are far more memorable. When you look at a picture like LETHAL WEAPON you see characters who are very flawed, very real. And I think that's why that picture was so successful.

So in addition to the 10-page "whammo" factor, a quality action film will feature a worthy, powerful antagonist and a vulnerable hero.

In fact, the ideal combination is an arrogant, cocky villain who is positive he has the perfect organization and the perfect plan. Against him you would pit an imperfect hero. And that kind of combination goes back as far as the Bogart pictures. Take a look at THE MALTESE FALCON and all of the hero's problems in that. His guilt over his partner's death, set against the arrogance and confidence of the Sidney Greenstreet character. It's perfect. Or look at ROBIN HOOD, certainly a bit of a comic book romp, but you look at the cocky arrogance of Basil Rathbone and Claude Rains, who of course run the kingdom, and run an army. Robin, on the other hand, has a bunch of guys in leotards.

The fact is, the audience loves to root for the underdog. And I think many current action films have gone too far in the other direction, where you leave the audience almost feeling sorry for the *villain* in some instances. Some of these heroes are absolutely invincible, with the camera creeping slowly up their biceps and pectorals the way it used to linger on Hedy Lamarr's legs. And you start feeling sorry for the poor, out-of-shape bad guy.

I've found it difficult in watching some of the films of this genre to clearly define a three-act structure. At times, it seems as if the plot kicks into high gear with an immediate conflict and action sequence, and simply continues to roar through a series of stunts until the final crescendo. Is structure approached differently in an action film?

I always use a three-act structure. I'm very conscious of where the act breaks are, getting my hero up a tree, throwing rocks at him, and getting him safely down. It's always in there.

70

However, television has influenced the motion picture industry, and I think it first became evident in the James Bond movies. In television we very often open with a "teaser," a self-contained sequence designed to pique interest in the episode. That format was standard throughout the fifties and sixties, and the Bond movies, to my knowledge, made it *de rigeur* in the motion pictures. They open with a sequence that takes your breath away, and now almost every adventure movie begins that way. I think, as a writer, you're pretty much obligated to do that, you have to open with that terrific sequence.

How long does a scene like that normally last?

Oh, roughly five minutes or so.

And that kind of opening has become an integral part of this genre?

Absolutely. If you go into a meeting at the studio, they're going to ask you, "What's the opening sequence?"

But is this scene also an integral part of the *story*?

In the James Bond movies, of course, it has nothing to do with the story at all. The sequence ends, and a guys says, "Very good, 007. Now that you've killed those poor devils here's the plot of *this* film."

I like that opening sequence to tie in somehow. I like all my loose ends to tie together at the end. So yes, for me that opening is a vital part of the story, although it may take fifteen or twenty minutes into the film to discover exactly *how* it ties in.

There is a constant debate I have with producers and studio executives, and that is, "Let's not make this movie 'dumb.'" I'm constantly having people say, "What's that joke, what's that remark mean, they won't get it." And my answer is, "Who are *they*? Who are the people who won't get it, the kids? What's wrong if some of the adults get it? Believe me, your mythical twelve-year-old simpleton is not going to leave the theater because there's a clever remark! You've got enough car chases and gun fights to keep *them* happy. (Laughter) So let's have the picture work on a couple of levels at once."

The other debate I always have with those people is over the structure of the plot. I'm the one, more than the producer, who says, "Wait a second, we've got to cover these story holes. There's no reason for the villain to tie up the hero, he'd kill the s.o.b. if he got the chance!" I'm often throwing out whole scenes that executives are happy with, saying, "I've got a problem with this draft, even if you don't."

So underneath all the car chases and gunfights, as you put it, the cornerstone must still be a strong story?

I look for a strong internal logic. It's very important that you have a plot that makes sense. A lot of times, when you analyze pictures you can't find a penny-weight of logic behind the villain's motivations. I mean, if he wanted to rob a bank, why didn't he just rob a bank, why did he have to kidnap the ambassador from Thailand's daughter, and do plastic surgery on the bank teller? Look for logical motivation, and logical sequences of events.

How detailed do you get in describing your action sequences?

I get very detailed. But you have to keep in mind that I've been a television producer for about seven or eight years now, and I've produced hundreds of hours of television, and I know what can and can't be shot. The Hollywood myth about the unshootable script goes something like this: some picture was being made about thirty years ago, and the script said, "Ext. Black Hills of Dakota. The Indians cross the ridge and attack the cavalry." That was it, Scene 122.

So the producer calls the director and says, "What are you doing, you've been there two weeks, it's only one eighth of a page!" When I write action, my experience as a producer and director tells me what can be shot, and I know that if I were to write this hypothetical sequence it would have to span six or seven pages.

If you're new to this genre it would be a good idea to obtain some scripts. You can buy them at Larry Edmunds [Ed. note: a bookstore in Hollywood and North Hollywood, specializing in books about and for TV, movies, and theater] or beg, borrow or otherwise get them any way you can. When you study some of these scripts, you'll see that a well-written action script goes into a lot of detail. You don't have to be camera-happy, but you do have to put those shots in there, and you have to realize that the camera is not some omniscient, all-seeing eye.

Take THE FRENCH CONNECTION as an example. You could not show the car under the subway, and the interior of the subway itself in one shot. That's going to be two different shots.

So you include basic camera directions in your scripts?

Yes. Be aware of what direction you're shooting the action from, whether you're inside or outside, and be sure to break it up. The first thing that's going to make someone reject an action screenplay is if they come across things that simply cannot be shot.

Does budget enter into consideration when deciding on action sequences?

Sure. If you're making a domestic comedy, or some type of hospital drama, it's not automatically an expensive picture. On the other hand, as soon as you start describing an action picture you have to exert some kind of control at the typewriter. Even if you know it's going to be a twenty million dollar movie, you still have to exercise control.

73

I'm in a situation now where I am often writing a
movie as part of a project that's already underway,
and a budget is basically in place. So, I don't have to
be as budget-conscious as I would if I were trying to
sell the script as a spec effort. On the other hand, I
know that the money that will be spent has to be
spent "smart"—you want to spend the money on two
or three big scenes, and the rest of the picture has to
show some restraint. And many of the little tricks are
the kinds of things you learn from producing.

Such as?

Well, it's cheaper to have bullets hit windows than
walls. That's because windows can just be replaced
with a new glass pane, whereas they have to go in
and patch and repaint bullet holes in walls. Those
kinds of little things add up.

**Does the prose in your action description read pretty
much the way a novel might?**

Yes, mine does. Some people do a very terse, tele-
graph style of action description. A script by Walter
Hill might read something like, "Int. Hotel Room—
Day." Then it says, "Sleazy." One word, that's the
entire description you get. But he's probably going to
direct the picture, so he knows what he's going to do.

However, in my case I realize that the first audience I
have to win over are the people who are going to read
the script. So I really try to make it a good read. In
fact, I get so compulsive I'll even manipulate my
prose to have a tense moment happen right at the
page break: "He opens the closet and out falls..." turn
the page. I actually contrive to have page-turners.

**Along the lines of keeping your reader in mind as you
write, do you break up the action descriptions into
bite-sized chunks, for easy scanning?**

I vary it. There's an old stunt that was demonstrated
to me many years ago by a good friend of mine, a

very accomplished producer named Frank Telford. When you pick up a script—and you look like a horrible Philistine when you do this—you pick it up and look at the number of pages, and say right off whether it's too long, too short, or just right. And the writer is dying, thinking what a cretin you are. But then you take it a step further, by flipping through the script backwards, and *upside down*. And you look at the margins, noting whether it's talky, stage, or a good mix. In a good screenplay that margin is going to be a good mix of dialogue margins and action margins. And it should vary back and forth—a stretch of three or four pages of dialogue with a couple snappy scenes, three or four pages of action only, or an equal mix of each. It's like a tennis game. A good tennis game will have some volleys, some fast and furious rallies, some slow shots, some aces, some lobs, but not all of one.

In fact, I will go so far as to say that you can pick up a script that's written in French, and even if you don't know French you can flip through it and say, "This movie moves," or "This movie is going to lay there." Writers should try looking at their own scripts this way. Another good test is to take your finished script and read only the stage directions, skipping the dialogue. How does the "moving" part of this movie strike you? Next, read only the dialogue. How does the sound track come across?

Are there any specific guidelines regarding dialogue in an action picture?

As I mentioned before, I don't think American heroes should talk too much. Go back as far as the movies in the '30s and you'll find heroes like Bogart, people who only say as much as is necessary, and let their actions speak for them. There are exceptions of course; Burt Reynolds, the Bond movies...but usually heroes are men or women of few words, and I think that's a good trait to emulate.

Also, everybody is always looking for those kind of pithy, deadpan remarks that will live on after you leave the theater. You know, "Make my day," "I stick my neck out for no one," those kinds of lines. I've gone into meetings at studios where five minutes is spent discussing the plot of the picture, and twenty minutes looking for that line that they hope and pray will catch on.

The line they'll put up on the billboard.

Exactly. And in at least one case I can think of the line is decided upon even before the picture is written! Stallone's movie, COBRA, had a line that went, "You're the disease and I'm the cure." They did that before they wrote the script.

Did you consciously try to come up with a catch-phrase in your movies?

Well, we have some snappy ones in DIE HARD, but I don't think they work as well out of context. From my experience, the lines of dialogue that really make audiences scream and yell are not necessarily going to work around the coffee table the next day. If it works in the scene, that's my main concern, I don't care if it works on the t-shirt.

Didn't COMMANDO have one?

"Let's party." That caught on. The other one was, "Remember I said I'd kill you last? I lied."

I remember seeing the "Let's party" line used in a fabulous episode of "Amazing Stories."

Right, the two kids quoted it just before they went out to terrorize their baby-sitter. I was thrilled to see that it had entered the vernacular.

I should caution writers not to let this catch-phrase business be an overriding concern in writing the script. Make each line work in the scene, that's the main thing, and that should be good enough. I've seen some movies with obvious, wholly inappropriate tag lines that stick out like a sore thumb, just have nothing whatsoever to do with what's going on in the story. That's no way to write dialogue.

How about some guidelines in terms of scene length, and pacing?

If you have a scene longer than three pages, it better be a damned good scene. Movies nowadays are paced much faster than they were years ago, primarily because audiences are in tune with the language and grammar of motion pictures.

When movies first began, and I'm referring to the very first single-reel silent films, they would show a train pulling into a station, and people would literally run out of the theatre in terror thinking the train was about to hit them. When Robert Flaherty went up to Alaska and filmed NANOOK OF THE NORTH, he showed the dailies to the Eskimos. It took the Eskimos two evenings to understand the concept of pictures that told a story. When close-ups were first used, people were completely disoriented. And action scenes had to really be spelled out. For example, if we were in a 30s movie right now, just the two of us talking, I'd say, "Kerry, let's continue this interview in Rome." And we'd cut to you going to an airport, and me going to a dock. They we'd cut to an airplane, and a boat. Then we'd cut to Rome, and a title would come up that said, "Rome" and then "Italy," so you wouldn't be confused. Then you'd see both of us arriving at a table and sitting down again. Nowadays, of course, I'd say, "See you in Rome," we'd cut to a close-up of a Cinzano ashtray, pull back and there we are in Rome.

Because the audience is so educated, movies all move at a much faster pace. Not just action pictures, but all pictures. But it's especially crucial in an action picture, and if you have a scene longer than three pages, you can bet you'd better be able to justify it because somebody is going to ask you about it. Of course, if you absolutely feel that they *need* to be longer, by all means do it.

Another point about pacing, with regards to plot versus subplot. I think that you can only get away from your main story, your central plotline, for one scene at a time, maybe two at the maximum. Any more, and your pace will sag, and your audience will become confused. Now, if that's your intention because your next scene is a shocking revelation that's designed to catch everyone by surprise, that's different. But if you don't have that as your intention, then don't leave your main plot for more than two scenes at a time.

Story Outline

DIE HARD

ACT I

JOHN MCCLANE white knuckles his seat as he flies into Los Angeles on an airliner. It's the Christmas season, he's a cop, and he's carrying a gun under his civilian clothes.

At a swank executive Christmas party in an LA high-rise (Nakatomi Plaza), a MR. TAKAGI gives his underlings a pep talk. A sleaze named HARRY is hitting on a pretty businesswoman—HOLLY MCCLANE—who blows him off and calls home to see if her husband has made it back from the airport. She doesn't have much faith in his arriving, but she asks her housekeeper to make up the spare room just in case.

At the airport John meets ARGYLE, his limo driver. They chat as they drive through LA, and we learn that John lives in New York. He had decided not to follow his wife to California as she pursued her career, because he didn't think she would make it.

When they arrive at Nakatomi Plaza, Argyle parks in the underground garage so John will have a ride in case he strikes out with his wife.

Inside the lobby, John uses a computer directory to find his wife's office. He discovers that she's going by her maiden name now. He takes the elevator to the thirtieth floor, the party, and his (maybe) wife.

At the ritzy party, John searches the party for Holly. He meets her boss, Takagi, and they catch the sleazebag, Harry, snorting coke on Holly's desk. Finally she arrives, and they have a nearly awkward reunion.

John and Holly get reacquainted in the bathroom as he washes up. She offers him the spare bedroom, and he accepts. But they end up arguing, and she storms back out to the party.

On ground level, a large truck pulls up in front of the Nakatomi building. Two gunmen shoot their way into the lobby and one of them goes to work on the computer that controls the alarms and elevators.

Meanwhile, a whole platoon of dark-suited terrorists with ominous-looking metal briefcases disperse throughout the corridors. Two of the men take out the phone system, while downstairs the computer whiz seals the building off from the inside.

From the executive washroom, John calls Argyle on his limo phone. But the line goes dead...

...And a squad of terrorists storms the Christmas party, machine guns blazing. The place breaks into a panic as John watches from the washroom, then escapes into a stairwell while the terrorists clear the offices.

John finds refuge above the thirtieth floor, in a part of the building still under construction. With his gun drawn, he's nervous and alone...for now.

Act II

Head terrorist, HANS GRUEBER, singles out Takagi and takes him upstairs as John slips through the building.

John ends up in the same office as Hans and Takagi. It turns out that Hans isn't a terrorist after all, but a high stakes burglar after $600 million worth of loot in the corporate vault downstairs. He wants the safe's computer code from Takagi, but the executive refuses, and Hans guns him down in cold blood. John witnesses the brutal murder, (although he can't see Hans) and Hans' henchmen launch their pursuit of him.

Down in the parking garage, Argyle is partying in the well-appointed limousine, oblivious to the situation upstairs, which includes gunmen rigging the roof with explosives.

The computer whiz goes to work trying to crack the vault's security codes.

John borders on panic as he hides upstairs, then pulls a fire alarm. He goes from euphoria to despair as the fire trucks approach, then are called off when Hans dials 911 and claims a false alarm.

But there's no time to get uptight—there's a terrorist hot on John's trail. He plays cat and mouse with the gunman, then takes him out.

The computer whiz breaks his first access code as John rifles the dead man's tool pack, then puts a Santa hat on the corpse and sends it down with a jeering note to Hans and his gang. John hides atop the elevator and gathers information on the terrorists' strength and positions as they talk.

Now Hans and the gang know John is in the building, and they know he means business.

John crawls out of the elevator shaft and checks out another hiding place, while a hulking terrorist with long blond hair goes crazy over the death of his brother—the corpse with the Santa hat. Holly watches the tantrum and knows that John is causing the trouble. To add to that, coke-sniffing Harry sounds like he's going to be a real problem.

On the roof of the Nakatomi Plaza, John uses a walkie-talkie he lifted from the dead terrorist to call for help. The police think he's a crank, but at that very moment a handful of gunmen are heading upstairs, ready to blow John away.

Down the street a few blocks, a cop (AL POWELL) is loading up on Twinkies when he gets a call to check out the Nakatomi building. He looks up at the high-rise from the parking lot of the convenience store. He can't see or hear the gun battle blazing away on the roof.

John puts up a helluva a fight with his stolen machine gun, and leads the terrorists back into the bowels of the building. But he's running out of options...he *barely* makes his escape down another elevator shaft.

But now he's trapped in an air duct, with the blond terrorist hot on his tail. Again, he barely escapes with his life.

As John crawls out of the air duct and looks down into the parking lot, Al arrives on the scene. The cop doesn't see anything out of the ordinary, but goes in for a quick look anyway. The impostor guard shows him around, and everything seems to be in order.

But tell it to John, who thirty-four stories up is in the middle of a shootout with two more gunmen. After a hellacious firefight, John kills them both.

Just as Al is backing his car away and calling in a false alarm, John sends a corpse flying down into the police cruiser's windshield. Al freaks out and calls for reinforcements as he spins out of control down an embankment, in a flurry of squished Twinkies.

Reinforcements arrive—every cop in LA must be there! But Hans is cool as a cucumber—cops are part of his plan. John, however, is not part of his plan, and Hans angrily dispatches another search and destroy mission.

John taunts Hans over the radio while digging through a bag of explosives he lifted from one of his latest casualties.

In a TV newsroom, a REPORTER argues with his boss for a chance to cover the Nakatomi situation.

Hans discovers that some detonators are missing and gets in touch with his computer guy—who has three out of seven vault security systems accessed.

John gives Al all the information he can over the radio, as Hans listens in, still ice cool.

The SWAT team arrives downstairs, along with DUANE ROBINSON, a bonehead cop in charge of the operation. Al briefs him, while a TV crew sets up and the terrorists tune in.

Holly demands bathroom privileges for the hostages, and Hans grants them.

Down in the limo, Argyle comes out of his party mode with a jerk as he watches the TV news report covering the hostage situation outside.

The cops take their positions and prepare to go in, against the frantic advice of John and Al.

Hans and his team brace for an attack as a police reconnaissance team approaches the building.

Argyle tries to find a way out of the parking garage,

but he's trapped.

The recon team gets shot to hell by the coldly casual assassins, who are guided by the computer wizard and his monitoring equipment.

Then the SWAT team sends in an armored car, which the terrorists promptly blow to smithereens with a pair of rockets.

John sends his own batch of explosives down an elevator shaft, setting off a series of explosions that rocks the entire building, much to the delight of the news crew, who gets it all on film.

Al tells John over the radio that he got two more bad guys with the explosives. Then Duane Robinson grabs the radio and tells John to cool it. John blows him off and says he wants to talk to a real cop. Robinson angrily hands the radio back to Al, who wishes John luck.

Inside the building, Harry slimes his way into Hans' headquarters, and offers to deliver John to him.

Al and John pass time on the radio, talking of their personal lives, and getting to know each other. They're interrupted by Hans, who, thanks to Harry, now knows all about John. The TV crews are listening in, and they scramble to find relatives for an interview.

Then Harry gets on the radio and tries to talk John into surrendering. Hans gives Harry a bullet in the forehead for his macho efforts.

Hans *finally* loses his cool, screams at John, demanding he give him the detonators he stole from one of the dead terrorists, and threatens to kill hostages until he gets what he wants.

Robinson and Al argue over John's fate, and Hans finally speaks to the police. He makes bogus demands for the release of political prisoners around the world—a ploy to buy time.

The computer whiz has been working like a madman, and he only has one security system left to penetrate, but it's a tough one.

As Al and John grow closer over the radio, the media analyze hostage psychosis and the FBI relieves Robinson of his command at the crisis site.

Hans goes looking for John himself, and finds him.

But Hans is separated from his gun, and, under the watchful muzzle of John's machine gun, thinks very quickly indeed and pretends to be just another hostage. In a psychological game of cat and mouse, John gets Hans to reveal who he really is, but the machine-gunning cavalry comes to Hans' rescue.

Another lead-filled inferno chases John through the building, but he manages to bring down two more gunmen before he is cornered in a computer room. One of the survivors shoots out all the windows in the room, sending billions of shards of splintered glass down around John, whose bare feet are sliced to hamburger as he makes his escape from the room under fire.

Hans gets the detonators back.

The TV crew gets Holly's home address, and the blond killer throws a temper tantrum, telling Holly that her husband is still alive and making life miserable for the terrorists.

Over the radio, Al and John talk about Al's past. John is hiding in a restroom, bleeding.

Hans and his evil crew watch and wait as the FBI cuts power to the building...which turns out to be a bonus for the bad guys.

When mainframe power switches to generator power, the safe finally opens. Hans floats inside in a nearly religious euphoria, and as his henchmen loot the vault's treasures, the FBI coordinates a helicopter strike on the building.

All alone and bleeding badly from his feet, John uses the radio to make what he believes is a final request—he asks Al to apologize to Holly on his behalf. Then he realizes that something might be wrong on the roof, and goes to check it out.

Act III

At Holly's home, the TV news crew intimidates its way into the house for an interview with her children.

Up on the Nakatomi building, John discovers that the whole roof is wired with explosives. But before he can alert Al, the blond killer finds him. As helicopter gunships bear down on the building, John is caught in yet another blinding firefight.

Hans sees Holly's kids on TV and makes the connection between her and John. He takes her as a personal hostage and orders the rest of the employees up to the roof. John continues his battle royale, while the robbers load the loot into a truck.

The truck is loaded. Meanwhile, John literally hangs his maniacal opponent out to dry, while the hostages are herded out to the helipad on the roof.

Federal agents scream ever closer to the building as John bursts out onto the helipad, takes out another terrorist, and sends the hostages scurrying back downstairs. He fires a few shots to wave off the choppers, but they mistake him for one of the killers and open fire.

As the roof explodes around him and annihilates the choppers, without a second to spare John grabs a fire hose and swings off of the roof, crashes through a window into an office several floors below. He then makes his way downstairs, through explosion after explosion, searching for Holly.

Down in the parking garage, Argyle spots the terrorists as they finish loading their truck. And John spots Holly, being slapped around by Hans and his cronies.

Argyle rams the getaway van with his limousine and takes out a bad guy of his own. And John confronts Hans, who holds a gun to Holly's head.

John prevails in a tense psychological duel, and the mortally wounded Hans makes one last grab for Holly's life. But he can't hang on, and falls to his death in the street below. John pulls Holly to safety and into his arms.

In the wreckage outside the building, John and Al recognize each other without having to say a word. When John introduces Holly to him, she uses her married name.

And just as Robinson saunters up to try and play the tough cop one last time, the blond killer, or what is left of him, bursts outside and levels his machine gun at the crowd. But before he can fire, Al empties his revolver into the gunman and finishes him off.

Argyle finally busts out of the parking garage unharmed, and the TV news crew tries for an interview with John and Holly. Holly decks the reporter.

Argyle drives John and Holly away. They are kissing in the back seat of the limo. It looks like John might not have to stay in the spare bedroom after all...

DIE HARD

THE MECHANICAL FLOOR-TIGHT ON HANS

He checks the plastique, not pleased. He turns, DROPS
to the floor.

LOW ANGLE

He lands, knees bent... looks directly at a PAIR OF
BARE FEET. A GUN BARREL DROPS INTO THE SHOT close to
his head.

> MCCLANE
> Lost?

NEW ANGLE
A moment. And then Hans turns, looks up.

The transformation in his expression and bearing are
mind-boggling. Hands shaking, eyes filled with fear,
he swallows, looks up at McClane and in a <u>perfect
American accent says</u>

> HANS
> —ohGodplease—don'tkillme—don't
> kill me—you're one of them, I
> know it—

                    MCCLANE
               (thrown, unsure)
          Whoa, whoa, easy man. I won't
          hurt you. Who are you? What
          are you looking for?

Hans' eyes dart towards—

THE BUTTRESS TEN FEET AWAY

Where a tiny piece of his Mac-10 sticks out, barely
visible.

BACK TO SCENE

                    HANS
          A way up to the roof... I
          thought I could signal for
          help—

He starts in that direction.

                    MCCLANE
          Forget it. They got a guy up
          there. You want to stay alive,
          keep moving. Hey? You hear me?

Hans realizes this tack won't work. He follows
McClane.

                    HANS
          You... you're an American?

                    MCCLANE
          Only if Brooklyn counts.
               (as they exit)
          You work for Nakatomi, huh?

AROUND THE CORNER

McClane and Hans walk together. Hans is still a
"nervous wreck."
                    HANS
               (nodding)
          There was a party—celebration—
          all of a sudden they were there—
          shooting—God, they... they...just
          slaughtered Mr. Tagaki—

CLOSER

McClane looks at this poor civilian, on the edge of
going to pieces. He puts his hand on his shoulder.

> MCCLANE
> Relax, man... you smoke?

Hans nods, still "frightened." McClane takes out his
spoils of war, the Marlboros. Two left. He sighs,
takes one, offers the other one with an expression
like a little boy forced to share a cookie. McClane
takes out a lighter, does his and Hans'. Hans is
shaking so badly McClane has to hold his watch hand
for him. Hans nods, grateful... then peers at McClane.

> HANS
> You... you don't work for
> Nakatomi...And if you're not
> one of them...

> MCCLANE
> I'm a cop from New York.

> HANS
> (puzzled)
> New York?

> MCCLANE
> (explaining)
> They invited me to the Christ-
> mas party. Who knew?

Hans' eyes take in his bare feet.

> MCCLANE
> Better than being caught with
> your pants down, right?
> (extending his hand)
> John McClane.

> HANS
> (shaking hands)
> William Clay.
> (smiling)
> Call me Billy.

McClane nods, friendly-like, and his eyes glance casually over at—

THE WALL—ROSTER OF EMPLOYEES ON THIS FLOOR

In alphabetical order. CAMERA MOVES OVER the "c's": CAMPBELL, S.; CLAY, WM.; CRAWFORD, L... PANS BACK TO CLAY.

BACK TO SCENE

> MCCLANE
> Billy, you know how to use a handgun?

> HANS
> (hesitant)
> One weekend I went to a combat ranch...
> (apologetic)
> You know, that game with the, the guns that shoot red paint? Must sound pretty silly to you...

> MCCLANE
> Sounds better than nothing.

McClane takes out his Baretta, pops out the magazine, jams in a fresh one and hands it to him.

> MCCLANE
> Time for the real thing.

Top Secrets:
MARY AGNES DONOGHUE

Mary Agnes Donoghue

PARADISE

WHEN SHE WAS 16 YEARS OLD and just out of high school, Mary Agnes Donoghue landed a job as a secretary at a company which manufactured turbine engines. She didn't last long; caught drawing pictures of Mickey Mouse on her desk, she was fired. She couldn't appreciate the irony of the situation for some 30 years... when she would find herself writing three movies for Walt Disney Pictures, and making her directorial debut on one of them.

PARADISE was Donoghue's eleventh screenplay to be optioned; out of twelve screenplays written, that's not a bad record. She began writing as a child in Queens, New York, and laughs as she remembers the Gothic novel she turned out when she was ten years old, complete with a governess, a Victorian-style house on a hill, and storms swirling around. Although she always loved to write, Donoghue didn't consider it a legitimate occupation. "The thought of taking it seriously, or of being taken seriously, was alarming, unnerving." Nonetheless she started publishing poetry in her twenties, and by thirty had sold her first screenplay. That's when she decided to start writing full-time. She hasn't looked back since.

PARADISE, which Donoghue both wrote and directed, was her third script for the studio (BEACHES was released in 1988; DECEIVED opened concurrently with

93

PARADISE in the Fall of 1991). A coming-of-age pastoral drama, PARADISE focuses on ten-year-old Willard (played by Elijah Wood) who is sent to live in the country during the final months of his mother's pregnancy. His caretaker is Lily Reed (Melanie Griffith), his mother's longtime friend. A warm, sad-eyed woman, she is dealing with her own personal tragedy, one which has driven a wedge between her and her husband Ben (Griffith's real-life husband Don Johnson). As both Ben and Lily separately take Willard to their hearts, the boy tries to effect a reconciliation between them.

Donoghue's greatest achievement in PARADISE— as both writer and director—is that, despite the rather predictable plot, the film still manages to be emotionally satisfying. Equally impressively, she accomplishes this while assiduously avoiding any hint of sentimentality or manipulation. Her direct, yet low-key approach keeps any cloying or maudlin moments at bay, especially in the scenes between Willard and his 9-year-old tomboy neighbor, Billie (Thora Birch). Billie is as spunky as Willard is shy, as fearless as he is insecure. Their friendship lies at the core of the film as surely as does the relationship between Ben and Lily.

Drawn to stories with a strong emotional content, Donoghue tends toward character-driven pieces in which plot grows out of character. With the exception of the thriller DECEIVED, in which plot predominates, relationships motivate and form the foundation of her stories. The "voluntary" bonds of friendship hold a special fascination for her because they're not, in her words, "compelled by passion" the way romance is. Like all relationships they come with their own set of rules and regulations. In PARADISE the children's friendship grows naturally and believably through shared pranks, adventures, and poignant conversations.

Although PARADISE was adapted from the 1987 French film LE GRAND CHEMIN, Donoghue insists it is not a simple remake. To begin with, disparate French and American sensibilities required a different emphasis and approach. PARADISE is very much a story about people overcoming a tragedy; although the couple in LE GRAND CHEMIN had also lost a child, the story focused more on the bickering and fighting between two unhappily married people. Donoghue considers the French version grittier, but also more whimsical (it has more of a "city boy comes to the country" feel), whereas her script offers a more dramatic base and tackles more emotional issues: overcoming fears, the process of friendship, coming to terms with loss and grief. PARADISE proves far more emotionally involving than its predecessor.

The directing job on PARADISE was not one she had planned for; actually, her goal was to be able to direct the project she had slated to follow PARADISE. However, when Disney chairman Jeffrey Katzenberg called and asked if she was interested in the assignment, she jumped at the opportunity. Not only did this afford Donoghue the chance to exercise every writer's dream— control over her own work— it simultaneously elevated her to a still-rare position in Hollywood: that of a successful female screenwriter and director.

Interview with Mary Agnes Donoghue

PARADISE

What was the genesis of PARADISE?

Actually it's based on a French film called LE GRAND CHEMIN, which Disney had the rights to. I owed them a screenplay so we met and talked about it. I liked the French movie very much, but the minute it became American it changed totally.

How did you go about adapting it?

I watched the movie maybe two or three times and then went off and wrote my script. I didn't follow the structure of it; my version is quite different.

When I adapted BEACHES, I used very little from the book—I'm sure the novelist would like to kill me, but it's true. Prior to BEACHES I'd written a play about a friendship between two women. It's a subject I'd wanted to deal with for a long time, which is why I adapted BEACHES, but I went about it my own way.

Once you've looked at or read the source material, what's the next step?

It depends, I suppose, on the source material. If you have something wonderful to start with then you'd want to stick closer to it. I never understood why

BONFIRE OF THE VANITIES turned out so badly. It's a fabulous book. You could read it, go to sleep, and in the morning find a way to link together what you remembered—and end up with a great script. You wouldn't need to do anything. I didn't feel that BEACHES was a good book, so I didn't feel uncomfortable about changing it for the film.

LE GRAND CHEMIN was set in the 50s in a provincial village in France, and the characters were peasants, little changed from their ancestors, who had been working the same land for hundreds of years. There's no such thing in American life. I realized I just had to leave it behind and do something different. And, oddly enough, the French people who came to see PARADISE ended up really liking it because it was totally different; it wasn't an attempt to create something that didn't exist in American life or a debasement of French life. I tried to make it true.

When you're writing your own original material, what's the period of germination?

Sometimes a long time. It can be a year, or a couple of years. I never go at anything directly. I never work from outlines. Suddenly I'll have an idea for a scene or situation, and it keeps haunting me. I keep going back, hunting for a way in. It's almost like trying to find a little door, and it's always through the characters. What I usually do is create the premise, the two main characters through their relationship to each other, the end. Then it starts coming to life in my head over a period of months—I'll hear snatches of conversations or confrontations. It has to come from that. I can't plan something from the outside, it has to come from the inside.

Is there a point, then, at which these internal dialogues reach a critical mass?

Definitely. I think I'm a very lazy person, so I need

something to get me going. Once I can imagine these characters existing, behaving a certain way, it excites me and I can start making my contribution. I give them a form, I give them a structure to move through, but it always comes out of the characters coming to life. It's almost as if I didn't do it, as if I'm watching snatches of a movie and I get so interested that I want to find out what happens. The only way to do that is to write it.

That sounds somewhat similar to the way an actor might create a role.

Actors go at their characters differently, but it's essentially the same process. I create characters through the way they come up against each other—it's the dynamic between them that brings them to life—whereas for an actor I think it's a matter of isolating a character completely alone in the world to understand who he is.

Do many of these scenes end up in the final script—is this a process of building the movie in your mind?

Yes, most of them are very key scenes, and the dialogue is complete. Nothing has come before and nothing is coming after, yet the scenes are quite developed and frequently reveal the story to me. The things the characters are saying to each other are critical, it's not just chit-chat.

Roughly how much of the movie needs to exist in your mind before you start writing?

Quite a bit. I'm starting to write a new one now, an original. It takes shape in a seemingly haphazard way, but by the time I start, I pretty much know all three acts, what the act breaks are, I have a lot of scenes, a lot of dialogue, and actually the basic moves of the script are already established. I usually know the end, too, but depending on how it goes, I might change it.

When these scenes occur to you, do you jot them down or make notes as you go along?

Some of it I write down, some of the dialogue is really specific and I don't want to lose it, but most of it I keep in my head. By the time I finish a script, I know it completely.

To what degree are these scenes already in the settings you end up using?

They're in a setting. The one I'm doing now is set in New York, it's a sophisticated setting. There's street life, you can use people bumping into each other.

That wouldn't work in Los Angeles unless their cars crashed.

That's right, you can avoid anyone in Los Angeles.

One reason I was asking about settings is that I'm interested in how writers use the visual qualities of film. For you, is that intuitive, or something you work on?

It's definitely something I work on. That aspect of it is more thought out. You have to think of how to keep something interesting visually, especially the kinds of things I write, which are character-driven. You could end up with two people just sitting in chairs talking to each other. And no matter how interesting the conversation, that's going to get tedious. You have to move, you have to use the place they're in. I always want a sense of movement in my scripts, but it has to be central to the development of the characters, not some arbitrary bit of business to keep things active.

Let's talk about the description of the action. In his book, *Adventures in the Screen Trade,* **William Goldman says that initially you have to create a reading script—one that reads well, that keeps the reader riveted. Yet a lot of film writers create very sparse stage directions. Where do you fall on that continuum?**

I don't write sparse stage directions, and I don't think you should. If you want to see what you imagine on the screen, you'd better be as clear as you can about what it is you see, or it's not going to appear. [Novelist] Graham Greene writes description of place brilliantly. In one paragraph, you can see and even smell the street he's describing. It's precise and so complete. That's what screenwriters should do.

Maybe the script is not going to be published, but it must communicate visually, and to do that you must write well. I think screenplays should be as well written as books, and that requires finding a very swift and telling way to describe what you imagine.

I was talking at a film school class, and one of the students said, "Oh, our instructors said not to put in any stage directions, not to describe the clothes people are wearing—"... But that describes who these people are: how they dress, where they live, what's in their house, whether or not they drink coffee. All those elements are critical to character. The setting of a scene is as much a part of the story as the things the characters are saying and doing.

I'm not suggesting, by the way, that writers put in every camera angle. But you had better put in the ones that establish pace and mood or you end up with nothing. Maybe there are some types of films in which none of this matters. Action films, in which the hero is going to come in and—

Kill people.

That's right. [Laughter] Spray the room with bullets.

Getting back to the process of writing your script, since it's fairly complete in your mind, does the actual writing then go quickly?

Not really. A first draft usually takes me four months, but my first drafts are fairly complete. You could shoot it—it may not be what you want to shoot, but you could. It's not 150 pages long and chaotic.

During that four months, what's your writing process like? Do you set goals for yourself?

Pages. I have to do at least three pages a day. I don't wait for inspiration or I'd never finish the screenplay. I work sort of like a bank clerk. I go to work at eleven o'clock, I finish at six or seven, every day. Those are my hours. But that's time actually spent at the computer. The rest of the time you never stop thinking about it, which can be intensely irritating to the people around you. But I'm not one of those maniacs who work solidly for 48 hours, driven by wild inspiration. One reason is, the more I write, the more critical I am of my own writing.

So you do a lot of back-tracking and changing as you go along?

Oh yes. I can't go forward until I think it's right. If you're writing something that's character-driven, you're not dragging your characters through some big sprawling plot. The characters are the plot. If what they say to each other isn't right, if what they think and feel and do is wrong, you're going to end up nowhere.

In the course of rewriting, how do you get over the problem of being too close to it to be objective? Is that a problem for you?

Not so much. The whole time I'm writing it, I'm being critical. Of course there are things I don't see. But I have met very few people who give me good notes. Those are the people I want to talk to, because they understand what's missing. In studio notes, the problems are usually found, but not defined, so in trying to sound knowledgeable they say all these authoritative but completely wrong things that make you furious.

That's not to say there aren't people at the studio who understand writing, but notes are composed by committees, and in the process the one good note is buried under thirty terrible notes. It can be fairly grueling to deal with.

When you've finished a first draft, do you put it aside for a while?

Not very long, usually for a few weeks. I tend to stay with something completely until it's out of my hands, one way or another. In terms of what I do in the course of rewriting, I do exactly what I do in a first draft: tell the story and follow my instincts. If I'm bored when I read a scene, I know something is wrong. You can tell when you're bored, when there's something wrong, when you've tried to cover up a big hole with tricky writing. You know when you're doing it initially and you really know it when you get to the second draft. Inevitably, it means that something is wrong structurally; you can't cover that up with dialogue or amusing little scenes. If the structure is right, you can think of a million ways to write the scene. If it's wrong, you can't think of anything.

It's a parallel to a situation in comedy writing, which is that if a punch line isn't working, it may not be the punch line that's wrong, it may be what leads up to it.

Yes, I had a play on in London, in which the first scene just didn't work. For the entire run of the play I couldn't figure out what was wrong. Then just before the end of the run I finally realized that each character was doing what the other one should be doing—if I flipped it, it was exactly right. The minute I realized that, it opened everything up. The odd thing is that the version that didn't play well, read well.

I wish there was a handy formula that you could apply to writing. It would make it so easy. Unfortunately, it's hard. One of the hardest things is learning to recognize and consciously understand your creative instincts. If you're a writer, you have to be guided by instinct. Even when it tells you to do a massive rewrite.

You've touched on the importance of having characters who are real both to the writer and the reader. What other hallmarks of good writing come to mind?

Well, I believe suspense is very important. If you are telling a joke, you don't give the punch line first and then tell the joke. I think that's what a lot of people do when they're writing drama. Maybe it's because so many writers are in therapy. A dreary examination of one's psyche in a deadly, well-meaning, earnest way is not interesting in a film, it's not drama. You have to be led into something, you have to be surprised. Keep them expecting, keep them wanting to know what's going to happen.

I've already mentioned structure. To me, structure is everything, and to get that right you have to think clearly. It has to come out of the nature of the thing itself; you don't impose structure, you find it. If you try to jam things into a structure, it turns into a formula. It's tedious, and it doesn't work.

I think it was Rodin who was asked how he could sculpt such wonderful statues out of blocks of marble, and he said, "I just chip away all the bits that aren't the statue."

He's right on the nose! [Laughter]. That's the structure. I think that's true in every single thing you write, which is why it's always so frightening each time you sit down. Each time you start over again, you know nothing. You just know how to get out of the messes quicker, how to recognize when you're in trouble.

Has the experience of directing influenced the way you write?

Yes, it was a great thing to work with actors. I discovered a great process. Once a first draft is finished, it's quite wonderful to read it through strictly from the point of view of one character. It could be a secondary character, but you read it as though that character is the star of the movie, and not there just to serve the others. You can then fine-tune in a quite amazing way. To me this was a great revelation.

Also, directing certainly has made me think more visually. I'm trying to think of some wonderful, purely visual way into the film I'm writing now. I started out writing prose and have never been to film school, so I've come at it from a different angle, and directing certainly has opened up the process for me.

A lot of writers end up directing, or wanting to, out of self-defense, to try to protect their work. But you also have strict principles about re-writing other people's work, do you not?

I won't do it. I've had it done to me, and I wouldn't do it to anyone else. I had recent discussions with some studio executives who said, well, what if we have a wonderful story from someone who can't write it, who would be grateful to have an experienced writer do it? That might be different. And I don't feel bad about adapting a book, going from one medium to another, but I think it's a terrible thing to rewrite someone else's work. Perfectly good scripts are slaughtered and people do it purely for the money. There's no other reason. It's a total waste of your time as an artist. I've never heard anybody say, "I did this rewrite out of love or passion for the material, I really wanted to make it better than the original writer did."

Life is short, and you might as well concentrate on your own work, rather than fall into the rewrite abyss. I don't have children; I suppose if I had a family to support I might have a different attitude, but I doubt it.

Even though there are only one or two names on the final writing credits, many films go through four, five, six rewrites with as many different writers. Why is there such a frenzy of rewriting?

I think a lot of it has to do with directors having to make their mark. They have to take the script over in some way, and the most obvious way is to have it rewritten, which completely eliminates the original writer as a player in the process. Half of the rewrites that happen are as a result of that. It's all about power, it's not about art. As is this business of directors having a possessory credit. Very few of them wrote the script, cast it, or put the project together. Many of them are just hired hands who come in at the end of the day and suddenly the entire film is their vision. Ludicrous.

Isn't that part of a larger phenomenon? Not only is the original writer forgotten, but market research is used to make a movie into what an audience thinks it wants. They do test screenings, and if the audience doesn't like the ending, they slap on a different one.

That's right. Originally, FATAL ATTRACTION had a brilliant ending—she commits suicide and makes it look like he murdered her. That's an incredible act of revenge. But the audiences didn't like it.

Those previews can be useful, too. There was a piece missing in PARADISE. I suspected it, but the previews made it clear. Melanie Griffith's character literally vanished from the third act, so her move to reconcile with her husband at the end was anticlimactic. You could feel the energy go out of the audience as well. When you lose them, there's usually a good reason. I wrote and shot a new scene on a sound stage, and it changed the whole last part of the movie. It's surprising how things can work on the page and even when you're shooting, and then when it's on the screen it's not right.

Previews can be useful, but as a way of helping you to make the film be what you want it to be, not so the audience can impose its own tastes on the film.

Going back to the notion of having principles in this business—doesn't it require being enough in demand that people will hire you on your conditions?

Exactly, but if you wait until you're in demand to have your own conditions, you'll never be in demand. Sometimes you just have to be out of work. I'm in a nice spot right now where I can pretty much do what I want to do, which is great. I did work hard and stuck to my guns to get there, and it may not last, but I'm also not that greedy. I have what I want, which is not to be the highest paid writer in Hollywood, but to have the kind of creative freedom I have now. If I can make $15 million movies that bring in $25 million or $30 million, then I'll be able to keep on making movies that interest me.

PARADISE

ACT I

The bell rings at an elementary school, and kids pour down the school steps. WILLARD YOUNG, a ten-year-old boy, bumps into another boy, both dropping their books. Willard asks the boy where he's going for the summer. The boy answers, "To my house in Colorado." When asked the same question, Willard answers, "Africa."

Willard exits the school bus and walks down the road. In passing through the lower-class, decaying urban neighborhood, Willard is jeered at by some local boys, and is eventually chased to his apartment, where he's barely able to slam the entry door in their face and escape.

Willard enters his apartment. His mother is on the phone in her room. He looks into the room; she sees him, and closes the door without acknowledging him. She is not having a happy conversation. Willard sits in a chair.

In a bus station, Willard is with his mother, ROSE-MARY, who we can now see is in the late stages of pregnancy. As they walk across, Willard notes that his friend's mom just had a baby, and she didn't send *him* away. Willard's mom reassures him that he's not being sent away, it's just a "vacation." They both board the bus.

The bus tools along through the city, out into the countryside. Willard and Rosemary eat bag lunches.

It's dark out, and both travelers are asleep on the bus as it continues to course along the highways.

Sunrise out the bus window, and Willard awakens to watch the world go by. The monotony puts him right back to sleep.

A little later, Rosemary nudges Willard awake, telling him that they've arrived in Paradise.

The bus pulls away, leaving Rosemary and Willard by the side of a dusty road in the tiny town of Paradise. They begin walking—Rosemary knows the way. They talk about the town. Willard is obviously not impressed.

Inside a diner, a waitress talks with BEN REED, telling him that she knows she's very attractive to men (Ben rolls his eyes) and she wants to get married, but she doesn't know to whom. She notes that it's tough raising two fatherless daughters on her salary, not that she regrets having them, even if they are just the result of physical attraction.

Willard enters the diner, asking directions of Ben. Ben wonders aloud why Willard wants to go to the street he's asking about, but gives the boy directions. Willard says he's going to see some people named Reed. Ben remarks that he knows those people, but doesn't like them much anymore. He used to, but he feels they've changed for the worse. Willard leaves, looking apprehensive.

Willard and Rosemary arrive at the Reeds', where they're greeted by LILY REED. Rosemary introduces her to Willard as, "My oldest friend."

In the kitchen, Willard is introduced to farm life as a chicken is neatly beheaded for dinner.

As they prepare dinner, Rosemary and Lily reminisce about old times, and how they wish they lived closer to each other.

Willard takes a walk down a dirt road, just shooting some time until dinner. In a tree above the road sits BILLIE, a nine-year-old girl. She introduces herself by asking if he has ever seen a dead body. After some give-and-take, she informs him that nothing fun ever happens around this town. He breezily states that he's from the big city, where people get killed all the time.

Billie insults Willard with a remark about his height, and after a brief spat attempts to make up to him by inviting him to the diner where her mom works, where they can get some free sodas. He turns her down, so she ups the stakes by offering to treat him to a view of her sister DARLENE with her top off. He takes her up on that.

Out on the Reed's porch, Lily and Rosemary talk about Willard's father. Rosemary suspects he's having an affair. But she hasn't told Willard; as far as he knows, his father's away on sea duty. Rosemary thanks Lily for taking care of Willard, and remarks on how much she envies her this peaceful life.

From a treetop, Billie and Willard catch a great view of Darlene doing her ironing sans clothing.

At the bus stop, Willard and Lily wave to the departing Rosemary. Willard is upset, but tries not to show it.

Later, at the house, Willard and Lily form their first tentative connection, when she teaches him how to shell peas. They talk briefly about Willard's school, but Willard isn't opening up. Then, when Lily opens a cabinet while fetching a basket, Willard spots a large model airplane, the kind you can fly by remote control. Lily quickly takes the plane from him and replaces it in the cabinet, this time on a top shelf. She explains that her husband Ben made the plane, and she doesn't think he'd like Willard to play with it.

Willard retreats outside to pick berries, which is where he is when Ben rolls up. This is the first time we see that Ben is the gruff, cynical man Willard had spoken to in the diner. Ben tells Willard not to worry about that, though, because he's not around very often.

Lily and Ben share a tense conversation about Willard. Lily's back is to Ben as he talks, and he blows up, asking her to at least look at him when he talks, at least acknowledge him. He also avers that he will not concern himself with entertaining Willard, and she assures him that she doesn't expect him to. Ben storms angrily out of the house.

ACT II

That evening, Willard finds himself stuck in the bathroom. The door won't budge, no matter what he does. He's pulling with all his might when Ben opens the door, sending Willard tumbling back. Ben asks Willard if he has everything he needs. Willard says, "I guess." Ben presses him for a more definitive answer, but Willard isn't very responsive. Willard goes upstairs to bed.

It's late at night in the Reeds' bedroom, and Lily arises, having trouble sleeping. She finally leaves the room, and we see that Ben has actually been lying awake the whole time.

Lily goes into the attic, where she finds an old box. Inside the box is a pair of child's boots, and a small jacket. She smells them deeply, and squeezes the jacket the way you'd hug a child.

Daytime, and Billie and Willard walk through the woods. They talk about their fathers, with Billie noting that she really doesn't know her Dad. Her father isn't Darlene's father; hers works at a roller skating rink, Darlene's does something else. Willard says he doesn't see his Dad much either, because he's a radio operator on a Navy ship. He notes that his Dad has been gone an especially long time this time, and Billie asks him, "What makes you think he's coming back?" Willard explains that he always does, and Billie accepts that.

The two hijack a small rowboat, and continue their conversation about their fathers. Billie relates a dream she has, where she goes to a roller-skating rink and sees her father. He doesn't recognize her, of course, since they've never met, but in her dream she does some amazing tricks, and he immediately knows that she's his daughter. Billie is interrupted when the boat's owner comes into view.

The two children climb a tall observation tower, the kind rangers used to use to spot forest fires. When they get to the top, Billie walks along the outside railing, an incredibly dangerous stunt. Willard is stunned, and when she invites him to try, he'll have no part of it.

The two chat some more on the tower, this time

about popularity. Willard assures her that he was the most popular kid on his block. Billie admits that she has no close friends, because people think she's a showoff. She says that if he's bored they could go to the mall, but Willard says he's not bored, and together they look out at nature's beauty spread below them, and Billie rests her arm across Willard's shoulder.

Inside a small church, a minister suggests that all in attendance reach out and take the hand of their neighbor, in a show of unity and friendship. In one of the pews sits Lily, Ben, and Willard. Their hands are all in their laps.

Leaving the church, Ben launches into a scathing attack on the church, calling it a room full of hypocrites and demonstrating his point by listing the shortcomings and failings of many of the folks in attendance. He can't believe she buys into all this. She says that going to church gives her a measure of comfort, and he replies that there's more to life than being comforted. Like living.

It's dead and quiet at the Reeds', and that's what Ben hates about Sundays. He snaps at Willard, and Willard finally asks, "Why do you always make things so hard?"

Later in the day, there's an unspoken battle for supremacy between Lily and her sewing machine and Ben and the televised baseball game. Willard witnesses it all. Ben wins, and Lily leaves. By now, Willard has headphones on, and Ben asks him what he's listening to. They chat briefly about music, then baseball (which Willard doesn't play), and Willard mentions he'd seen the model airplane Ben had made.

The two are outside, flying the airplane. Ben hands the controls over to Willard, and tells him that the airplane is now his.

Ben comes into the house, and there's a brief moment when we see the depth of his feelings for Lily. He reaches out to her, but she reflexively jerks away— then apologizes. He leaves.

Using live night-crawlers for ammo, Billie and Willard stage a bomb run on some old women at a funeral service. After chasing off the mourners, Billie and Willard have a chat about ghosts and her mother's new boyfriend.

Sally prepares herself and her kids to go to the show, where the boyfriend can get them all in for free.

Willard spends an introspective moment in the tree over the cemetery. He sees Lily place flowers over one of the graves. Willard checks the headstone after Lily leaves, and reads the name of a little boy, James Benjamin, who was just over three years old when he died.

Lily gives Willard a letter from his Dad. Willard wonders why every letter from his father is missing an envelope. He's starting to suspect something is not quite right about his Dad. Willard and Lily seem to be forging a nice friendship.

Ben decides to take Willard to work with him on the shrimp boat. Lily is a bit apprehensive.

Willard watches as Ben prepares the boat for a fishing run.

Lots of seafaring action, as the shrimpers haul in their daily catch and Willard watches with great interest, and ends up diving right in to help, elbow deep in shrimp. At one point, he earns a pat on the back from Ben.

At the end of the trip, Willard holds Ben's hand, and thanks him for taking him on the boat. Ben apologizes for his rough manner. They're getting along much better now.

Lily is there to meet the boys when they dock the boat. She was obviously worried, and feeling protective about Willard. She wants to take him to a coffee shop; at the suggestion, Ben pushes off on his own.

In the diner, Lily and Willard have a chat about the female anatomy, and specific parts thereof. It's the kind of conversation you might expect a boy to have with his mother, or someone else he feels close to.

Lily helps a completely exhausted Willard get into bed. She's starting to become quite attached.

In the church, Lily sleeps through the service.

Ben and Willard go fishing. Ben remarks that the last time he'd been to this spot was with Lily— and they didn't come to go fishing. He and Willard share a man-to-man laugh.

Ben reminisces about Lily, a girl who was unafraid, bold, full of life. Willard asks him about James. Ben explains that the boy died an accidental death when he was three. And then cuts the conversation short.

The two fish together. Ben looks down at Willard, but you get the feeling he's thinking about another boy, a son he might have had but lost.

Sally and Lily talk about Sally's new boyfriend, who is okay in spite of chronic bad breath. Sally's decided that since this guy really doesn't turn her on, he must be the right one. They're interrupted when Willard comes in after a triumphant day of fishing.

There's a chink in the protective armor of both Lily and Ben, when she admits to having slept through the sermon, and he offers to clean the fish for her. Willard tells Lily, "Ben thinks you're beautiful."

Billie and Willard spy on Darlene as she has sex with her boyfriend. They're spotted, and they take off laughing.

Billie and Willard discuss "the curse," and Billie claims Willard as her best friend.

Willard and Billie frolic in a water hole. They talk a bit about how Willard is something of an outcast at home, and he claims her as his best friend.

Willard looks through a photo album, talking about the past with Lily. He asks her, "Don't you love Ben anymore?"

Willard's relationship with Ben is growing, as they share a conversation about history. Lily is happy to see it.

A mass swim-in at the water hole, with Willard, Ben, Lily, and Sally are there, all having fun. Ben talks with Lily, but only briefly.

That night, Lily talks with Ben about the loveliness of the evening. It looks like something's about to happen, but after a promising start, she pulls away, crying. He's angry, frustrated, and confused.

Ben slugs down a couple of shots of whiskey at the local tavern, toasting "The ice queen."

It's apparent later that night that Ben had more than a couple shots, as he runs his truck right into the side of his barn.

115

An argument develops between Ben and Lily. He wants to finally get everything out in the open, and she can't. He drags her up into the attic, where he grabs a hunk of lumber and starts destroying all the baby's furniture. She begs him to stop, but he can't, he's enraged, screaming, "You're not the only one who lost a child, Lily!" He grabs her, shakes her, and begins tearing at her clothing, sexually attacking her. She submits passively. He stops, stunned at his behavior. That's when Lily admits that she heard the baby cry, just once, and ignored it. When she went in to wake the child, he was dead. She blames herself, and can't get that cry out of her head. All she can do is be sorry, every moment of every day. She can't stand to feel, and can't stand to be touched. Ben realizes he can't help her, and decides he must leave her.

Morning, and Billie is all dressed up for something special. Willard is there to meet her at her house.

The two kids get on a bus headed out of town.

They head for a large roller-skating rink. Outside is a picture of the roller-skating champion. Billie asks Willard if she looks like the man in the picture.

Billie introduces herself to the man she thinks is her father, a surly, cigaret-smoking jerk who chases her off the ring when he learns she isn't booked for a class. She tells him he's her dad, and he responds by skating away.

At the diner, Sally sees Billie return, and knows right away what happened. Billie cries, as Sally comforts her.

Willard visits with Ben, who is living on his boat. Willard confesses to missing Ben. They play poker, and talk about Willard's dad. Ben says that he misses Willard, too.

That night, Willard looks at pictures of his family, while downstairs, Lily taps disconsolately on the piano keys.

The next morning, Willard and Lily talk about how she misses Ben. He can't understand why she doesn't just ask him to come back. She says she's afraid to.

Billie investigates some strange music coming from a house way out in the woods, and meets an elderly woman who is an artist. She's the owner of the boat Billie always swipes. They part as friends.

It's a birthday party for Sally, and we meet her new boyfriend, a well-meaning geek with bad breath who announces their plans for marriage. At this, Billie explodes, and takes off.

After the party breaks up, Willard and Billie talk about the boyfriend. It sparks a fight, in which Billie points out that Willard's father has probably left for good.

Willard tears up all the letters from his father.

Act III

Lily looks for Willard. She finds the letters all torn up. She sets out to find him.

Lily goes for Ben to help find Willard.

Together, they search for the boy.

After checking the hospitals and driving around town, the two are back at the house. Sally shows up. Ben decides to continue looking, and goes out into the darkness with a flashlight.

Sally and Lily talk about Sally's impending marriage— which may not ever happen, as Sally has second thoughts.

Billie searches the woods for Willard. Ben searches for both of them.

It's morning, and Lily and Sally are asleep in the living room. Ben is behind them, staring out the window.

Billie wakes up from her nighttime perch in a tree to the sound of the buzz of a model airplane.

Billie alerts the adults, and leads them to Willard.

Willard is on the outside edge of the observation tower the kids had played on earlier. Ben is climbing up, trying to calm him. In defiance of his fear, Willard stands, and teeters on the railing that runs around the structure. He walks around the entire outside of the tower, and when he finishes, shouts, "I did it!" The sudden movement causes him to lose his balance, but Ben grabs him in a bear hug.

Billie has fainted.

Later, Willard calls his Mom, and asks for the truth about his father.

Willard gets into bed and cuddles with Lily. They talk about his dad, and his walk on the railing, and Willard explains that he had just gotten sick of always being afraid. He did something that had always scared him, and now he wasn't afraid of it anymore. Lily listens carefully.

Willard and Billie say their goodbyes. They're still best friends.

Ben and Lily say goodbye to Willard.

Ben gives Lily a ride back to the house. She asks him in, he says no. But it's raining, so he walks her to the door, and they embrace— hesitantly at first, then passionately.

PARADISE

INT. UPSTAIRS HALLWAY-ANGLE FROM TOP OF STAIRS-
NIGHT
As Lily quickly turns and goes into the house,
Willard scampers up the stairs and moves to the side
of the bannister nearest his door. He crouches down
and watches them from around the newel post.

                    BEN
                 (loud, hard)
            Don't walk away, Lily! It's
            bad manners to walk away when
            someone asks you a question!

She turns to look at him as he comes in the back
door after her.
                    LILY
              (calm, controlled)
            Leave this until the morning,
            Ben. I don't want Willard to
            hear us.

As she starts up the stairs Ben comes after her and
Willard quickly darts into his room, leaving the
door open a crack.

> BEN
> (savage)
> But I don't want to leave it
> until the morning, I want to
> settle it now. I've left all
> of this for more than two
> years and I can't leave it a
> single minute longer.

INT. WILLARD'S ROOM - NIGHT
Through his partially opened door and beyond his
crouched figure we can see them in the hall. Just
as Lily reaches their bedroom door and starts to
open it Ben comes up behind her and grabs her by
the wrist. She spins around on him, frightened.

> LILY
> (harsh)
> What are you doing?   Get away
> from me!

As she struggles against him he drags her past
Willard's room to the little attic door and yanks
it open.

> LILY
> Stop it!   You're hurting my
> arm!

Without a word he starts pulling her up the stairs.

INT. ATTIC - NIGHT
Shafts of silvery light filter in through dusty
windows. Still gripping her wrist, Ben reaches the
top of the stairs, lets her go, then CAMERA
FOLLOWING quickly walks to where the child's
furniture and boxes are kept, grabbing a stray piece
of lumber as he goes. As he starts smashing the
furniture to bits with the lumber she rushes over
to him, with a cry of pain and outrage, and tries
to stop him.

LILY
(crying, frantic)
Stop it! Stop it! Please
stop it!

He throws down the wood and grabs her by the
shoulders, out of his mind with anger and pain.

BEN
(raging)
You're not the only one who
lost a child, Lily! I did too
and that pain will stay with
me for the rest of my life,
but Jimmy's dead and you can't
bring him back by turning this
house into a grave! He's dead
and I'm alive and I won't
pretend to be dead anymore
just to keep you company!

He suddenly pulls her to him and kisses her
violently. As he releases her slightly she looks
at him with cold contempt.

LILY
Get your hands off me!

Pure hatred fills his eyes.

BEN
Why should I? I'm your husband, aren't I? Doesn't that
give me some rights? Wouldn't
the Reverend Close agree?

He suddenly pushes her against the wall, then as
he begins to make love to her as an act of violence,
ripping savagely at her nightgown, she becomes
completely passive, simply enduring his brutality.
In the middle of it, he suddenly stops and looks
at her, then shoves her from him and turns away,

horrified and shaken.

                    BEN (cont'd)
                    (tortured)
          My God, what am I doing...?
          How did I get to be this
          person...?

She stays very still for a moment, her face blank,
then she slowly pulls her torn nightgown around her
and looks at him.

                    LILY
               (soft, flat)
          I heard him cry.

Pause. He slowly turns to look at her, not
comprehending what she is saying.

                    BEN
          What...?

                    LILY
          In his crib. I heard him cry
          and I didn't go. I never told
          you. I never told anyone.

He stares at her, his body absolutely still with
shock.

                    LILY (cont'd)
          I was sewing and I heard him
          cry. Just once. I waited, but
          he didn't make another sound
          so I went on sewing and when I
          went in to get him from his
          nap he was dead.
                    (looking away,
                     soft, amazed)
          It was such a small thing...
          just a piece of candy hidden
          under his pillow...

> LILY (cont'd)
> (pause, she looks
> at him, shattered)
> If I'd gone he wouldn't have
> choked. If I'd gone when he
> cried he wouldn't be dead.

He stares at her, then leans against the wall and
begins to cry softly. She stares at him, numb.

> LILY (cont'd)
> (soft)
> I can't stand to be touched. I
> can't stand to feel anything.
> All I can stand is to be numb
> inside and to be sorry, every
> minute of every waking hour,
> because when I'm not I hear
> his cry. Over and over and
> over.

He finally turns to look at her.

> BEN
> No one can answer every cry,
> Lily. It's not your fault.
> It's still just a terrible
> accident.

She stares at him, then shrugs helplessly.

> LILY
> It doesn't matter what it is.
> An hour doesn't pass when I
> don't hear his cry inside my
> head.

They stand frozen, then Ben looks back out the
window.

                    BEN
              (soft, tortured)
          I can't help you, can I...?

                     LILY
               (shaking head)
               No.
Pause.

                    BEN
          I also can't go on living like
          this, Lily.
               (pause, defeated)
          I'm leaving.

They stare at each other, then she finally looks
away.

                    LILY
                 (dully)
          I guess it's time.

He looks back out the window.

                    BEN
                 (lost)
          Yeah. I guess it is.

She turns and silently goes back down the stairs.

_____

Top Secrets:
NICHOLAS KAZAN

Nicholas Kazan

REVERSAL OF FORTUNE

O THER THAN SUNSET BOULEVARD (in which William Holden narrates the story despite floating face-down, dead, in Gloria Swanson's swimming pool), REVERSAL OF FORTUNE must be the only major film whose voice-over narrator isn't conscious. That's only one of the unusual aspects of a script that won its author, Nicholas Kazan, Golden Globe, Academy Award, and Writer's Guild Award nominations.

Kazan's hereditary credentials are impeccable: his father, Elia Kazan, was a noted stage and film writer and director whose best-remembered film probably is ON THE WATERFRONT. The famous name didn't help the younger Kazan break in: "Quite the reverse was true," he says. In fact, as is true of many of the writers profiled in this book, Nicholas Kazan's original writing goals were in another field, in this case journalism. He served as a stringer for *Newsweek* and now considers that he wasn't a particularly outstanding news writer.

Kazan's transition to film writing came when he was one of ten writers recruited to pen the sequel to the under-ground comedy hit GROOVE TUBE. That set him on the course of comedy writing, and he wrote a number of spec scripts, none of which sold. However, it was a spec comedy/horror script (later rewritten and produced with his name removed) that brought him to the attention of the producers of FRANCES, who hired him to do the screenplay. The success of that script set him down a new path: writing films based on real people, including Patricia Hearst and, in REVERSAL OF FORTUNE, Claus and Sunny Von Bulow, based on a book by Claus' attorney, Alan Dershowitz.

The challenges that Kazan faced in adapting the book were numerous and formidable. For one thing, none of the protagonists were particularly likable. Claus may be witty in a ghoulish way, but he definitely wouldn't win any Mr. Congeniality awards. Sunny is in a coma at the time of the action, but what we see of her in the flashbacks suggests she was a deeply troubled and difficult woman. Dershowitz is the best nominee for a likable character, but even with him one gets more than a whiff of arrogance and self-centeredness.

Secondly, the legalities involved were complex—the case portrayed is the appeal, not the original trial, yet in order to understand the appeal the audience has to understand all of the issues raised previously. If this had been a television film merely "inspired by" or "based on" a true case, a writer could have played around with the facts in order to create a neater dramatic reality, but this was a case well known to the public and based on a successful book, whose author was looking over Kazan's shoulder. Undoubtedly lawyers representing the principals were hovering just out of sight as well, ready to send down a hail of writs. Under these circumstances, fudging the facts would have been dangerous even if Kazan had wanted to do it. Finally, possibly the biggest drawback in conventional movie terms is that there's no clear-cut answer to the mystery of how Sunny really died. The outcome of the case is that Claus Von Bulow is innocent, but the audience is left with more questions than are answered: was he guilty but freed because of a lack of evidence? If he didn't take action to bring about her death, did he abet it through his inaction? Lacking even that, from a moral standpoint how responsible was he for the psychological disintegration of Sunny?

Up against these problems, Kazan did what Kierkegaard characterized as the hallmark of the man devoted to freedom: instead of wasting time fighting reality, he extols reality. The reality was that this was a complex case featuring complex people, and the best way to deal with that was to fashion a complex film.

When there is a complicated story to tell, the unskilled writer will assume that he or she has little time to devote to characterization. The skilled writer, however, will understand that fully-realized, fascinating characters are the best tools for guiding an audience through the complexities of the story. Accordingly, Kazan takes the personality of Claus Von Bulow and Alan Dershowitz as his focal points. Outwardly very different, certainly in terms of their class origins, both are arrogant and vain. The interaction as well as the parallel action of these two unlikely allies leads us through the thicket of exposition necessary if we are to understand the case. It also makes important points about the system of justice we enjoy: that it is about the enduring principles of the law, not about personalities, and that its results are based not on doubts but only on what can be proved beyond a reasonable doubt.

Absent is Sunny, the victim. But although she was physically removed from the case, she was the center of every allegation and every denial. Again, embracing this reality, Kazan took the bold step of having her be present after all, via a voice-over that anchors the story. Speaking from her permanent coma, she brings us back after each flight into alternative possibilities.

Kazan takes the curse off the ambiguity of the ending as well, by giving the audience as much information as anybody else (other than Claus and Sunny) has and saying, in effect, "go home and make up your own minds...and if you can't, consider about how difficult it is to serve the black-and-white demands of justice in a world that is made up of myriad shades of gray." As David Denby pointed out in his *New York* magazine review, "The movie is great because it uses an ambiguous case to explore the ambiguities of personality and character, and because it suggests that mysteries, if richly enough developed, can be more satisfying than certainties."

Certainly Kazan was well-served by all the actors and the director. Jeremy Irons received the most attention for his smiling-skull portrayal of Claus, but Glenn Close deserves equal credit for, in a relatively short period of on-screen time, portraying the disintegration of Sunny. Ron Silver, as Dershowitz, makes his character one whom you have to admire at the same time you think he's probably a bit of a jerk. Director Barbet Schroeder's degree in philosophy from the Sorbonne was good preparation for helming this film; undoubtedly ambiguity and the moral corruption of the upper classes so scathingly portrayed in the film were hot topics of student discussion. At the same time, Kazan and Schroeder don't load the deck. The passion of Dershowitz and his disciples ultimately comes off almost as disembodied as Claus Von Bulow's outlook: for everyone in this film, life seems to be about principles, ideas, or status more than it is about flesh and blood.

All these are notions seldom explored in popular American films. The writer or film-maker who aspires to take them on in his or her work will find much to learn from in REVERSAL OF FORTUNE.

Interview with Nicholas Kazan

REVERSAL OF FORTUNE

One of the problems that you had to deal with when writing REVERSAL OF FORTUNE was that most of the audience coming to the movie knew the outcome already, since it's based on a true story. How do you make a movie like that compelling?

The most difficult thing for me about that movie was that this case was about an *appeal*. Most "legal" movies are about trials. And there is something inherently dramatic about a trial. You end up in a courtroom with a verdict, and that's very exciting. It's like the judgment of God, and it has a natural dramatic quality.

But REVERSAL is about an appeal. Now, a real appeal is approximately the length of a script. It's about a hundred pages, and it's submitted to judges and then the lawyers get up and they each have a half-an-hour to talk in front of the judges. *Months* later a decision is announced, again on paper. Not dramatic at all.

An appeal is also based on a case that has already been decided. That is, there's been a trial, the defendant has been convicted, and an appeal attempts to show that the person was unfairly convicted. Well, I had a terrible problem because I knew that of the people who saw the film, many would know a great deal about the

131

case, and many of them would know nothing or next to nothing.

Somehow or other, I had to summarize the case at the beginning of the film, which seemed like an impossible task, because the people familiar with the case would be bored by what I said, and yet if I didn't provide sufficient information, the people who knew nothing about the case wouldn't understand the film.

And then I realized there was one perspective that no one had, and that was Sunny's.

You feel that brings the audience closer, makes a more compelling story, because they're getting someone's viewpoint they hadn't gotten before?

As I say, I was sort of forced to use it in the beginning. Then I found as I was writing the script it provided additional benefits.

Normally in a film about a murder, or an attempted murder case, you quickly lose sight of the victim and of the reality of that person's demise. In this case we're talking about someone who's not physically dead, but she is mentally. For all intents and purposes, Sunny Von Bulow is dead. And by cutting back to her comatose body, it was a way of emotionally reinforcing the stakes in the film. And then, of course, in the end it enabled me to be like Houdini to escape the film in a somewhat satisfying way.

Even though the ending is morally ambiguous and the audience feels a little ambivalent about it, they can leave feeling that whichever side they believe in, they are right.

Yes, exactly. And part of what was exciting about the case was that people aren't sure. By not saying he's guilty or innocent, I sustained the mystery of the case.

In effect what you have is a murder mystery that isn't solved, and may even raise more questions by the end

of the story than it settles. Yet there is a sense of closure and satisfaction there.

Many people told me that by the end of the film they didn't care whether he was innocent or guilty. They cared when they went in but they didn't care at the end, which to me was a very gratifying comment.

The way that I solved the problem that you asked me before is, I thought it was kind of a juggling act. Once I had laid out the case against Von Bulow, I started throwing balls up in the air. What about this? What about that? And the idea was to create many little mysteries. This film obviously does not have a so-called conventional three-act structure, to the extent that such a thing can be said to exist.

In a sense, you have three different movies going on. Sunny telling her story from the coma; Claus dealing with his appeal; and Dershowitz and his team gathering the facts and getting their case together. It almost seems like all three stories were adversarial to each other, because they were fighting for screen-time, and also fighting for your attention and emotional involvement.

That's right. Drama is essentially about secrets. In the classic Greek drama, the secret was that Oedipus had killed his father and slept with his mother and he didn't know it. And you get the sense of this secret. In any film or any play, when you have the sense that there's something you don't know, or the characters don't know, you want to find out—and you want to see the characters find out—what those things are.

In REVERSAL, I tried to have as many secrets as I could. Little pieces: you wanted to know what happened to parts of the medical case. You wanted to know why this person said that. You wanted to know who Claus was. You wanted to know how the relationship between Dershowitz and Von Bulow would work out.

In the place of conventional structure, which I think is mostly bullshit, I had these other mysteries because I think it's *that* which really excites people. The human desire to know. That's what sustains a film.

Assuming that Dersh is your main character... what difficulties did you find in working with a character who is a real person?

Dershowitz is a real person. He's a person I admire. But I was in kind of a double bind. An interesting character has flaws. Basically, in the most simplistic terms, you want every character to learn something. During the making of the film, we were joking around and I said that Hollywood is sustained on the illusion that human beings are capable of change. Because in all these story classes you are taught that every character *has* to change.

In reality, as one of my shrinks said, human beings come off the rack. You can do a little nipping and tucking here and there, but more or less they are who they are. In a film, a character is supposed to undergo a profound change. And, if not a profound change, at least a slight change. Claus does not change, but, by the end, Dershowitz has clearly undergone something, and that's good.

Coming back to flaws, what's supposed to happen in film is a character has a flaw and then over the course of the film, he grows and he more or less doesn't have that flaw in the end. In any case, a character is more interesting if he's flawed. The boy or girl who is a goody-goody at school, and the teacher's pet who gets straight "A's" is not very interesting to anyone. Whereas, the guy who cracks up a car is certainly the subject of great conversation. And, is much more likely to have a film made about him.

I was caught in this double bind, as I mentioned, because if I gave Dershowitz flaws which he did not really have, then he would be outraged and say, "You know I'm not like that at all." And, if I gave him faults which he DID have, then he would still be outraged and say, "I'm not like THAT at all." No one wants to be seen for their real flaws, and you certainly don't want to have someone make up flaws about you. He is not perfect in the film, but it was hard to give him the minor flaws that I did.

Let's talk for a moment about the original spark, the first time you are struck by a story idea. You have the idea— now, what is the process from there?

I write notes until I am ready to start writing the script. In those notes I write about the characters. I don't write where they go to school and all this other stuff that a lot of people do. Because when you dream, you don't know where characters come from and where they're going. I don't have to know what Dershowitz does when he leaves that apartment for the last time in the film. It's not important.

Going back to process: what I do is write notes, lines of dialogue, scenes. In one case I wrote the last scene of a film before I even got the job.

You knew where and how the film was going to end before you started writing it. Is that typically what you do?

No. Whatever I get excited by, I write. I just write notes, and I write a kind of rough outline. I don't use cards and all that other stuff. I do write notes about scenes, but I always change it as I'm going, because rhythm is every-thing and there's no way to judge rhythm until you string scenes together, fully written.

Do you have to know everything that a character would do under any given circumstance, or do you like to be surprised when you're writing?

I'm a big believer in surprises. I write until I can't write notes anymore, until I'm just going crazy with the sense that I don't want to write notes anymore, I've got to write the script. That initial stage might last as little as 10 days or as long as 5 months. And then, I do a first pass (draft) in 10 days. I know people who write scripts in nine months, and I believe you're a different person at the end of nine months. I don't know how you can keep a coherent view of life, a coherent mood.

I write, obviously, very quickly, often very badly. Then I take a few days off and then do another pass, which takes about 10 days. Then I take a few days off, and then I do ANOTHER pass in 10 days. By the end of that 36-day period, I have a draft which is hopefully good enough to start showing to my friends. Then I adjust it according to their comments. Now, I might also show it to the people I'll be working with (producers, directors) and depending upon how much I trust them, I'll involve them somewhere in that process or only at the end.

Hopefully, when I hand the script to the producer they'll have comments too, and I'll make further revisions. I mean, I've worked with producers that will just accept the script, and then I've worked with producers that force me to do more. It's great to be forced to do more. I believe that it's the work you do at the end, the last five percent, that matters the most.

It's easy to start a script strong, it's finishing that's difficult.

It's just that at a certain point you're burned out, your vision is blurred, you don't see how to improve it anymore. Then someone says, "You know, if you cut out the first 20 pages and begin here," or "These characters are wonderful but you haven't paid any attention to this character..." And you say, "Of course!"

I often find that I have to go back and enrich. I have to go back and improve one particular character. Or rethink the character. I wrote a script once where I had a character who was a Haitian taxi driver, and he was a very enthusiastic character. I wrote the character and I really liked him, but then I realized that I could improve the character: I didn't change a line of his dialogue and I left in all the exclamation points, but I changed his affect, so instead of being enthusiastic when he was saying these lines, he was very downbeat. He was almost like a piece of jazz music. He was someone who had an air of mystery about him, he was almost four-dimensional, not just three-dimensional.

You've written with partners and by yourself. What are the advantages and disadvantages, and which do you prefer?

The fun of writing with other people is that you form a kind of joint unconscious. Instead of coming out of your conscious, the work comes out of both of you. You see the way you blend together and you begin to write things that you would never find on your own. And when you're stuck, sometimes the other person can get you unstuck, so it's wonderful.

The disadvantage is that it's not as personal and rewarding. When I write something that comes from me, I am all the characters, and when I put all those people together, I have some strange version of myself. Whereas, when you write with someone else, you have the way you interact with them, but it's less personally fulfilling.

You're very prolific. Do you ever get writer's block?

I think you only have writer's block if you stop, so I never stop. If you take a six-month vacation and you come back, you're going to have writer's block. I think writing is a process, and if you keep the process going, you simply can't get blocked.

The most exciting time of that process is when I'm very hot, and I'll write 10, 20 pages in a single morning burst. And then I'll walk to buy lunch. Then I'll walk back, and on the way back I'll try to think of what I wrote and I just can't remember. I have no idea. And I'll come back to my office and read what I wrote and say, "Wow. Where did that come from?"

When you're really going well, you unleash your unconscious, and there's this exciting and incredibly liberating feeling.

Would you go back and rewrite past scripts any differently?

If I were to go back and rewrite an old story, I don't think I would be able to do it any better than I did then. I think that the most important thing is to just keep doing it. I've written a lot of scripts and most of them have not been produced. But you learn by writing, and by watching movies. Of course, it is an enormous help to have things produced, because you learn how and where you can rely on an actor, and what kinds of things you can and can't give an actor.

On FRANCES I had one actress who was wonderful, and I had a speech that was perhaps 8 lines long that took perhaps a minute-and-a-quarter for her to deliver, because she invested so many varied emotions in it. I thought, "My God, I'd better really watch it and not give characters very long speeches. And if I do I'd better note in the script that the lines are to be spoken quickly." I'm a writer and a person with a really fast metabolism, and I often write characters that speak quickly and energetically with a flow and rush of ideas. If those things are performed in a careful, measured dramatic way, it would seem endless, and the rhythm of the film would be thrown off.

Do you write with specific actors in mind?

I like to write a character. You write a character, and an actor will come in who IS the character.

Like Jeremy Irons was chillingly dead-on as Claus?

Yes, and as Glenn Close was fabulous. Ron Silver was wonderful. Those three were all fabulous. There's really no need to write for a particular person or actor because somewhere out there, there's an actor who will become the person you create. And when that chemical process happens, it's completely exhilarating.

To touch on the business end of scriptwriting a moment—do you feel that the trend of mega-buck scripts will spell the demise of independent filmmaking?

Independent films will always be made. I think it's wonderful that scripts sell for a lot of money. Until a year or so ago, the films were being entrusted primarily to film school directors, and everyone was enamored with the auteur theory. People were only concerned with how beautiful a film looked. And they found that action films last summer didn't do quite as well...

They rediscovered storytelling?

Yes, exactly. They rediscovered storytelling. I mean, DRIVING MISS DAISY is a wonderful story, certainly one of the best films of last year. Another was MY LEFT FOOT. A wonderful story, and it was an independent film. People are rediscovering that it's a lot easier to make a good film from a good script. You can fuck up a good script, but it's a lot harder than with a bad script. AT CLOSE RANGE, which I regarded as badly done, well, many people love the film. They compliment me on it. Now, if as much damage had been done to a *bad* script, you wouldn't be able to watch the movie.

It's great that writers are getting paid good money. It's a sign of respect. In all frankness, on REVERSAL, they replaced the first director because he didn't want to shoot my script.

Now I have two scripts which are shooting, both of which I rewrote: both of which don't have the original director. In one case the original director loved the script, but the more he got into it the more he didn't understand it, and so he bowed out.

The other case, the director wanted the script rewritten and the studio said, "No." In both of those cases the studio backed the story. It wasn't me, or my reputation. It was just that they felt they had a good script, and they knew if they made that script, they'd stand a chance of making a good commercial film.

Is there anything you can suggest to our readers about improving their writing?

Well, it's very helpful to have actors read your stuff. I used to be very involved with a playwright's workshop and it was very helpful. The most helpful thing, as I've said, is to keep doing it. The hardest thing is to listen to criticism. Criticism is *always* destructive. It's destructive to the creative spirit.

In a certain sense we're all crazy. The screenplay is a revelation of exactly how crazy we are. If you can't eliminate the manifestations of your own idiosyncrasies and your own craziness, then your screenplay won't be appreciated by other people. You have to smooth out your flaws. For instance, if you're a person who compulsively makes a certain kind of wisecrack, your friends may like that, but you can't have *all* your characters making wisecracks all the way through every script. You can have *one* character in any given film doing that. Maybe two if they're both in a certain kind of world, like the newspaper world, where that might be appropriate.

What else does it take?

You must be aware of your limitations and able to change them. Besides that you need two things: talent and stamina. I don't know any writer who hasn't had an enormous amount of shit dumped on their heads—any number of times. The hardest lesson that I've learned is to be patient and sympathetic to other people. The executives doing their job are trying to deal with ten projects every day in great detail, maybe more. They barely have time to read the reader's report and make a quick analysis, so they often make suggestions off the top of their heads. The suggestions usually come from a good place, but in my opinion, are usually wrong.

Criticism is symptomatic. Just like a patient comes in and tells the doctor his arm hurts. The doctor does a little more investigating and finds out the person is actually on the verge of a heart attack. What the studio executive would say is, "You need to get your arm massaged."

The criticism is a symptom. Yes, there's something wrong, but don't always take the suggested cure. Get a second opinion and diagnose it yourself. *You're* the person who created it; you're God for this script. You're also the doctor, the person who knows this body best, and knows that the reason the arm is hurting is the result of something you planted 50 pages earlier. You may have to change *that*, so the arm won't hurt any longer.

So the answer lies in the process, and the key to being a successful screenwriter is to get in touch with your ego and then let it go.

You have to have a tremendous belief in yourself in order to survive the criticism you take. You have to believe in your vision in order to write anything at all. And, you have to believe that it's going to be the greatest thing. And then, painful as it is, you have to accept the comments of others and make alterations. Change it. The weird thing is, often you end up with something that you don't love as much as you loved the first impulse, but it'll be better, because the first impulse is largely neurotic; you write to express something inside. Then, as I said, you refine what you've already written so that it becomes intelligible, and tolerable, to other people. It retains its personality, but it is transformed into something with a more universal language.

Story Outline

REVERSAL OF FORTUNE

ACT I

We fly over a posh stretch of coastal New England real estate, and slip into a hospital, on into a private, guarded room, and we listen to the disembodied voice of SUNNY VON BULOW, who lies in a deep coma. She calmly gives us a brief prologue to the story we are about to see...

She has slipped into a coma twice, both times under suspicious circumstances.

She takes us back to when she fell into the second coma, and shows us how her children, suspicious of their mother's husband, CLAUS VON BULOW, hired a Manhattan attorney (BRILLHOFFER) to look into the case.

Claus' stepson, ALEX, and a private investigator searched the von Bulow mansion, and found a hoard of drugs in Claus' closet. One of the drugs, insulin, which was found in a vial and on the tip of a hypodermic syringe, was fourteen times the normal level in Sunny's bloodstream.

During this investigation, Claus was vacationing with his mistress, whom he told he would inherit fourteen million dollars from Sunny if she died.

Based on evidence and testimony from the mistress, the stepchildren and a medical lab, Claus von Bulow was convicted on two counts of attempted murder.

The present. ALAN DERSHOWITZ, a respected attorney and Harvard law professor, receives a phone call from Claus von Bulow.

Alan meets with Claus, who wants to hire him to handle his appeal. Alan thinks Claus is guilty.

Alan discusses Claus' case with his son...flashback to the maid's testimony...she found Sunny lying in bed next to Claus, unconscious, and urged him to call a doctor. Claus did not do so until much later, and when he did talk to a doctor, he lied about Sonny's condition. Mrs. von Bulow had slipped into her first coma.

Just prior to Sunny's second coma, the maid found the bag of drugs with insulin in it. She thought that was odd, since Sunny didn't have diabetes.

Flash forward—Alan figures his odds of winning an appeal for von Bulow are 100 to 1. But he takes the case.

Alan gathers a crack team of former students and colleagues, to include his ex-lover, SARA. They have 45 days to make a nearly impossible case for appeal.

Claus meets with Alan and offers to gather affidavits testifying to Sunny's drug abuse. Despite his own declarations of innocence, even Claus isn't sure if they can win.

Alan briefs his associates, who think Claus is probably guilty. But that's the challenge, since it *is* possible that Claus was railroaded. They agree that in order to have a chance at an appeal, they will have to discredit the witnesses and medical evidence. Alan gives research assignments to the team members.

Act II

Alan interviews a small time hustler, and finds a connection between Sunny's drug supply and her son, Alex.

The legal team members descend on Alan's house, and the case is in full swing. The attorney Brillhoffer won't release his notes from the original case. Alan suggests that Sunny's children might have framed Claus.

Claus gives Alan the affidavits he gathered. He swears there was never any insulin in the house, and denies rumors that he killed his mother and aunt as well. Claus has a bad reputation. His smug attitude, along with the fact that he had a new girlfriend two days after the trial, doesn't help any.

The comatose voice of Sunny von Bulow admits to her abuses of drink, drug, and sugar (she was hypoglycemic.)

Claus visits Alan and his legion of associates. Von Bulow's very presence leaves a cold cloud of suspicion hanging over the legal workers.

At dinner, Claus tells cold, calculating jokes about Sunny and his case.

Flashback to the trial—the mistress Alexandra testified that she wasn't sure if she still loved Claus. Claus maintains she does, and that she wrote many letters to tell him so.

Flash back even further, to three weeks before the second coma—Sunny was upset after discovering Alexandra's love letters, and overdosed on aspirin. She fell down and cut her head on the bathroom floor, but forbade Claus to call a doctor.

Back to the present—Alan's team members grill Claus on every point they can think of. They're a crack team, and very skeptical of him.

Alan decides they won't be able to win on legal technicalities. They will have to enter new evidence and prove that Claus is innocent.

Claus flashes back to Christmas, where despite her hypoglycemia, Sunny had been hitting the eggnog rather heavily. She had been out of sorts; she and Claus had been discussing divorce.

He recalls that his wife knew about his mistress, and flashes back further, to a previous summer, where he very casually told her about Alexandra. Sunny merely asked if the affair was any better for him than the prostitutes he usually visited.

Flashing forward to Christmas again, Sunny was so drunk that Claus and the children had to haul her stumbling off to the bathroom. Claus and Sunny argued in bed that night. She was upset that despite marrying into her millions and being able to join the idle rich, Claus preferred to work. She chain-smoked and popped more pills, and he turned away to go to sleep.

It was the next day that the maid said she found Sunny unconscious in bed next to Claus, who tells Alan that the woman's testimony was greatly exaggerated.

Flashback to the hospital—Sonny was upset because Claus did not let her die when she went into the first coma.

In the present, Alan has two team members submit drug samples to a lab, to see if the insulin samples used in the first trial could have been wrongly identified. Alan learns that there shouldn't even have been insulin on the needle after an injection—unless it had been dipped into the solution and then left to dry.

Claus is convinced his stepchildren framed him, but Alan is more cautious, because of other discrepancies in the case.

Claus flashes back to just after the first coma—Sunny was in a frenzy as she searched for her pills. She found them in the room of her maid, who had hidden the drugs in an attempt to save her employer from herself. Sunny ground the pills into powder and mixed them with liquid, so they would be harder for the maid to find. At the first trial, the prosecution had assumed that Claus mixed the solution so he could inject his wife with it.

Back in the present, Alan is worried that Claus might sacrifice him to get off the hook. The meeting takes a nasty turn, but Von Bulow is unflappable.

The comatose voice of Sunny von Bulow tells us about her past days as the wife of an unfaithful Austrian Prince. It was in the Prince's castle that she met and fell in love with Claus. She remembers the passion, the tenderness of the younger von Bulow—we're almost tempted to like him a little.

Back at legal headquarters, Alan argues with team members over an illegal search technicality from the first trial. It quickly turns into a personal argument between Alan and Sara, his former lover. Later, one of the other team members digs up a precedent that will allow them to present new evidence at the appeal, which is only seven days away.

The two-bit hustler that Alan interviewed earlier shows up in the middle of the night and wants to change the testimony on his affidavit. He tape-records the conversation without Alan's knowledge.

Over a feast of spaghetti, one of the young lawyers becomes convinced that Claus was framed. One of the others suggests that they framed an already guilty man.

Alan receives a phone call—the opposition has an ace up their sleeve that could blow Alan out of the water.

Claus and Alan talk about the second coma. Flash-back to Claus trying to explain to the children that he and Sunny were splitting up, because she couldn't tolerate his wanting to have a job. The kids were sure she'd get over it.

At dinner things seemed normal enough, except that, despite warnings from her doctor about her hypoglycemia, Sunny had nothing to eat but an ice cream sundae. Claus retired to his study after supper, Sunny retired to her pharmaceuticals, and later they congregated in a sitting room, with Sunny falling slowly into a stupor.

Later that evening, one of the children summoned Claus to help with Sunny, who was in pretty bad shape. Husband and wife argued some more.

They were calm by bedtime, but still arguing. Claus ignored her and went to sleep. Early that morning, the dogs woke Claus to be let out. He went through his morning routine, and only at breakfast did he realize that Sonny hadn't gotten up yet. He found her sprawled face-down across the bathroom floor, unconscious, her skirt hiked up over her waist.

In the present, a team member arrives with news of the prosecution's ace in the hole: the two-bit hustler who recorded his conversations with Alan has doc-tored the tapes to make it sound like Alan is offering money for witnesses to alter their testimony.

ACT III

Most of the legal associates now believe Claus is innocent—they learned that at the medical lab, the test syringes they submitted came back with positive read-ings for insulin, even though there was actually no insulin on the needles.

Alan suddenly realizes a flaw in the maid's testi-mony. The incriminating tape recordings of Alan's conversations with the hustler are discredited. When

147

he meets with his client, Claus flashes back to when Sunny overdosed on aspirin after reading Alexandra's love letters.

Claus wonders if Alexandra was trying to drive Sunny to commit suicide, or was his former mistress in cahoots with the step kids he believes framed him?

The comatose voice of Sunny von Bulow sarcastically introduces the appeal proceedings, and Alan makes his case before the appellate judges. While Claus watches the proceedings on a television screen, the prosecution plays into Alan's hand by arguing the new evidence instead of von Bulow's guilt.

At home that night, Alan suggests to Sara that on the day Sunny fell into the second coma, it was a simple case of her passing out as she went to urinate, which would explain why her skirt was up over her waist when Claus found her on the bathroom floor.

Sara thinks Sunny took the barbiturates the night before, that Claus knew about it, and helped along her suicide attempt by dragging her into the bathroom and placing her on the floor, underneath open windows that let in the freezing outside air. Her nightgown would have come up over her waist while Claus was dragging her across the bedroom carpet.

After class the next day, Alan learns that they won an appeal. He meets with Claus to tell him the news, and announces that the notes from the lawyer who first looked into the case (Brillhoffer), show that the witnesses had changed their stories—nobody had mentioned insulin when they first talked to Brillhoffer, so the stepkids probably did set Claus up.

Von Bulow comes as close to being overjoyed as we have seen him. And while Alan claims a legal victory, he tells Claus that he still doubts his moral integrity.

The comatose voice of Sunny von Bulow comes back one last time to say, "Claus von Bulow was given a second trial, and acquitted on both counts. This is all you can know, all you can be told. When you get where I am, you will know the rest."

We also see the unflappable Claus one last time, still his arrogant, spooky, chilling self, as he makes a final joke about his close call with the penitentiary.

REVERSAL OF FORTUNE

INT. DERSH'S HOUSE. NIGHT.

Sara cooked; she's serving Elon and Dersh.

>   ELON
>   So. Now it's up to the judges,
>   you can tell me what you
>   really think.

>   SARA
>   I think... some couples are
>   meant to be, and some aren't.
>   (glances at Dersh)
>   Some people love each other,
>   but they don't know how to be
>   together.

>   DERSH
>   You gotta learn.

Subtle smile exchanged between them: they've
learned.

>   SARA
>   And some people can't learn.
>   (more)

                    SARA
                  (cont'd.)
          their time passes, and they
          can't accept that.

                    ELON
          You're saying Sunny couldn't
          accept it, so Claus tried to
          <u>kill</u> her?

                    SARA
          Maybe. Face it: all we had to
          prove was that the state made
          a lousy case. We <u>didn't</u> prove
          he was innocent. We <u>couldn't,</u>
          we didn't have to, and he
          probably <u>isn't!</u>.

                    ELON
          He isn't...? You mean—

                    SARA
          I mean he didn't inject her
          with insulin: so what? Break
          it down. First coma: no prob-
          lem. The <u>attending doctor</u>
          thought it was caused by
          hypoglycemia, loss of air to
          the brain, so on. But the
          <u>second</u> coma? Why does Claus
          act so guilty?

                    DERSH
          Wouldn't any man feel guilty
          if his wife was suicidal?

                    SARA
          Yeah. Say Sunny took those
          sleeping pills with the inten-
          tion of killing herself. *But
          how did she end up* lying on a

marble floor in a freezing
bathroom with her head under
the *toilet bowl?*

ELON
Playing with the dogs?

DERSH
How about this?

INT. CLARENDON COURT. DAWN.

Empty room. <u>Fast</u> FADE IN: Claus getting up with the
dogs, exiting. At the sound of the door shutting,
Sunny's eyes open—

DERSH (VO)
Sunny wakes up miserable.

Lying on her back staring at the ceiling.

DERSH (VO)
<u>Second</u> marriage is over;
children are leaving home.
What's to live for?

Claus returns with the flashlight, weaving his way
past the rawhide bones. He does not look at her.

<u>But she's staring at him...</u>

When he exits again, she sits up.

Ginger ale on her night table. She pours some into
a glass.

Sips.

Stares.

Unscrews the cap on her Neo-Synephrine bottle.

<u>Pours the entire contents into the glass.</u>

Drinks. Savage thirst.

Screws the cap back on the Neo-Synephrine and plops the empty bottle into the wastebasket.

Looks around the room: lavish and desolate.

Climbs out of bed. Shivering. Heads toward the:

BATHROOM. DAWN.

<u>First time we've been inside it. It's stunning:</u> the size and cost of many New York apartments. Walls entirely mirrored; floor of Italian marble; sink, tub, and fixtures suggest Versailles. Yet somehow personal, feminine. No wonder she took refuge here.

She turns on the light, runs the water in the sink...

Rinses her glass.

Stares into the mirror... Face neutral. Like she doesn't care. Or as if she's searching for something that isn't there...

CLAUS' STUDY. DAWN.

He's doing his pushups. Vaguely sexual suggestion...

BATHROOM. DAWN.

She blinks; her mind beginning to cloud...

With enormous concentration, she focuses on the mirror... on her own image...

And breaks into a huge smile of relief—

Falls—

Spinning—

Landing face down, head under the toilet.

Immobile.

DERSH'S HOUSE. NIGHT.

> ELON
> But when she was found, her
> nightgown was hiked over her
> waist.

> SARA
> Exactly. How did it get there?

> DERSH
> Let's say as she's...

CLARENDON COURT. BATHROOM. DAWN.

She's back facing the sink again, smiling...

> DERSH
> (cont'd)
> Standing at the sink...

Suddenly, before she falls, she shuts her eyes,
wincing—

Convulsing. Hands tensing... some kind of physical
reflex... fingernails digging into her thighs...
pulling up her nightgown—
This time, when she falls, she lands the way we saw
her originally, with her nightgown hiked up...

DERSH'S HOUSE. NIGHT.

> SARA
> I don't buy that.

                    ELON
         It <u>does</u> seem far-fetched.

                    DERSH
         So's the truth sometimes.

                    SARA
         Bullshit. I think she took the
         barbiturates the previous
         night.

INT. CLARENDON COURT. BEDROOM. DAWN.

Sunny apparently sleeping as Claus leaves with the
dogs.

                    SARA (VO)
              And let's say he <u>saw</u> her take
              them, or she told him she was
              going to before they fell
              asleep.

Claus returns with the flashlight, starts weaving
his way among the rawhide bones... and then stops,
looks at Sunny. Something peculiar in her breath-
ing... he approaches her:

                    CLAUS
              Sunny?

She does not stir.

He shakes her slightly; her body flops.

Shakes her harder. Still no response.

Pulls open an eyelid, aims his flashlight: pupil
is dilated.

                    SARA (VO)
              This time he <u>wants</u> her to
              succeed...

                    154

Claus looks around the room...

> SARA (VO)
> Is there some way to help her
> along?

His breath is <u>steaming</u>...

> SARA (VO)
> Of <u>course</u>. The open windows.
> Zero degrees. How long could
> she survive...?

Claus lifts her body, drags her out of bed... onto
the floor.

Looks at her body... turns to look at the door:
unlikely, but someone just <u>might</u> come in...

Ah, the bathroom!

He opens the door, drags her toward the bathroom.

> SARA (VO)
> The action of carrying her
> would naturally pull up her
> nightgown.

INT. CLARENDON BATHROOM. DAWN.

He sets her down.

Examines her:

Feet toward the door. Looks like she's been dragged
in there. No good at all.

He shifts her around, awkwardly, until her head is
toward the door, beneath the toilet bowl.

He adjusts her position slightly.

Considers it...

Adjusts again.

Now she looks okay: awkward, but not excessively so.

He starts to pull the door closed behind him...

Wait... No... Something's missing...

He runs the water in the sink...

Finally satisfied, he starts out of the room.

CLARENDON BATHROOM. DAWN.

His hand on the doorknob. Overcome with the enormity of what he's just done. His eyes glaze as we hear:

>   SARA (VO)
>   Remember what Sunny said? "Why
>   did you call? I would have
>   been better off, <u>you</u> would
>   have been better off..."

Claus pulls the bathroom door <u>shut</u>. <u>The deed is done</u>.

Top Secrets:
WILLIAM KELLEY

William Kelley

WITNESS

WILLIAM KELLEY LEARNED THE WRITER'S CRAFT by writing television shows. Lots of them. About 180 of them, in fact, including episodes of the classic *Gunsmoke* and *Route 66* series, *Kung Fu, How the West Was Won, Judd for the Defense, Petrocelli,* and *Serpico.* Many would assume that a writer with this background would develop a slick style that skates over the surface. Kelley admits, "an awful lot of that takes place in T.V." But Kelley is also an acclaimed novelist (*The God Hunters, The Tyree Legend,* and the best-seller, *Gemini*), and he is intensely interested in knowing everything about his characters. He has also been an editor at Doubleday, McGraw Hill, and Simon & Schuster, perhaps a useful preparation not only for writing but especially for rewriting.

The crowning achievement of his long and distinguished writing career was the Academy Award-winning screenplay, WITNESS, co-written with Earl Wallace (Pamela Wallace, Earl's wife, shares the story credit.) It was an immensely successful and admired film, and it fulfilled Kelley's own desire: "If we're very lucky," he says, "We (writers) steal a little fire from Heaven. The real writer recognizes when that happens...he preserves it, and cousins it, and protects it as though it was his own small corner of madness. It's a matter of secret pride that we are touched by this fire. Especially if you're going to ride yourself to do that one great screenplay."

Earl Wallace brought to the collaboration a background as a newsman and a lot of television writing experience on *Gunsmoke* (where he become a story editor and where he met Kelley), on movies of the week, and serving as Story Editor on the miniseries *The Winds of War,* and co-adapter of *War and Remembrance.* WITNESS was not only their first collaboration but also their debut screenplay. It was that rare creature: a spec script that is produced and attracts a major cast, major director, and the backing of a major studio.

The genesis of WITNESS was an idea that occurred to Pamela Wallace. She and her husband were renting a house from a woman who had grown up in Amish country and had left behind some written material about that sect. "Pamela was looking at the stuff," Earl Wallace recollected, "and she said 'wouldn't it be interesting if one of these women got involved with a tough, urban type?' We evolved from there."

Earl Wallace began writing the script during a Writer's strike (traditionally, many television writers use that period of enforced idleness to get around to writing their "Great American Novel" or a spec screenplay). As Kelley recounts in the interview, ten pages into the script, Wallace called him to see if he wanted to collaborate. When the first draft was done, they showed it to a number of people, including producer Ed Feldman. He optioned it and paid for a re-write. The biggest change was a slimming-down of the first draft, which had come in at 140 pages instead of the standard 120. As Wallace recalls of the leaner draft, "That's the version he took to Paramount and that's the one that got Harrison Ford's involvement."

The next step was the involvement of director Peter Weir, who is known as an active director not adverse to having major input to stories and scripts. This initially worried the writers, and a major bone of contention did develop. As Wallace recalls, "Peter's original position was that Book (Harrison Ford) and Rachel (Kelly McGillis) should not make love. When you're talking a love story, either it happens or it doesn't happen, there's no middle ground. That's what we had to fight for. Fortunately, Paramount stood behind the script. And on 95 percent of the points, Peter came around."

What sets the script apart is its unique setting: the Amish society. A tough urban cop comes into this world, ignorant of it but drawn to a woman who has grown up in it. In short, a classic "fish out of water" situation, but in this case one that respects the setting, instead of just using it. The co-authors pride themselves on the accuracy of that element of the story. An Amish man served as technical advisor, and according to Kelley, "The Amish didn't make one change in the script as to Amish practice."

Many viewers found this sensitive portrayal of a way of life that shuns what most people consider progress the most interesting and compelling part of the film. The middle part of the film depicts the timeless rituals: a barn-raising, a funeral, and the peace of a way of life that seems to be operating outside of time itself. Weir's visuals tend to high-light the purity of these people—Rachel seems to emanate a white glow whenever she's on screen. The script itself hinted more at the dark side of any society that is so rigid, but Weir undercuts those hints whenever they arise. There's a certain irony to Weir's worshipful treatment, of course, because the Amish are opposed to commercialized entertainment like movies, and resent the tourist intrusion into their communities that the movie undoubtedly increased. Nonetheless, they have cause to be grateful that the story was made by Kelley, Wallace, and Weir rather than by any one of a dozen filmmak-ers who would have had the pacifist Amish take up AK-47's in the final scene.

There is considerable violence in the film, and some critics felt that the two elements didn't mesh. The reviewer for *Daily Variety* wrote that, "Too often...this fragile romance is crushed by a thoroughly absurd shoot-em-up, like catsup poured over a delicate Pennsylvania Dutch dinner." How-ever, the majority viewpoint was that the contrast served both aspects of the story. The *Hollywood Reporter* review noted that "the pastoral, pacifistic surroundings make the threat of impending violence almost terrifyingly palpable."

Harrison Ford's interest in the script was what immediately propelled it into the big leagues, and his performance
was outstanding. Previously best known for action roles in
STAR WARS and INDIANA JONES, in this film he had the
opportunity to reveal a deeper side of his acting. The *Hollywood Reporter* complimented him for creating "a persuasive
portrait of a hunted man trying desperately but unsuccess-
fully to fashion a new life for himself."

One element worth considering in any film is what is
referred to as the "character arc," the growth or transformation the character undergoes. Both the script and Ford's
performance are masterful in this respect, as John Book starts
out as a gruff, expletive-spouting, confident cop who considers the Amish with amused interest. Gradually, by way of his
attraction to the Amish widow Rachel and his liking for her
son, Book begins to like and respect these people. By the end
he has come to envy their sense of community, their peace of
mind, and their principled stand, and to depend on them for
his very life. But, to his palpable distress, he is destined to
remain an outsider.

Rachel's character arc is more subtle, but equally
well-handled. Critic Kirk Ellis wrote, "her growing independence—and her blossoming beauty—are perhaps the movie's
greatest pleasure."

The nuances of their transformation is one aspect of the
film that makes it a useful text for aspiring film-makers, and a
vindication of William Kelley's insistence on knowing his characters inside-out. He found himself returning to his extensive
notes when he did the novelization of the screenplay. In many
cases, novelizations are hack work, knocked off in a week or two
by a writer who had no involvement in writing the screenplay.
Kelley's pride as a novelist made him want to make the novel
also as good as he could, and anyone interested in appreciating
the difference between the two forms will benefit from reading
the novel and watching the film.

Interview with William Kelley

WITNESS

How do you go from idea to finished script?

As quickly as possible. And I mean that. But how quickly that is, depends upon the story. For instance, I have an idea for a new way to tell the story of Joan of Arc. That will take a hell of a lot of research, including a trip to France and trips to certain libraries. I would probably write the idea up in two or three pages, take it to a producer I thought might be interested and try to get the trip financed and get certain financing for a treatment, etc. You feel safer about finishing then. The fact is, I'm going to do Joan Of Arc all by myself and then try to just sell it as an original screenplay. But, I have to wait until I can get to France and walk the ground.

Do you develop an idea into a treatment and then an outline?

I hate treatments, but sometimes, especially if you are assigned an idea, the producers really need a treatment. I think what they do is cause you to lose a lot of energy, not to mention time, that might otherwise have gone into the screenplay, just to convince them that you can do what you already know you're going to do. Which

163

seems a little ridiculous. So mostly I resist treatments, but I do a step outline for myself anyway.

A step outline is just an act breakdown with scenes listed 1, 2, 3, 4, 5 and then usually an indication—for my own use—of how long each scene is going to be so that I'll know that I have about a 30-page first act, a 45-page second act, 30-page third act. So you have to have a pretty good notion of each scene, and any good screenplay requires four or five good dramatic scenes.

You have to lay out the scenes and usually the key scenes are the longer ones, four or five or up to eight pages long, but generally not more than that.

I do a step outline and then add it all up and make sure it comes in at around 120 pages. Then I begin. The step outline isn't ironclad, of course, and you can change as you go along, but I think it's necessary for your own purposes to do a step outline.

You collaborated with Earl Wallace on the screenplay, WITNESS. How do you feel generally about collaborative screenwriting?

I feel that for some people it's almost essential. I think of great teams like Billy Wilder and I. A. L. Diamond. Once they teamed up, I don't know that they ever did a screenplay separately. It is an added strain in one sense depending upon how well you get along with the other person. But I think you more than make up for that in the ease of having someone there who's talking about the same scene you're talking about. You can work out scenes, ways around difficulties and especially you can work out pace better when you're working with someone else. The other person will say, "Well, why don't we just jump from this or that" or you may say to that person, who has a long scene in mind, "Let's jump over this, why don't we do that." You tend to spark one another with ideas depending on how compatible you are. Earl and I were extremely compatible. Had no problems at all.

Which leads into the next question—how do you work with someone?

Earl started WITNESS during a strike. He did the first ten pages, then he called me and said, "I'd like to collaborate with you for various reasons, especially because I'm stealing a story you did for *Gunsmoke*." Then I read the pages and liked them very much and said, now, Earl, I'm doing this thing (I was doing something else, a novel). I said, "Why don't you go ahead and finish the first draft." He said, "I can't. I don't know that much about the Amish." So I got him a book on the Amish and he read it, while I really ripped through the middle part of the screenplay and gave it to Earl. Then he sat down armed with that and his reading and did a first rough draft. Earl liked an awful lot of what I'd done so then he skipped through that and added and corrected some of the police work. Then we got together for one long weekend, Thursday through Monday, and did a re-write in that time just as fast as we could go, because we both believe that energy comes from working under fierce, hard time conditions. Energy shows up. We'd done so much of the work already, there wasn't that much to do. It wasn't like writing a whole screenplay, but we wanted to do it fast and furious. It helps two things, the energy in the screenplay and the pace.

So, how do I work with someone? Having only worked with one person in collaboration, I can only answer to that. Earl and I are still very good friends. I think you should work respectfully, you listen. Early on it's determined that one of you is going to have to take care of pages and scenes and all the rest. And Earl was terrible about that. I had to number pages and make sure where the hell we were, but on the other hand, he said I was terrible about sticking to the subject. That is, I would jump all over the place and eventually come to a conclusion. He seemed to think it took longer than necessary, but in the end he said, "I think it's a good way because there's nothing we haven't covered from every God damn angle by the time you get done talking about it."

Referring, I assume, to your passion for "back story;" the complete history, even ancestry of a character. You're very particular about that, true?

Yeah. I think I am uncomfortable with surface writing and an awful lot of it takes place in TV. And of course Earl and I came out of TV. Earl was not a surface writer, but he readily admits having learned in our collaboration to pay more attention to background and characters and back story. For example, what did John Book's father do, and what was Rachel's background and why did an Amish woman only have one child? As a matter of fact these things didn't have to come out in the screenplay, but it was necessary for me to know them because I knew Amish women generally have a child every two years. And she only had one child and she's maybe married ten years or more.

Things like that are important to me, I suppose partly because of my self-training as a novelist. And when I did do the novelization of WITNESS, I had to then refer back to all the characters, because there are certain ways — there are certain things, when you are doing a screenplay that you simply don't have to know, when in the novel you do have to know them.

So, in a way Earl was right in saying, what the hell do we have to know that for. But, because of my training, I had to know, or I wanted to know. I keep index cards on my characters right down to even assigning them astrological signs. And even though I may reject the whole damn thing, at least I can bounce off it and determine what my character would do. How she's different. She may have something rising, maybe a Leo with Venus rising. I don't know a damn thing about astrology, but that's just one of the little things I do so that I can get to know my characters upside down, inside out. That made Earl very impatient, but

I know that I'm generally very much admired for my characterizations. And I know why. It's that I walk that ground, too.

What's more important to you, narrative, dialogue or characterization?

Boy, that's a bitch. It's like asking what's more important, inhaling or exhaling. Especially talking about the dialogue or characterization. One comes out of the other so completely. Narrative is important to me when I'm doing screenplays. It keeps me in touch with, and keeps me involved in narrative style, which is very important to me, because I know I'm going back to a novel and that's where I need it. And I don't want to lose touch with it. And you can lose it. As for dialogue and characterization, they're hand in glove, and I just don't know how—I wouldn't know how to say which is more important. They're both extremely important. Character comes first, but characterization is mostly done through dialogue.

How do you handle exposition so that it tells the audience what they need to know without impeding the narrative?

This reveals the amateur writer faster than anything I know. Exposition is necessary. There's no question about it. But, you do it as unobtrusively as you possibly can; and as you get on through a screenplay, go back through and wherever there's exposition see if you can possibly leave it out. Or have it appear in any other way. I mean, a newspaper, an old yellowed newspaper article, or a radio broadcast or some other thing in any way you can, try to get exposition out of your dialogue.

Try to get it into present action. Think of relatives meeting for a funeral. And they don't stand there and say, you remember when? What you're trying to reveal, let's say, is an event in Tupelo, Mississippi that may bear on your story that happened twenty-five years ago. So one character says, "You mean to tell me you can't remember? I can remember the exact God damn day." And then the other character says, "What was the day?" "It was July 8th. For Christ's sake, don't you remember that? It was my birthday." In other words, you can turn it into an argument and make it entertaining simply by artifice. You can reveal something in a dramatic way that you have to get into the story, but do it through a funny sequence or an odd-ball sequence. You say, "What's the matter?" "That woman." "What about that woman?" "What about it? She's wearing the same dress that Aunt Maggie wore da-da-da-da." What you have is an object to refer to. A distraction from the expository stuff.

You must always remember that you are dealing with a camera. And you can get around exposition in so many ways, by using the camera, by using an expression, by having another object or just have a dog run up and bite somebody and the guy says, "For Christ's sake that's what happened to me thirty years ago." And you suddenly realize these people were together thirty years ago. That sort of thing.

Just think of anything you can possibly do to avoid putting direct exposition in dialogue.

How carefully do you work out your plotting and pacing in the changes of successive drafts?

I work them out extremely carefully and, of course, pacing is the whole point. Your plot, once you've got it, is pretty well there, but pacing may very much eliminate what you thought was absolutely necessary to your plot, in successive drafts. You may find that you don't need things. We lost all kinds of things from the beginning of WITNESS. For example; how the dead man died, the dead husband in the opening scenes. That was in one of the first drafts because we wanted to know how he died. He died in a silage cutting machine accident. As you go along, you realize for pacing we don't need to know how he died. I do as a writer, but the viewer doesn't need to know.

The main thing — after you have the plot established and the characters set — is pacing. To see how you can cut every scene down and lead one scene into the next as quickly as possible until you think, well this thing is only going to be thirty-three pages long, if I'm not careful. But, it'll never be that. The pacing is extremely important and I must say I learned more from Earl Wallace about pacing than I had learned in the previous twenty years of screenwriting. He's a pacing master.

Are there ever problems in your completed scripts that you couldn't fix, things you do not feel good about?

My answer is, no. If I couldn't fix it, I'd consider myself a fairly incomplete writer. When I'm finished with a script everything is fixed or I don't submit it.

Do you enter into a project with a particular theme in mind?

This question really puzzles me. Absolutely. I mean, I don't know how to get started, even about, say, Joan Of Arc. And you can say the theme was religion or da-da-da. My theme in going into Joan Of Arc is why I'm going to write it in the first place, which is to correct a lot of errors and to do a better and more honest movie about her than has been done. So, the theme therefore is the true story. The theme is her real life, not a crazy girl, who heard voices; but a noble person, who truly was a saint and who probably was entirely sane.

The word theme is much disputed even in academic circles. What the hell does that mean, theme? What is the theme of the movie, say, GLORY? Most people start by saying, well the theme is about the black men who took part in a war. That isn't the theme, that's the story. The theme is probably courage, grace under pressure, whatever you want to call it. What would you say the theme of GLORY is?

169

I would say that a movie like GLORY may have more than one theme. Certainly one of themes would be learning to look beyond your own prejudices to learn respect for other people. Which is what I think happened to the white soldiers. They were standing by when the 57th marched to the front. Another theme would deal with the young lieutenant played by Matthew Broderick. A theme of rising above expectations your friends and family might have for you. They expected him to be a gentleman soldier and he was not. He took the toughest, dirtiest, meanest job that was available and rose above his family's expectations to become a hero, even though he died.

You just answered your own question better than I could. Most people would not be that bright about it and go to the heart of the matter.

Most people won't give a hoot about *my* answer. [Laughter]

I think almost invariably writers enter into screenplays and everything else with a story in mind and then develop a theme out of the story, but they go so hand-in-hand that it's hard to say. But if I were to say, do I think of the theme first, the answer is definitely no. I think of a story and then I think, where does this lead me, what is my theme?

In story conferences the producer has a certain view of what you can do and what you'd like to do and they'll say, well, what about you doing one about a nun? A story about a nun because he knows I'm interested in religion. And I could say, okay, my theme will be how nuns were mistreated in the old West and rose above it. That's not really a theme, but he thinks of it as theme. Or, "Do one about a faith healer." He thinks of that as theme. It's gotten very confused in Hollywood.

Let me give you a straight answer to this. I think the word theme is the most useless word with reference to screenwriting and novel writing and story telling that I know of. I think a lot of people mean message, but a lot of others mean story. It's a very confused word and I've learned this at USC: that the kids say theme when they mean message. What is it supposed to mean? So I could say the message of *Gemini* or of *The Godhunters* very easily [Kelley's first two novels]: The search for God takes innumerable directions and it doesn't really make a whole hell of a lot of difference how you go at Him, just so long as you go at Him. That's *Gemini*. And if you fail, which was Gemini's case, that's fine. *Godhunters* is the search sort of in mid-process. But the theme, if anything, was the search for God.

How much control does a screenwriter have over his script once a deal is made and the producers are on the project?

As much as the screenwriter's personality can enforce. I told my students at USC that we ought to have a course in arrogance and in fact I tried to teach them that. Maybe not to be arrogant necessarily, but to be forceful and to either charm or terrify or otherwise inconvenience the producers so that they don't dare leave you out. And also, when you make your deal to say, "Now I want to be on the set, I want to be in on casting, I want to be in on the selection of director, I want to talk to the director and then I want to talk to the stars, or the actors, when you've selected them."

The last writers' strike went on for five months over what is called *creative control*. And it's extremely difficult. It can't be legislated. I am of the opinion that it really is just force of personality and style, personal style. That you let them know that only the writer is going to do the writing on this movie or let's forget it.

But it sort of depends. If a studio buys it then the first thing you've got to do is find who is going to be the executive assigned to your movie. And then get to know him or her pretty well. Let that person get to know you. Get a working relationship established very early on. Even before I agreed to sell a screenplay I would do that.

If I'm assigned a movie, it's slightly different. I mean, it's their idea, but then, you know, most people in Hollywood, most successful producers, are reasonable people and there's very little skullduggery that goes on, and they're not going to try to rip you off. Unless you're a jackass or a personality disaster. Then they want to get you the hell out of the way as soon as possible.

To what degree does the success of a freelance screenwriter depend on his verbal skills as opposed to his ability to write a good script? The ability, that is, to pitch an idea.

There's no way to stress too much the preparation for a pitch. That is, to know exactly what you're going to say and go in and get it said. If you have the impression that they like it, the thing to do is to get up and get out of there before they have to start easing you towards the door. Plan what you're going to say, go in and say it, be polite; and then get the hell out. They'll appreciate the saving of time and they'll appreciate your directness and positive approach, and your positive departure.

What one piece of advice is the most important piece of advice you can share with writers?

Write the best you possibly can every time out. And that includes walking the ground, that is, doing your research. If it takes place in a certain location, walk the ground, get out there even if it's at your own expense, make sure you are accurate and be a bulldog for research. In other words, if you want one piece of advice it would be to do the very best script that you

172

possibly can do given what you've decided to do or what you've been assigned to do. And, if anything, surprise the producers with the quality of the work.

Also, when you are beginning a screenplay, write and rewrite one scene until you've got it perfect, until you think you know the characters. And you will, if you do it right. You will learn how they speak, you will learn their limitations, etc. Just in doing one scene until it's perfect, but you must have the scene—the key scene of the screenplay.

Then you will find that you will write to that high level for the entire screenplay and, perhaps, for your whole career.

———————————————————————

Story Outline

WITNESS

ACT I

Opening credits over a montage of daily life in an Amish farming community.

The Amish farmers gather in a church for the funeral of one of their own.

At the wake, the mourners voice their respect for the deceased, and a young blond man, DANIEL, offers his very friendly respects to the widow, RACHEL.

More glimpses of an Amish farming day—glimpses into the past, for the Amish shun modern technology and still use the equipment and methods of the mid-nineteenth century. The plain, simple farmers stand out amidst the hustle and bustle of modern day Pennsylvania, especially as they drive their horses and buggies into the city.

Rachel and her son, SAMUEL, ride into town to catch a train to Baltimore. Daniel and other friends see them off, then Daniel races his horse and buggy against the train (and loses) as they pull away. Samuel looks with wonder out the window as the train speeds through the scenic Pennsylvania countryside.

Samuel and Rachel's train is delayed in Philadelphia. Samuel is in awe of the huge, crowded train station and its modern gadgets, and wanders off to investigate.

Some time later, Samuel and his mother are still waiting. There are few people around now. Sam wanders off to the restroom, and from the concealment of a stall he witnesses the murder of one man by two others. One of the killers, a very cool customer, nearly discovers Samuel.

The police are on the murder scene. Enter JOHN BOOK, a rugged-looking cop who immediately takes charge. He tries to talk to Samuel, who had reported the murder, but Samuel is scared and hesitant. John finally breaks the ice with a joke about his partner. It turns out the murdered man was an undercover police officer.

John drives Rachel and her son, against Rachel's wishes, to have a look at a suspect. John reminds her that her son is a witness to the murder of a cop, and the law says they will do what he needs them to. But Rachel wants nothing to do with "the English laws."

John and his partner enter a seedy bar, where the patrons seem to know and despise the two cops. John grabs a suspect and forcibly hauls him outside, smashes him up against the police car for a frightened Samuel to take a look at. Rachel grows more upset, especially since the suspect is not the right man.

John takes Rachel and her son to his sister's house for the night. Forty years old, and the siblings still don't get along very well.

Rachel and Samuel try to settle in for the night, but they are strangers in a strange land; John's sister says an awkward goodnight.

John has Rachel and Samuel, who want to leave *now*, at the police station. Samuel looks at a police lineup, but doesn't recognize anybody.

John takes the mother and son to lunch at a greasy spoon. He plows right into his meal and feels like a clod, as the two Amish stop to pray. Rachel relates her conversation with John's sister, who described him as an idealistic loner who thinks he's the only one who can do anything right.

Back at the police station, Samuel pores over mug shots, but doesn't find the man who murdered the cop in the train station. When John is distracted by a phone call, Samuel takes the opportunity to wander around the offices. He finds a picture of the killer—and correctly identifies a narcotics officer (McFEE) as the murderer.

Act II

John tells his supervisor (SCHAEFFER), that the boy fingered McFee. It makes sense, he says, because of McFee's involvement in a years-old drug bust. Schaeffer and John are the only two who know of the connection, and John asks him to keep it that way.

In an underground parking garage that night, McFee ambushes John and wounds him. Schaeffer must have clued the killer in.

At his sister's house, John scrambles to bandage himself up and get Rachel, Samuel and himself to safety. He can't trust anybody but his partner, his sister, and the Amish.

John calls his partner at the police station and asks him to lose the train station murder file for a few days, and warns him to be careful.

John's partner lifts the file from the records.

McFee and his crew tear John's car apart looking for clues to his location, while Schaeffer interrogates the sister, telling her that John is the dirty cop. She angrily defends her brother's integrity.

In his sister's car, John drives Rachel and her son back to Amish country. They don't know he's been shot. He drops them off and drives away, but passes out at the wheel and crashes into a birdhouse. He couldn't go to a hospital—gunshot wounds have to be reported to the police, and that would endanger Samuel, who McFee and Schaeffer are sure to be after.

Rachel and her father haul John to town in a wagon, to her house. Rachel's father and the friend think John should be taken to a hospital, but Rachel argues the unconscious John's case for him, and wins. John can stay.

With a team of horses Rachel and her father haul John's car into the barn.

Rachel tends to John's wound. He's delirious and in great pain. She is visibly shaken when he finally falls asleep, and she fears he may be dead. But by morning he is improving.

In his search for John and Samuel, Schaeffer tries to put the heat on a small town cop in the Amish country. But the local cop is unflappable, and besides, there's nothing he can do—Samuel's last name is a common one, and the Amish don't have phones, so they won't be listed in any directory.

John wakes up to see the Amish community elders staring over him. They wander outside and wonder what to do about the strange, wounded "Englishman." Inside, Rachel warms up a little to John, who has been unconscious for two days.

Samuel finds John's gun in a drawer and starts to play with it, but John catches him. He tells the boy how dangerous guns are, but takes out the bullets and lets him have a better look at the weapon. Rachel is mortified to see her son playing with a gun, and hides it and the ammunition.

Rachel's father lectures Samuel on the evils of guns and fighting.

Rachel lends John her husband's old clothes, to help him blend in, and they get to know each other a little better. She's a pretty woman, and she catches him staring at her.

Whether he's healthy enough to travel or not, John needs to get to a phone. He looks like a goof in his high-water Amish outfit; even Rachel laughs. But she sobers up when he asks for his gun and bullets to take with him.

John rides the wagon into town with Samuel and his GRANDPA. He calls his partner in Philadelphia, who warns John that McFee and Schaeffer are hot on his trail.

Back at the house, John puts the gun away and hands the bullets back over to Rachel.

Samuel shows John around the farm. John tries to start his car, but the battery's dead.

Grandpa rousts John out of bed at 4:30 the next morning. It's time to milk the cows. The city cop is sound asleep and all thumbs after getting his milk from a carton his whole life, but he gets the hang of it and manages to soften up Grandpa a little.

At breakfast, John tries to tell a joke, but bombs. He's still from a different world, though he and the Amish family are beginning to appreciate each other.

John meets Daniel, the blond Amish man who talked to Rachel at her husband's funeral, and saw Samuel and her off at the train station. Daniel is in a courting mood as he walks off to visit Rachel.

Daniel and Rachel sit awkwardly on the porch swing; Rachel's eye is on John as he putters around the farm.

John is rebuilding the birdhouse he crashed into when Rachel brings him a glass of lemonade. With shy admiration, she dismisses Daniel as a friend of the family.

In the barn that night, Rachel helps John try and get his car running, but the only thing that works is the radio. When an old Sam Cooke tune comes on, he steals a quick dance with her. The possibility of a kiss is there, but he doesn't follow through.

Then Rachel's father bursts into the barn and scolds her for listening to the "modern" music. She argues back, telling him that she's capable of thinking for herself, and to hell with the rumors about her and John and what the elders might do to ostracize her...she's committed no sin.

Back in Philadelphia, John's partner gets the third-degree from McFee and Schaeffer. It's a tense meeting, and the bad guys are in control.

At an old-fashioned barn-raising (a frequent event for the Amish), John holds his own as a carpenter. Daniel is a bit jealous of his glances at Rachel, but it's a friendly rivalry so far.

At lunch, all eyes watch to see how John and Rachel interact. Daniel's playful jealousy becomes a little more serious.

After lunch, while the men work, the women gossip with and about Rachel.

Back at the farm that night, John deliberately walks in on Rachel as she bathes. She is his if he wants her, but he hesitates and the opportunity passes.

The next morning, John tells Rachel that if they had made love the night before he would have had to stay in her world, or she would have had to join him in his.

John wades through the Amish-watching tourists in town to make a phone call. He discovers that his partner has been "killed in the line of duty." Then he phones Schaeffer at home and tells him he's coming after him.

As the Amish leave town in their wagons, a bunch of rednecks harass the farmers, Daniel in particular. The Amish are pacifists, but John can't stand to see his new friends being humiliated, and he decks the rednecks.

A citizen tells a local cop where this unusually violent "Amish" man is staying—just the clue Schaeffer and McFee need to find their prey.

As she watches John erect the repaired birdhouse, she realizes that he is leaving and rushes to him. Their suppressed passion finally bursts forth, as they embrace out in the open, where anybody might see them.

Act III

Later in the day, Schaeffer, McFee, and another thug, all armed to the teeth, stalk Rachel's farm.

The crooked cops storm the farmhouse; Grandpa sounds a warning to John, who locks himself in the barn with Samuel, then tells the boy to run and escape to a neighbor's farm.

John tries to start his car, but no go. One of the thugs hears the commotion and storms the barn. Samuel looks back as he hears the shooting, and back in the barn, John leads a wild chase that ends with one dead gunman in a silo, buried under tons of corn.

Samuel has run back to the farmhouse and hidden inside; as Schaeffer hauls Rachel and her father outside, Grandpa gives the boy a hand signal.

McFee hears John digging for the dead man's gun in the silo. McFee attacks, but John drops him.

Meanwhile, Samuel is ringing a bell that can be heard all across the valley. With Rachel at gun point, Schaeffer talks John into dropping his own weapon.

In response to the ringing of the bell, every Amish person within earshot descends on Rachel's farm, just in time to see John pushed out of the barn at gun point by Schaeffer.

But Schaeffer's number is up; after all, he can't murder everyone in the village. John disarms him without a struggle.

Dozens of uniformed police mill around the farm, gathering statements.

Back in his city clothes, John says good-bye to Samuel. And then to Rachel. It's a wordless good-bye, but filled with thoughts of a love that can never be.

With a wish of luck from Rachel's father, John drives away and passes Daniel, who gives him a friendly nod as he walks down the dirt road to Rachel's house.

William Kelley's Pick

WITNESS

INT. SICKROOM

As SAMUEL comes in with a fresh bedpan. BOOK is lying
asleep on the bed.

Samuel puts the bedpan down, checks to make sure
Book is indeed asleep, then quietly crosses to the
foot of the bed and opens the clothes chest.

ANGLE

Book's big .38 revolver lies holstered atop his
folded clothes. Fascinated, Samuel picks it up,
admiring the heavy burled pistol grips. Unable to
resist, he starts to remove the weapon from the
holster, then pauses to steal a look. o.s...

BOOK

His eyes are open and watching Samuel icily, which
gives the boy something of a jolt.

                    BOOK
          Give me that.

Mutely, Samuel hands Book the pistol from arm's

length. He looks on as Book takes the pistol out
of the holster, shoots the boy another look, then
snaps open the cylinder and shakes out the heavy,
copper-jacketed bullets into his palm. He snaps the
cylinder closed again, then nods to Samuel.

>   BOOK (CONT'D)
>   Come here.

The boy edges closer.

>   BOOK (CONT'D)
>   You ever handle a pistol like
>   this Samuel?

>   SAMUEL
>   (swallows)
>   No pistol. Ever.

>   BOOK
>   Tell you what—I'm going to let
>   you handle this one. But only
>   if you promise not to say
>   anything to your momma. I've
>   got a feeling she wouldn't
>   understand.

>   SAMUEL
>   (grins)
>   Okay, Mr. Book.

Book smiles. Then he gives the boy a playful, John
Wayne-tough guy wink as he cocks and uncocks the
pistol, demonstrating the action. He finally hands
it over to Samuel, butt-first.

>   BOOK
>   Call me John.

The boy tries to imitate Book's one-handed
expertise, but his hands are too small. Book smiles.
Samuel finally manages to get the thing cocked,

using two hands, and Book reaches over to guide the
muzzle away so that it's not pointed at him.

>   BOOK (CONT'D)
>   You don't want to point that
>   at people you just started
>   calling by their first name.

Samuel levels the pistol at the door and, just as
he snaps the trigger, RACHEL enters, pulls up short
in some dismay to find her son has a gun pointed
at her. Samuel blanches and Book winces, knowing
there's heavy weather ahead.

>   RACHEL
>   (snaps)
>   Samuel—!

Samuel quickly hands the pistol back to Book, who
holsters it.

>   RACHEL (CONT'D)
>   Wait for me downstairs.

Samuel exits, and Rachel angrily advances on Book.

>   RACHEL (CONT'D)
>   John Book, I would appreciate
>   it if, during the time you are
>   with us, you would have as
>   little to do with Samuel as
>   possible.

>   BOOK
>   Nobody meant any harm. The boy
>   was curious. I unloaded the
>   gun—

>   RACHEL
>   It's not the gun. Don't you
>   (more)

183

                    RACHEL (CONT'D.)
          understand... It's you. Your
          anger... your violence!
                    (and)
          That's not for Samuel.

Books looks at her thoughtfully:

                    BOOK
          Okay, right.
                    (and)
          He's a fine little guy.

Rachel softens a bit:

                    RACHEL
          Please, it has nothing to do
          with you personally.

He hands her the holstered gun and the loose
bullets.

                    BOOK
          Put it someplace Samuel can't
          get it.

A beat, then Rachel takes the pistol and starts to
go. Book stops her:

                    BOOK (CONT'D)
          Friends?

Rachel glances back at him, smiles and nods. And...

                                        CUT TO:

INT. KITCHEN- LAPP FARMHOUSE- NIGHT

Book's holstered gun and bullets at center table.
Eli sits on one side, a chastened Samuel on the
other. Rachel looks on from the b.g.
Eli knows that this is as important a dialogue as

he will ever have with his grandson: at issue is
one of the central pillars of the Amish way.

>   ELI
>   The gun—that gun of the hand—
>   is for the taking of human
>   life. Would you <u>kill</u> another
>   man? Eh?

Samuel stares at it, not meeting his grandfather's
eyes. Eli leans forward, extends his hands
ceremonially.

>   ELI (CONT'D)
>   What you take into your hands,
>   you take into your heart.

A beat, then Samuel musters some defiance.

>   SAMUEL
>   I would only kill a bad man.

>   ELI
>   Only a bad man. I see. And you
>   know these bad men on sight?
>   You are able to look into
>   their hearts and see this
>   badness?

>   SAMUEL
>   I can see what they do.

Now he meets Eli's eyes:

>   SAMUEL
>   I <u>have</u> seen it.

Eli expels a deep sigh; then:

>   ELI
>   And having seen, you would
>   (more)

>   ELI (CONT'D)
>   become one of them? So that
>   the one goes into the other
>   into the other, into the
>   other...?

He bows his head for a moment. The he fixes the boy
with a stern eye and, driving the heel of his palm
firmly into the tabletop, with enormous intensity:

>   ELI (CONT'D)
>   "Wherefore come out from among
>   them and be ye separate, saith
>   the Lord!"
> (indicating pistol,continuing from Corinthians
> 6:17)
>   "And touch not the unclean
>   thing!"

His intensity tinged with righteous anger, is
hugely impressive.

Top Secrets:
TODD W.
LANGEN

Todd W. Langen

TEENAGE MUTANT NINJA TURTLES

IT'S NOT TOO SURPRISING TO KNOW that when Todd W. Langen came to Hollywood in the early 1980s, he was a young man with stars in his eyes. What might be surprising is that the stars he saw were the real ones, the kind that twinkle in the nighttime sky.

Los Angeles, besides being home to Hollywood and Disneyland, has also been the aerospace mecca for the nation, and Langen, who had obtained a Bachelor's and a Master's degree in aerospace engineering in only 4-1/2 years at the University of Michigan, was hired at Hughes as a systems engineer in the launch vehicle integration group, working with commercial systems division.

Almost immediately upon being hired he realized that this career was not going to offer the personal fulfillment he desired, and his lifelong interest in entertainment began to manifest itself in the form of spec scripts. He wrote, as he puts it, "Many, many, many, manymanymany" spec scripts, to the point where writing came to take up nearly all his spare time. Not that his daily work was so dull: Langen worked directly with the Shuttle program in setting up satellite communications networks for Australia, Mexico, and other countries and companies. He met with astronauts, traveled to Florida for launches, manned a position on the Mission Control console, and other rather exciting stuff. But still, it wasn't what he wanted. So, for

189

three years he labored away on his spec scripts, targeting his writing towards television mostly because he felt it offered the most accessible avenue into the business.

Finally, with a reasonable nest egg in the bank and several spec scripts tucked firmly under his arm, he walked into his boss' office one day and said, "I quit. I'm going to become a screenwriter."

Looking back on that decision, Langen shakes his head with amazement. "Fortunately, at the time I didn't know what a cliché I really was," he says. "I wasn't aware that every cab driver and waiter in town had a screenplay, or was working on a screenplay. Had I known... well, who knows?"

As one might guess from a guy who'd spent his academic life mired in equations and theorems, when Langen first began writing scripts he had received no formal training in writing, and had no experience or knowledge whatsoever about the craft or business of screenwriting. "I just came home nights, pulled out a writing board, a pad of paper and pencils, turned on the high intensity lamp and started writing," he says. "I had no idea what I was doing, but I just felt like giving it a shot. And you know, it was my feeling then—and remains so today—that the best way to do anything is to just sit down and do it. It's the best way to learn."

Eventually, though, he did pick up some books on structure, characterization, and the basics of storytelling, and was pleasantly surprised to find that he had instinctively followed most of the rules. "That was a real confidence builder, it made me feel good," he recalls. "It made me think that maybe I was on to something, that this might be something I could do."

The business side of show business, however, proved a bit daunting at first, as Langen found every query he launched thudding back to Earth like a fallen satellite. So complete was his initial failure that he not only couldn't get anyone to respond to his stories, he couldn't even convince them to send him a simple release form. When Stephen J. Cannell Productions became the first to actually enclose a blank release form in Langen's SASE, he rejoiced: "At the time, that was a real milestone!"

He submitted his scripts, and a woman in the story

department later informed him that while those scripts weren't quite ready, they were indicative of some real talent, and encouraged him to try some more. He did, and eventually was able to use several of these efforts to land an agent. "I spent all of 1986 and half of 1987 continuing to write spec scripts, all the while hoping my agent could get me in to *Family Ties*. I really wanted to write for that show." As it happened, he never made that show, but the show's producer, Michael Weithorn, did read one of Langen's scripts and offered him an assignment on his new show, *The Pursuit of Happiness.* "That was my big break," Langen says. "The show was shot, it aired, and it got me into the Writers Guild. And immediately thereafter we went on strike!"

Ironically, Langen sees the period of the writer's strike as being extremely beneficial, because he used that time to write a spec screenplay which eventually helped him land the TEENAGE MUTANT NINJA TURTLES project. During that time he also penned the "Square Dance" script for *Wonder Years*, a spec effort which not only sold, but went on to win the Humanitas Award. When the strike ended he found himself with the go-ahead to write another *Wonder Years* episode entitled "Coda," which went on to win a Writers Guild award and an Emmy nomination—and earned him a staff job on the highly respected show.

Meanwhile, Langen's life was about to be permanently changed by a band of pizza-gobbling, skateboard-riding adolescent reptiles.

In a chorus of the most sweeping understatements imaginable, critics predicted that TEENAGE MUTANT NINJA TURTLES "...should go over big with subteens," (*Daily Variety*), and "...should appeal to young fans." (*Hollywood Reporter*). They might just as well have included, "And it might make a few dollars, too." History has shown the trusty terrapins to be a genuine phenomenon, both in their debut and the sequel. Langen received shared credit (with Bobby Herbeck) for the original, and was the sole writer on the sequel.

Surprisingly, few people seem to remember that the Turtles had been around long before their story hit the big screen. Creators Peter Laird and Kevin Eastman conceived the critters about five years before they became the biggest animation act on television, and it was two years later that Turtlemania was packing theaters across the nation.

It is Langen's belief that the success of the film was very much due to its self-deprecating humor. It's almost as though every character in the movie knows the whole thing is pretty silly, and they're playing it strictly for laughs. The light-hearted tone and smart-aleck attitude keeps the adventure as fun as a brand-new comic book, and offers something for the adults as well as the kids to enjoy.

Certainly one of the challenges Langen faced was to keep the characters recognizable and distinctive. So, strong character traits were ascribed to each Turtle, since audiences couldn't really rely on physical differences to tell one Ninja from another. Also, the vulnerability of these superheroes was obvious from the start: they were young, inexperienced, brash and cocky kids who felt they could take on the world, but had no idea of the strength of the forces of evil.

The fairy-tale dimension of TEENAGE MUTANT NINJA TURTLES can probably be credited for much of its appeal, especially towards its youngest fans. In a dark, scary world, magical powers (radiation) are bestowed onto a helpless gang of kids (the baby turtles), and they survive only through the help of a stern, yet patient and understanding father/teacher, Splinter. It's an improbable netherworld as unpredictable and unlimited as a child's imagination, and the Turtles must learn, as every youngster must, the difference between right and wrong, the importance of education and practice, and the need for self-discipline. The heroism of the Turtles is the heroism each child dreams of demonstrating, and unknowingly personifies during the everyday struggle to grow up.

The Turtles are highly accessible superheroes that every child can relate to—and like most kids, they'll do practically anything for pizza.

And just think: most of us grew up thinking the only way to get that strong was to eat spinach. Where were the Turtles when *we* needed them?

Interview with Todd W. Langen

TEENAGE MUTANT
NINJA TURTLES

Did you find it tough to make the decision to quit a very promising career, and gamble on your writing skills?

Well, it certainly wasn't a decision I arrived at lightly, and you can imagine how well it went over with my parents. [Laughter]

You say you had been writing spec script after spec script with no success—and suddenly, things started happening. So why did it finally click? What changed in your writing that suddenly made it a higher caliber of work?

The more you do something, the better you get at it, and I simply had reached a point where my writing was getting more polished. Also, I started taking some chances. I had always taken some chances with my stories, but I began taking even more chances, and in the case of *The Wonder Years* spec, I was injecting even more personal memories and emotions into the script. I was trying to do something different and eye-catching. That was also true of the spec feature I wrote.

You see, during the strike I kept hearing writers saying, "Yeah, I've had this idea floating around in my head for thirty years now, and (because of the strike) I'm finally going to get a chance to write it." So I figured that when the strike ended there would be this tidal wave of scripts cascading into the readers' offices all at once. I wanted to write a script that was going to stand out, and give the readers a break from the RIVER'S EDGE kind of scripts, the ones fraught with insight and introspection, that I suspected they would be seeing a lot of. So I wrote a flat-out broad comedy called, I DO.

I meant for it to stand out, and that's exactly what happened. So, taking the long route to answering your question, I saw my writing improve due to an injection of more personal feelings and experiences into my stories, and a willingness to take some chances.

By doing both those things, you really were putting your butt on the line, risking rejection at a point in your career when almost all you had known was rejection.

I was truly enamored with the first season of *The Wonder Years*, I really wanted to be a part of that show. So I decided to put everything I had into that script, and that meant I had to take the chance of having a very personal story rejected.

In discussing writing techniques, many writers focus on the need for rhythm and tempo. Some talk of story arcs, and how each scene should have a beginning, middle, and end. Tom Schulman tells us about layering his work with multiple plot lines. What do you expect from your work? What is unique about your style?

I've been told that one of the things people notice about my work is it's pretty lean, there's not a lot of extraneous stuff. I get into the scene as late as possible, do what needs to be done, and move on, without too much filler. What do I expect to see in my work?

Yes, how can you tell when it's the best you can do? Is it something you can articulate, or is it just a feeling?

Certainly that gut feeling is part of it. But I go back and reread a lot of the stuff I've written before, and I always judge it by whether the emotional pull that I originally tried to put into that script is still as strong. That's a very difficult thing to put into scripts, and to tell the truth there have only been a few times that I feel I've succeeded. But in those scripts I can feel that emotional tug even when I read them years later, and that's a sign of success for me.

As far as the comedy goes, I also apply the test of time. Does the humor hold up, or was it funny at the time, but now seems a little forced, a bit contrived? Of course, it's tough to tell at the time you're writing the script—you just have to trust your instincts.

You know, I think at this early stage of my career, at least, I have this dread fear of over-analyzing what I do. I worry that I'll find out that it's all just been crazy luck, and I really don't know what the hell I'm doing. And ohmyGod, I should have been worrying about arcing those scenes, and now I don't know how to do it! [Laughter]

In fact, I've always avoided seminars and conferences and the like, if only because I have this morbid fear of finding out how many people are really out there writing scripts. I still think about the film schools, and the people coming out of those programs, and I still get paranoid about that. So, I really haven't spent a lot of time analyzing my work, apparently because of fear.

Well, do you have any idea of what you expect from your writing in the future? How do you see your skills growing and maturing?

One of the best things about working on *The Wonder Years* was the chance I had to work with some extremely creative and skilled craftsmen, people with the ability to put a great deal of depth into their writing. To really make the stories resonate with emotion, and communicate strong feelings to an audience, not only getting them to understand, but *experience*. And that's the area I would like to see improve in my own writing.

Certainly you achieved that strong emotional underpinning, that personal recognition factor, in "Coda" and "Square Dance". Is it frustrating for you to be able to do that sometimes, but not always?

Sure. But you have to realize that there are certain times it's just not going to happen, and there are other times when it's not even appropriate. No matter what, it's never easy. I keep waiting for that script that writes itself. I hear people say, "I just sat down and the whole thing seemed to flow right out of my pen." I'm still looking forward to that experience. I work at my writing.

How will you go about improving your writing along those lines?

Nothing magic. For me it's just a matter of writing, and writing, and writing. That's the way to improve. Sure, I read other people's scripts to a certain extent, I continue to watch television, I continue to watch movies, and I continue to read. In fact, sometimes reading a good novel or a collection of short stories is a real inspiration, it fires me up to get back at my own work. It encourages me to demand more, to do something more responsive. To do something better.

What goals have you set for yourself?

Complete world domination.

And on your way to achieving that goal?

I have two long-term goals. I want to create and executive produce my own show on television. And in terms of features—and I'm sorry to sound like such a cliché—I want to write and direct my own script.

I'm at a decision point right now in my career. I have had a certain amount of success in television, and a certain amount of success in features, with the TURTLE movies. I could go either way right now. I wish that I could continue to balance the two—work on a series, write a movie during hiatus—but I just can't keep that up. While I'm not sure you have to concentrate on one to the total exclusion of the other, it does seem that you have to concentrate on just one for a period of time. I really haven't decided which way to go.

As far as features go, I really want to direct because, like most writers, I guess, I don't want to always be in a position of turning my work over to someone else. Not that other people do bad things with it, but it's the old creative control thing, wanting to bring your original vision to a screen.

Having written for both television and features, what do you see as the main difference?

Well, the obvious thing is that in television you're working with predetermined characters, and unless it's your series, they are other people's characters. So you are working with a lot more restrictions, especially if you stay with that series over a period of time. The advantage to that, however, is that you get to live with and know those characters, and tell several stories with those characters—instead of just one story, as in a feature. And that can be very satisfying.

In some ways—and I don't want to come off as the final word here, since I'm still relatively inexperienced—movies allow more personal stories, and more complete stories. You can throw everything you want, and everything you've got, into that one story, without the restrictions of television. For instance, in television you can't kill off your main character, but it's been done many times in movies.

Does the "group grope" aspect of TV writing bother you?

At times it bothered me. But we were fortunate on *The Wonder Years*, because we never "tabled" scripts. It wasn't written like a multiple-camera sitcom. Instead, usually a person would come up with a story, go off on their own and write a first draft, and then receive notes.

They'd go off and do a second draft incorporating those notes, and at some final point in the process the executive producers would do a rewrite or polish. So I haven't really been exposed to the hard-core group rewriting sessions common to many other shows. And I don't think that is something I would want to do over a long period of time.

What about the difference in the time element, the pressures that are more prevalent in television writing?

Last season on *The Wonder Years* we were facing some very tight time limits.

I would imagine so, if only because the production time has to be so limited, due to the age of the cast.

We also had trouble with script deadlines, but that's just the nature of the business.

Sitcom producer Michael Warren likens television comedy writing to playwriting, except the typewriter is on a conveyor belt headed for a hole in the wall, and once it's gone, that's it.

I wish I could come up with lines like that! But it's true, television can be very demanding in that regard. The thing is, though, I love television. I grew up with it, it's a part of my life, and so at this point I really am having trouble deciding which area I want to concentrate on. But I'm beginning to lean toward features, though I don't know why.

Let's talk a little about the feature arena. You mentioned that a spec comedy you did was very instrumental in landing the TEENAGE MUTANT NINJA TURTLES assignment.

That, and a writer named Bruce Joel Rubin. I met Bruce on the picket line, and whenever I hear people talking about how this is a business full of backstabbing, manipulating, unscrupulous people, I just think of Bruce Rubin and I know it's not true. He read I DO, for me, and then handed it to the powers that be at Paramount. So, when the TURTLES people were looking for someone to do a rewrite, I was recommended.

Bob Herbeck wrote the first version, correct?

Right. He got everything underway with the comic book creators, he wrote a first draft. He was really under the gun, because the producers needed a script to set up a distribution deal. And to show you how quickly people in this town can move sometimes, when I was called in to do the rewrite I noticed that Bobby's first draft was dated *one day* before my initial meeting with the producers.

The first thing that struck me about the film was texture versus content—that is, it's a comic book tale that is shot so...well, dark.

Yes, that was one of the problems we encountered. But you can understand the logic. In one of my initial talks with the director, I voiced my concern about shooting these four guys in rubber suits in brightly lit rooms. What was remarkable, and what we didn't find out until afterwards, was that the Turtles actually looked pretty good, even in the exterior scenes, or the close-ups.

Were you surprised by the success of the film?

The producers were pretty sure it was going to open well. They were literally turning people away from the test screenings, which is quite unusual. I felt the built-in audience due to the cartoon series and the merchandising would ensure a solid opening too, although none of us really believed it would open so tremendously, or continue to have such "legs." I kept thinking that each weekend would be the one where it finally flattened out, but it just kept going. That surprised me, yes. Because don't forget that a large percentage of the admissions were half-priced admissions for kids, so for the film to make the kind of money it did—it was amazing.

It's very gratifying, too. This might get on the sappy side here, so bear with me...but the idea of being able to reach so many people, to have millions of people watch an episode of *The Wonder Years*, and maybe laugh at one of your jokes, well, that feels good. I've sat through TURTLES many times just to be with the kids, and hear their reactions. And you know, it's great to hear them using lines you've written, repeating jokes—and even hearing the press turn some of your lines into buzzwords. It's an exhilarating feeling.

What elements of the script are most responsible for that kind of impact and success?

I treated the movie not as an action/adventure film, but strictly as a comedy. I wrote it as a comedy with action elements, not the other way around. I'd like to believe, therefore, that the humor is one of the elements that helped set the movie apart. And I intentionally tried to appeal to the adults as well as the kids, by working in a higher level of comedy now and again. It was nice to hear the adults laughing in all the right places, too.

Along with the humor, I feel that in spite of what some critics have said, the Turtles each had a distinct personality of his own. I had some fun with that, and I think it added to the fun of the film. Certainly it helped the kids in the audience identify with the characters.

It seems to me that one of the challenges of writing a movie for kids—or a TV show for kids, for that matter— lies in the need to write believable, age-appropriate dialogue, and yet accomplish roughly the same amount of humor, and character development required in any *adult* story.

I found in reading a lot of spec *Wonder Years* scripts that many writers had difficulties writing realistic kids' dialogue. It was much more "sitcomy" kind of stuff, firing off straight lines followed by a kid saying something so witty and sophisticated it was beyond belief. In my mind, that's not the way to get the humor. It's a little harder to get the humor through more credible dialogue, but it's more satisfying, because it's more organic, and real.

I enjoy writing for kids. It's great fun to sort of harken back to my younger days and try to remember how we talked. Howard Rosenberg (*Ed. note: Los Angeles Times* television critic) once wrote a piece on *The Wonder Years*, and in it he mentioned that he was sort of taken down memory lane by a simple conversational thing I'd thrown into the "Square Dance script. Remember when you were a kid, and one of your friends would say something obvious, or a little dumb, and everyone would go, "Duhhh!" Rosenberg loved that, and that's the kind of thing that is not only fun to recall, but adds a certain realism and texture to the dialogue.

Any advice to offer before we close?

I recently received a letter in which someone asked me, "How can you keep going, keep trying, when you aren't sure you will ever make it? How do you face that uncertainty?" Well, I used to be an engineer, and the equation seems very simple to me; if you write you have a chance. If you don't write, you have zero chance. So, if you want to succeed, you're going to have to write. And that's what keeps you going.

TEENAGE MUTANT NINJA TURTLES

ACT I

A crime wave is sweeping the city, according to newscaster APRIL O'NEIL, and it looks like the perpetrators are silent, stealthy, lightning-quick ninja thieves.

After her newscast, April is accosted in a dark alley by a gang of the thieving youths she had reported on. But she's saved by mysterious, unseen rescuers, one of whom leaves a weapon behind. April grabs the odd-looking sword.

Opening titles over the TEENAGE MUTANT NINJA TURTLES gloating over their victory, as they slosh through the sewers.

In their hideout, the wisecracking Turtles report to their master, the rat SPLINTER. They do a little rock and roll meditation, then call out for pizza. RAPHAEL is the one who dropped his sword while saving April, and he takes off to do a little meditation of his own.

Two of the other Turtles collect their pizza through a manhole cover—at a three dollar discount for late delivery.

MICHAELANGELO, DONATELLO and LEONARDO pig out on the pizza pie, while Raphael wanders incognito through the city. He trips up a couple of purse snatchers, then fights a quick ninja duel with CASEY JONES, a hockey stick-wielding vigilante. Casey slam-dunks Raphael in a garbage can, then disappears into the shadows.

Back underground, Splinter has a talk with Raphael about dealing with his anger.

April's boss, CHARLES, and his son, DANNY, are in April's apartment. Danny is one of the youths who was stealing stuff in the opening scenes. And while his father talks to April, Danny steals twenty dollars from her purse.

April interviews CHIEF OF POLICE STEARNS. The Turtles are her biggest fans as they watch on TV, but SHREDDER, head of the crime ring, wants her silenced. As Danny is hauled in by the cops, the Chief hauls April into his office and has a good shout with her.

Raphael follows April down into the subway, where she is jumped by a gang of Shredder's ninja warriors. Raphael steps in and holds the bad guys at bay, but April is injured and the Turtle has to spirit her away to the underground hideout.

April wakes up, freaks out, and tries to deal with meeting a four foot tall rat and four huge teenaged Turtles named after Renaissance artists. Splinter tells how he learned ninja from his master YOSHI, then passed his skills on to the Turtles after they were all contaminated by radioactive ooze.

That night, April invites the boys into her apartment, and they all have a good time over frozen pizza and other assorted junk foods.

When the Turtles return to the hideout, the place is trashed and Splinter is missing. In shock, they go back to April's apartment for the night.

Act II
Chief Stearns finds Danny's file, calls Charles and tells him to keep April off his case.

In the morning, Charles stops by April's apartment and tells her she's off the crime wave story. The Turtles hide, but Danny sees one of them.

In traffic, Danny and his dad argue about the boy's clandestine activities. Danny bails out of the car and disappears.

He goes underground to the ninja thief hideout, where a hoard of juvenile delinquents indulge in booze, gambling, and cigarettes, not to mention the stolen goods they've been piling up.

This is also where the young ninjas train, and Shredder calls a meeting to bestow warrior status on one of the boys. Then he orders the elimination of the Turtles, who Danny squeals on.

Meanwhile, Splinter is in pretty bad shape, shackled and hanging from a wall in the warehouse.

The Turtles watch TV in April's apartment as she reports on the mysterious ninja thieves, aka the FOOT CLAN. She's violated her gag order, and Charles and the police chief are plenty ticked.

At the apartment, Leonardo and Raphael get into an argument while trying to come up with a strategy for rescuing Splinter. Raphael goes up on the roof to blow off some steam, while Donatello and Michelangelo munch on some pork rinds.

Casey Jones spots Raphael on the roof, just as the Turtle is jumped by ninja warriors from the Foot Clan.

April comes home bummed about her job to find the other three Turtles watching cartoons in her living room. The four of them go downstairs to check out the antique store while Raphael gets his chops busted up on the roof.

April and the three Turtles make it back to the apartment just in time to have a wounded Raphael and a herd of ninjas crash the place. A free-for-all erupts, and the fight moves downstairs to the antique store when reinforcements arrive.

Pretty soon the Turtles are outnumbered about a zillion to one, and even with some serious help from Casey Jones, things get way out of hand—all five make a tactical withdrawal as the building burns to the ground.

As he leaves, Casey overhears a telephone message for April, telling her she's been fired.

At the home of the Foot Clan, Shredder knocks Splinter around, trying to find out more about the Turtles.

Shredder's right hand man knocks the kids around for letting the Turtles get away, and in his rage he kills one of the youths.

Danny has a chat with Splinter, and starts to have second thoughts about his adopted family.

April, Casey and the Turtles arrive at an old farmhouse, just as their transportation breaks down. April and Casey get into a shouting match while the boys try to keep themselves busy.

April sketches pictures of the Turtles, while she tells us a little about who the Turtles are and what they're up to. Donatello's helping Casey try and get a vehicle working, while Leonardo watches over Raphael, who is in a coma and soaking in the bathtub. April almost warms up to Casey, but he blows it with a burst of chauvinism.

Raphael finally comes to, and he and Leonardo apologize for their earlier argument. Then all four Turtles go out into the fields to practice ninja.

Back at Foot Clan HQ Danny turns up missing, and Shredder is disturbed by the familiarity of the Turtles' fighting techniques.

At the farmhouse, the Turtles get into shape for the coming battle. And Casey manages to finagle his way into giving April a shoulder rub.

While meditating, Leonardo finds out that Splinter is alive and rushes to tell the other boys the good news. That night, the four of them join in meditation and call up Splinter, who tells the Turtles that he loves them and that they must stick together.

Next morning, while Casey and April chat on the front porch, the Turtles announce that it's time to go back to the city.

They drive back to the old sewer hideout, where they find Danny in hiding. While the gang gets ready to spend the night underground, macho claustrophobic Casey heads back up to sleep in the truck.

Danny takes one of Aprils' drawings of Leonardo, then sneaks away in the middle of the night, with Casey tailing him all the way to Shredder's hideout.

Danny sneaks back to see Splinter, who tells about his life with Master Yoshi and Yoshi's rival, the man who has become Shredder.

Casey goes undercover to rescue Splinter, and Shredder finds Danny talking to the large rat. Shredder also discovers the picture of Leonardo in the boy's pocket, then orders the rat killed.

Meanwhile, the warriors of the Foot Clan invade the Turtles' sewer hideout.

Act III

Casey and Danny free Splinter, but have to fight their way past Shredder's right-hand man, then talk their way past the his juvenile delinquent ninja wannabes.

The Turtles hold their own against the mob of ninja warriors, and the battle moves from the hideout to the sewers, to the street, and to a rooftop. The Turtles finally take everybody out, but then Shredder shows up...

The Turtles take turns at Shredder, and are repulsed one after the other. Down on the street, Danny, Casey and Shredder's delinquents show up to watch the battle. Casey hot wires a garbage truck and derails Shredder's reinforcements.

Up on the roof, the Turtles are exhausted as they gang up on Shredder. They manage to wound him, but they just can't take him out. Then the bad guy pins down Leonardo, and talks the other Turtles out of their weapons. Things are looking pretty grave...

Until Splinter shows up and reveals that Shredder is indeed Yoshi's old rival. Shredder flies in a rage at Splinter, who, with a little help from Casey, eliminates the evil ninja master.

A joyful reunion for the rat and Turtles, and then the cops show up, wondering what in the world could have caused so much commotion.

Danny finds April and gives back the money he stole, then searches through the crowd to patch things up with his father Charles, who kowtows to April to get her to come back to work for him.

And April and Casey finally lock lips, as Splinter and the Teenage Mutant Ninja Turtles cheer them on.

TEENAGE MUTANT NINJA TURTLES

The police look down at APRIL, and she up at them with her mouth lolling open in amazement, while nearby, a

MANHOLE COVER

slowly rises, revealing a pair of masked eyes. The eyes spot a single Sai (Ninja Dagger) on the ground next to April's purse, but so does April, and while the police return their attention to the thugs, she quietly stuffs the Sai into her purse.

> VOICE
> Damn.

And as the cover drops over the masked eyes

                                    CUT TO:

INT. SEWER - NIGHT

where three shadows, long and thin on the sewer wall, move in a line, splashing through shallow water. The shapes are almost human in form. Almost.

But they talk just like teenagers.

                    SHADOW #1
          We were awesome, bros! Awesome!

                    SHADOW #2
               (as a sportscaster)
          Yes, dudes and dudettes, major
          league butt-kicking is <u>back</u> in
          town!

                    SHADOW #3
          <u>Oh,</u> yeah.

They turn a corner and into full view for the first
time.

THE TEENAGE MUTANT NINJA TURTLES

Powerfully built. Heavily armed. Definitely green.

The first is LEONARDO, with blue mask and "katana"
(Ninja swords), the unofficial leader of the group.
Disciplined. Calculating. Cool under fire.

Next is MICHAELANGELO, with orange mask and
"nunchuckus," the happy-go-lucky, rock 'n' roll,
wisecrackin' surf Turtle. Slightly chubbier than
the others.

The third is DONATELLO, with purple mask and "bo"
(Ninja Staff), the intellectual of the group with
a knack for fixing things. Introspective. Often
soft-spoken. He views the world with a sense of
wonder.

                    LEONARDO
                 (pumping fist)
          Awesome!

                    MICHAELANGELO
          <u>Right</u>-eous!

DONATELLO
Bossa nova!

The other Turtles turn and give Donatello a look.

DONATELLO
Chevy Nova?
(more looks; he
imitates Mike)
Ex-cellent!

Much better. The other Turtles pat him on the back
with "All right!"s and a "Gimme three!" as they
`high three' (a Turtle three-fingered version of
a high five), and continue happily along.

MICHAELANGELO
Come on, let's hurry it up,
I'm starvin'.

They come upon the same boarded-up door seen
earlier, which swings open with unexpected ease as
they enter.

A fourth shadow, and then Turtle, steps into view
wearing a red mask. This is RAPHAEL. Mr. Intensity.

He looks at his single Sai, then back down the sewer.

RAPHAEL
Damn.

He, too, then enters the

INT. DEN - CONTINUOUS

a converted storage/maintenance chamber that, for
a sewer dwelling, has been made very warm and
comfortable. The place is filled with furnishings
and items that have been swept down the sewer and
bandaged together. Donatello has even rigged
lighting, a beat-up telephone half-booth, an old

211

black-and-white TV, and a heating source that taps
into the visible subterranean steam pipes. A tide
mark from earlier floodings accents the walls. A
picture of the Turtles from a photo booth is proudly
displayed.

Leonardo—energized, but trying to control it—
rushes TOWARD CAMERA and kneels.

> LEONARDO
> We have had our first battle,
> Master Splinter. They were
> many, but we kicked... we
> fought well.

THE CAMERA SLOWLY TRACKS AROUND TO REVEAL

SPLINTER

an aging, arthritic rat who stands about four feet
high and wears a patched-up robe and slippers.
Exuding the wisdom of his years, his voice is a balm
of tranquillity, his eyes serene, yet sharp.

And half of his right ear is missing.

> SPLINTER
> Were you seen?

Leonardo shakes his head "no."

> SPLINTER
> In this, you must never lapse.
> Even those who would be our
> allies... would not under-
> stand. You must strike hard
> and fade away. Without a
> trace.

Donatello flashes the slightest look at Raphael,
but this is more than Splinter needs. He turns to
Raphael and waits.

> RAPHAEL
> (finally bursting)
> I lost a Sai.

> SPLINTER
> Then it is gone.

> RAPHAEL
> But I can get it <u>back</u>, I
> can...

> SPLINTER
> Raphael. Let it go.

Raphael quietly burns while Michaelangelo moves to
the phone.

SPLINTER	MICHAELANGELO
(addressing them)	(in b.g.)
Your Ninja skills are	You got the address?
reaching their peak.	(beat)
Only one truly important	All right, good,
lesson remains, but must	yeah, I wanna large,
wait. I know it is hard	thick crust, with
for you here, under-	double cheese, ham,
ground. Your teenage	pepperoni, mush-
minds are broad, eager.	rooms, onion, sau-
But you must never stop	sage, green peppers,
practicing the art of	and <u>no</u> anchovies. I
Ninja- the art of invis-	mean no anchovies.
ibility. You are still	You put anchovies on
young, but one day I will	this thing and
be gone... Use my teach-	you're a <u>dead</u> man,
ings wisely...	okay? <u>Oh</u>, and...

> SPLINTER
> Michaelangelo!

He gives Splinter a little "sorry" smile and quickly
finishes.

>   MICHAELANGELO
> Uh, that'll do.
>   (sotto)
> An' the clock's tickin', dude!

He hangs up the phone and rejoins the others.

>   SPLINTER
> I suggest we all meditate now
> on the events of this evening.

Splinter closes his eyes and begins to meditate, but only a few seconds go by before they pop open again to the BLARING party song, "Tequila".

He turns to see Mike and Don dancing near a piecemeal stereo, their frenetic movements a living homage to "Two Wild and Crazy Turtles." But when the break cadence arrives, the part where everyone usually shouts, "Tequila!" the brothers stop, point, and substitute,

>   MIKE AND DON
> Nin-jit-su!

before picking up again. Mike finally spots Splinter.

>   MICHAELANGELO
> Uh, well, this is
> "like"...meditating...

Splinter turns back with a slight roll of his eyes before closing them again. But the hint of a grin on his face belies his knowledge that "boys will be boys."

Leo, sitting on a couch and "dancing" with his upper body, sees Raphael don the standard Turtle disguise—trenchcoat and fedora—and head for the door.

LEONARDO
Hey, Raph, where ya goin'?

RAPHAEL
(still peeved)
Out. To a movie. That okay
with _you_?

Leo raises his hand as if to say, "Hey, sorry I
asked."

And as Raphael exits

                                        CUT TO:

_____

Top Secrets:
Bruce Joel Rubin

Bruce Joel Rubin

GHOST

X

THE BIG DAY HAD COME. BRUCE JOEL RUBIN, his wife and two kids were finally leaving Illinois and heading for Hollywood. Rubin had misgivings, to say the least: "I was afraid, you see. I was afraid that if I made the move, and it didn't work out, my dream of being a screenwriter would be over. And I could not afford to lose that dream. It was all that motivated me. So better to be in the midwest and pray, than to go out and find my prayers weren't going to be answered."

But his wife convinced him that this was the right move. After all, hadn't he wanted this all his life? And hadn't they just returned from the Hollywood premiere of BRAINSTORM, his first spec script sale? Now was the time, and he who hesitates is lost, she'd said, and Bruce was finally convinced. The house was sold, the boxes packed, and the phone rang with a last-minute call. It was Bruce's agent.

"Bruce," the agent said, "I don't want to represent you any longer."

"But I just sold my house!"

"I'm sorry, Bruce, but what can I tell you, your work is just too metaphysical. And besides," the agent went on, "nobody wants to make a movie about ghosts."

Which once again proves that William Goldman was right. Nobody knows anything.

Bruce Joel Rubin (he uses the middle name to differentiate himself from another writer named Bruce Rubin) began his pursuit of a film career by enrolling at New York University's film school. There, he and classmates Brian DePalma, Martin Scorcese, and others developed their craft, and waited impatiently for the day they would burst onto the Hollywood scene.

"I figured once I left film school I would be immediately successful," says Rubin. "Little did I know that it would be twenty years before my first film was made!" What he has since learned, however, is that is more the norm than the exception. "In fact, the most common thing is to never have a film made at all!"

Finding himself in a predicament familiar to many writers—that is to say, broke—Rubin was quick to take the local Illinois university up on their offer to teach part-time. "I offered to teach screenwriting," he says, "but for some reason they didn't want me to do that. Instead, I was hired to teach public speaking."

It's an interesting image to contemplate, this vision of Bruce Joel Rubin teaching public speaking. His physical presence is nondescript; average height, average weight, thinning hair. His voice is quiet, his speech calm and measured. Powerful oration would not seem to be his forte, and yet, there he was, teaching school while writing spec scripts.

His first script sale would go on to become a movie that will probably make its biggest mark in trivia books: What film was Natalie Wood working on when she died? Rubin's complete disappointment in BRAINSTORM was only barely mitigated by the excitement of having a movie made, since extensive rewriting of the script by a parade of writers resulted in significant changes. In fact, the movie's final form retained not one word of Rubin's original dialogue, and he was forced to go through the Writers Guild arbitration process for credit. "In the end, I decided I didn't want a screenplay credit, because it wasn't my screenplay," says Rubin. "But I wanted a story credit, because it was my story." He settled for that, only to learn later that "story credit means nothing in Hollywood, or at best, has very limited value. But in this case it told the truth, and I have always been better served by the truth. Of course, this particular truth never got me any work, but on the other hand it never hurt my career, either."

Something else that certainly didn't hurt his career was his spec script, JACOB'S LADDER. Once featured in *American Film Magazine* as one of the ten best unproduced scripts in Hollywood, JACOB'S LADDER served Rubin well long before it was even bought. "People who'd never met me already knew of me, because they'd read the script," says Rubin. It was a script that opened the doors for Rubin to pitch another film idea—a little something that existed only in treatment form. A little something called *Ghost*.

Termed by one *Daily Variety* critic as, "An unlikely grab bag of styles that teeters, spiritlike, between life and death," GHOST was not taken too seriously at first. The review went on to say, "GHOST could nonetheless be a hit for Paramount..." To say the least. Projections are that when they finally stop counting GHOST will pull in around half a *billion* dollars.

Long after many of its contemporaries had completed their run and were out in the video stores, GHOST continued to fill the theaters, in some cases even seeing the earnings go *up* each week instead of down. It's a film that clung to life even more tenaciously than its star, Patrick Swayze, in his role as a banker who is killed, but is unable to completely sever his ties to the world of the living.

GHOST is very possibly the perfect commercial film. All the elements are there: a romance between a good-looking couple, a couple of very nasty bad guys, some exceptionally fine comedy relief in the person of Whoopi Goldberg's Oda Mae, lots of well-choreographed action, and a sweet, clear message. And, to top it all off, a relentlessly romantic and nostalgic theme song, *Unchained Melody* by the Righteous Brothers.

In taking aim at the mainstream audience, Rubin, along with director Jerry Zucker, went to great pains to keep things simple. Symbolism (the angel statue being hoisted in the air, the erotic claymaking, the smashing of barriers in the opening scene) is anything but subtle, and therefore not likely to pass over the head of the average viewer. The comedic tone of all of Oda Mae's scenes is strategic and eminently crafty; as Rubin himself says, it goes straight for the commercial jugular, and prevents GHOST from becoming a film that takes itself too seriously. It also keeps the tragedy of the story from weighing the movie down; after all, for most of the film the main character is dead, and won't ever be throwing phallic clay pots with his girlfriend again.

In dealing with a supernatural character, care must be taken to find limits to their power. Just as the seemingly invincible Superman could be easily felled by Kryptonite, so must a ghost have an Achilles heel of some sort; otherwise, any conflict is no contest, and therefore not dramatic. In GHOST, Sam's powers are extremely limited at first, because he has no idea how to go about being a proper ghost. As he learns to walk through doors and move objects through the focusing of pure energy, he becomes a force to be reckoned with, and certainly one who could make mincemeat of a mere mortal. So, how did Rubin create dramatic tension for the final confrontation with Carl?

He foreshadowed the idea that ghosts who invade someone's body are weakened almost to the point of paralysis. As soon as they depart the body, the ghost is limp, and powerless. The concept is first presented to us when Oda Mae's room is packed with spirits waiting to talk to the living, and one finally gets so impatient he leaps into her body. Later, Oda Mae is again possessed, this time by Sam, as he shares a last dance with Molly. Enter a murderous, maddened Carl, and Sam, shocked out of Oda's body, is forced to watch helplessly as his best friend-turned enemy chases the women outside.

It's interesting to note in Rubin's interview that his initial draft had Oda Mae being killed before Sam could recover and rescue her. Zucker insisted that the audience just wouldn't sit still for that, and Rubin eventually acquiesced. It was a change he was later quite thankful for, as were thousands upon thousands of moviegoers.

With GHOST and JACOB'S LADDER now finished projects, has Rubin finished writing about the hereafter? "I could never say everything there is to say, if I wrote for the next hundred years," he says. "These are stories about life, and about one experience we all, at some time or another, will share: the moment we have to give up that life, and let go of all we hold most dear—right down to our desire to breathe. Now, what could be more important or worthwhile to write about than that?"

Interview with Bruce Joel Rubin

GHOST

Like many screenwriters, you began by writing industrial films.

Yes, I did films for Wausau Insurance, Morton Salt, the local library, and for anyone else who would pay me. It was not very lucrative, but considering the level of need my family was in at that time, it was wonderful.

Did you find that the process of writing those films was beneficial in terms of your writing skills? In other words, did they help you write better screenplays?

The only thing they did was show me that I could probably write industrial and corporate films as a career if I wanted to, but I really wanted to be a Hollywood screenwriter. And in order to do that you have to write screenplays—complete, feature-length screenplays. A lot of people have asked, "Well, can I just write a short one, to demonstrate my talent?" No. If you want to write a feature film, you have to write one. It has a very defined form. It's like writing a sonnet; you can't write a six-line sonnet, because that's not a sonnet. And you cannot learn how to write one unless you write the full fourteen lines.

There is structure and flow to learn, and while you have

great freedom within that, you have to obey the structure. And learning the structure of film is the essence of writing a screenplay.

And so you pursued your desire to write feature films, and were rewarded with the option of your spec script, BRAINSTORM.

Yes. This was a film that I had intended to make on my own—in fact, I was one week away from shooting, with actors flying out, sets built, locations booked—when the financier, a wealthy shopping-mall magnate, got cold feet at the last moment and pulled the plug. One week away. It was a very devastating experience.

But it must have been gratifying to see the film finally made.

Well, it was actually a bit sad, because the film was totally taken away from me. This is a complicated story, but there was another writer on the film, a friend of mine named Philip Messina. He did a rewrite, and though we didn't officially collaborate, we certainly conferred and tried to work together.

At any rate, Philip's rewrite was wonderful. The version that he wrote, that had both of our names on it, was the movie that should have been made. Unfortunately, MGM and the film's director went to other writers, and the film began to devolve into something quite different from what it had been. A lot of the basic conceptual elements survived, but the drama, the story, the potential, all the fullness and richness of it just began to somehow abort. And I couldn't believe it, but every draft they would send me was worse than the last, and the worse it got, the closer it got to production.

Sounds like a disillusioning experience.

Hollywood is about disillusionment. It's about illusion and disillusion. And you have to learn how to deal with all aspects of illusion if you want to be a screenwriter.

Being a writer in Hollywood—and you've probably heard this in interviews before—is one step down from janitor in terms of the studio power structure. And you have to understand and appreciate that. The only time you are not below the janitor is when they want you. And for that period of time when they are talking about doing your film, you couldn't be replaced by God in terms of their affections. However, once they have made the deal, suddenly you learn all the things they don't like about your script. They don't tell you about them until they buy it, and then they go into the whole process of, "Well, this should be changed, that should be changed, we never really liked the second act, you've got a real problem with this character, that should be a woman instead of a man," and so on.

And you say, "But you just paid me all that money for this script!"

Exactly, but once they own it, the relationship changes very quickly, and the janitor's position becomes enviable.

Now, BRAINSTORM was finally made, and my wife and I flew out—at our own expense, I might add—to the premiere. And probably the most important thing that happened while we were here was that we had lunch with Brian DePalma, one of my NYU classmates. And Brian urged me very strongly to move out to Hollywood if I was serious about a screenwriting career, something I had heard numerous times but never wanted to consider.

What changes in your writing do you credit with causing your breakthrough into the ranks of professional screenwriting?

My writing has always come from the same space inside of me. It really is a metaphysical world view, and my best writing has always been motivated and inspired by that. It is a postulation of a vision of life that is not bookended by the experience of birth or death. It's a bigger experience, a bigger world, than we perceive, and I feel drawn to addressing those issues, and informing people that life is a more extraordinary and wondrous experience than a lot of people manage to remember on a daily basis.

But those are your own feelings and beliefs. Most of us have strong feelings and beliefs—it's getting them down on paper that can be so damn difficult, and requires certain skills.

Yes, it requires skills, but more than that it requires the basic motivation. And having something that inspires you to write, rather than just weaving a tale... merely weaving a tale is for me, not satisfying. I can make up stories, but to what end? For me, they have to be about something, they have to have purpose. And that purpose inspires me, drives me, to write. BRAINSTORM, GHOST, and JACOB'S LADDER, are all very much driven by this urge to enlighten.

In terms of writing skills, I have to admit that I never studied writing. I took a class at NYU in the early '60's, and I nearly failed the course. The teacher kept talking about something he described as "triangularity," which is something that, to this day, I haven't grasped.

In all the interviews I've done and all the writers I've talked to, I've never heard of "triangularity."

It was the idea that there are three points of conflict in every scene, even when there are only two people on the screen. That lost me. I still don't get it.

What did you do at NYU Film School, if not writing?

I concentrated on directing. But to answer your question concerning the honing of writing skills, it's my feeling that writing is rewriting. I rewrite and rewrite my scripts, and keep working them until they get better. I go over and over until they lose the fat, until I find that kind of condensation and shorthand of expression that makes the movie work on the page.

How do you know when it's working?

To me, a movie that I can read over and over and still find interesting is working. If I start to nod off during the reading of my script or anyone else's script, obviously that's a bad sign.

In this process of rewriting, do you use friends or colleagues as sounding boards? In other words, do you send out rough drafts, and get critiques, and then incorporate their comments, or is this a strictly solitary process?

I rely totally on myself. The only exception is that I let my wife read scripts-in-progress, mostly because I want some kind of affirmation.

Writing, ultimately, is the battle with myself, and it is my personal struggle. And it is a struggle. Sure, sometimes it flows beautifully, but more often I find I've gone in the wrong direction, or the material hasn't coalesced the way I wanted it to, or I've written five degrees lower than I was aiming for. And when that happens, I enter into a kind of sacrificial moment, and there follows a terrible bloodletting where I go in and do terrible damage to my material. I slash it to pieces. I've done that many times, and it seems to me that it is *that* moment when the movie becomes *mine*.

You see, first the story emerges on its own terms, and I'll kind of like it here and there, but there comes a moment when I say, this just isn't working. And at that moment I have to—and I'm sure you've heard this a million times—I have to "kill my babies." The *best* scenes, the *best* characters, *the* best dialogue, must all at one time or another be sacrificed in order to get what is really desired from the material. It's a very ritualistic process, and it always depresses me. I always get angry, and I am impossible to be with during those days when I'm destroying some of my best work. On the other hand,

227

out of that ritual, and from those ashes, the Phoenix always rises. It has never failed me.

The real movie finally reveals itself.

Yes. It's a process of digging deep. If you write a superficial movie, you get a superficial script. And I can't be happy with that. I can write superficially, off the top of my head, with no problem, and I have done that. I hate it. I want to write from depth, from my heart, from my soul, if you will. To do anything but that is a waste of time.

You spoke earlier about structure, terming it the essence of creating a story that works. Let's talk about structure a bit. It would seem that GHOST would lend itself quite easily to the traditional three-act breakdown, while JACOB'S LADDER seemed an almost literal translation of the mythological model, the journey of the hero as espoused by Joseph Campbell and other mythologists. Was this intentional?

I'm never intentional. I'm totally intuitive. I don't understand structure, at least in the academic sense. If you asked me today what a denouement is, I cannot tell you. I don't know my first act break from my second act break. Now, granted, I have to go back and identify them with the help of producers and directors, but I don't write that way. I just write from the gut, let it come out, and it tends to shape itself. I know what I think is a good movie. I know when a film works, and when it's not working. All I try to do is make it work.

I am a member of what I call the "Carpet-laying" school of screenwriting. I keep trying to get the carpet to lay flat, and every time there's a bump, I have to do whatever I can to push it toward the corner. And the film is not done until there are no bumps, and it's a clean ride right from the beginning to the end. The carpet lays perfectly on the floor, and it looks great. At that point I've discovered that I have nailed down a successful structure for that particular film.

228

Let's apply that school of thought to a specific film, say, JACOB'S LADDER...

JACOB'S LADDER was written very much as an act of faith. I didn't know where it was going. I just started writing it.

It began as a dream, a nightmare, really, which is the second scene in the movie. A guy leaves the subway, only to find that all the exits are locked. And in my dream I realized that the only way out for this guy was down. And down implied, very clearly, to Hell. And so I understood that in order to find freedom, I had to go through Hell.

I woke up in a terror from that experience, and the first words in my mind were, "What a great opening for a movie!" That's where it came from. I think a lot of great movies come from those spaces inside you, those dream realms. So when I started writing the script I knew nothing more than that one scene: a man on a subway who starts out with this experience.

At one point early on my wife looked over my shoulder and said, "What in the world are you writing?" And I said, "I have no idea." It was unlike anything I'd ever tried before—it was dark, frightening, and emotionally violent.

You just wrote page after page, with no outline, no road map of any sort?

I began writing an outline. In four days I created a sort of direction, but even that was written blindly, I really had no idea how this movie would come together. And as I immersed myself in the writing process, the real movie began to emerge, becoming something quite different from what I had begun. By the way, I don't think that experience is all that uncommon for writers.

Many writers say that they write an outline, and then throw it out once they begin the screenplay.

When I begin writing I always write a character biography for my main characters, and the minute I start the script I throw it out the window.

Why?

Because they become somebody else. The voice of the character has nothing to do with the voice I was planning when I wrote the biography. Another voice emerges, and you have to pay attention to that voice. You can't force it to be what you wanted it to be; you have to see what *it* wants to be. And when that happens, in a sense your characters write your movie. You simply become the vehicle, and in a way you're just transcribing. It's quite wonderful, as you become the first person to see your movie. It's very much—and forgive me, Shirley MacLaine—very much a channeling type of experience. You're allowing something to pass through you, and JACOB'S LADDER was that way for me.

While watching that movie I tried to visualize the actual script, and it seemed to me that it would be a fairly confusing ride for a reader. Was it? And if so, did you find that to be an obstacle in selling the script?

People loved it. The power on the page was palpable. The screenplay was so intense that people read it, and told me stories of literally getting hallucinations while they read it. One woman told me that she took the script with her on a whale watch, and never looked up to see the whales because she couldn't take her eyes off the page. It was completely engrossing. Very frightening, very provocative. And it kind of did what the movie does—bypass the intellect, going directly to the psyche. Because you never really knew where you were. Part of Jacob's struggle is that he's losing his mind; part of your experience is that you're losing it with him. And so you are put into a state of terrible paranoia, which for me is as frightening a condition as you can be in.

Because nothing is real, and no one can be trusted.

Everything you believed to be true suddenly isn't true. That was the kind of fear, and the level of dread, I wanted to show in the script.

There was something that puzzled me about the film, and that was the drug experimentation angle—it seemed thrown in, or if not thrown in at least placed in there in order to offer something more geared toward a mainstream mode of thought.

It was to give me a second act. I had to figure out the particulars of how Jacob died. I vaguely thought it was a Mafia killing, but I didn't like that, didn't want to do it. And then it hit me that he was a soldier in Vietnam, which was still fairly fresh terrain in 1980.

So I decided he would be killed under strange circumstances, and that the movie would be about the unraveling of those circumstances. That offered a plotline for the basic thriller aspect of the movie. The truth is, when you get to the end of the movie, you discover the story you were watching is an entirely different movie than the one you thought you were watching.

Right, it wasn't about that at all. Which is why the final graphic at the end puzzled me.

The graphic at the end was not my idea.

I had no idea why that was there.

Because Adrian Lyne felt there was a segment of the audience who would be desperate for some reality. That they couldn't make the leap to the higher element of the movie. I was pretty outraged by it, and said that to Adrian, and we fought about it a lot. But I wasn't the director. The only ultimate power is directing. As someone once said to me, directing is writing the final draft of your movie. And so I am determined and am planning to direct my next movie.

In spite of being a sort of roller coaster nightmare for the audience, JACOB'S LADDER ends on a very positive

note, an optimistic note—in a way, the same note you struck at the end of GHOST.

They're the same movie told from different perspectives.

Did you set out, in either case, to write a commercially successful film? Of course you wanted it to succeed, but did thoughts of commerciality affect your writing?

I don't think about those things. I just want to write an entertaining movie, a good movie that would entertain *me*. I don't mind being commercial. My themes are hopefully buried within some sort of commercial pill that you can swallow, so the message might detonate inside you later, or even during the movie. I'm always trying to get at something inside people, and I love to be commercially successful in doing it.

The success of GHOST is a shock, a wonderful shock. In the eighteenth week the grosses were going *up*, not down. That's pretty amazing. Now, I never knew what JACOB'S LADDER would do, either. I knew there would be people outraged by it. I knew there would be people who would hate me for writing it, if only because it requires you to do work. It's a movie that doesn't leave you, just because you leave the theater. You still have to do work with it, and there's a lazy factor in American culture that keeps some people from wanting to expend that energy. They want to walk out of a movie and say, "Hey, that was great!" and then move on.

At the showing I attended, there was complete silence in the audience as they left the theater. Not a sound. And I remember thinking, now that's called making an impact.

There are some people who have been profoundly affected by it, and they're the ones I was trying to reach. I suppose I'm sort of teacherly in my writing, and my reason for writing, and some students I will get this way, and others I'll get another way, with GHOST, perhaps.

What about practicality in terms of production? Do you keep that in mind as you write?

Yes. I want the movie to get made. I want people to see my movies, and I want people to like and be engaged by them. Even JACOB'S LADDER, which a lot of people have some trouble with, is certainly pretty engaging. It's hard to simply dismiss.

Well, it succeeds on a number of levels. You can watch that movie and give it no thought whatsoever, and it works as a thriller.

I was trying for that, with the hope that, when it climbed to a higher level, the audience would be willing and able to take that ride also.

JACOB'S LADDER was one of the best-known spec scripts in town for a number of years. GHOST, on the other hand, began as a treatment. Did you sell it in that form?

Hollywood does not respond well to treatments. Hollywood—particularly a few years ago—is based on the pitch. I had to go around town pitching GHOST. And I learned a lot. First of all, I learned how to become a storyteller with a four-minute deadline. Five minutes at most.

I went from office to office, and as I told the story I could see moments where their eyes would lose focus, where I would lose their interest. And so I realized I had to work on my pitch. And I worked on my presentation, with special attention to those parts of the pitch that I observed were losing my audience. Every time I saw an eye start to drift a little bit, I would go home and change that part. Finally I got that pitch to a fine, honed product. I went to four producers one week, and every one of them said yes, they wanted to do it. And I was in the enviable position of having to pick. One of the producers, Lisa Weinstein at Paramount, cried when I told her the story, and I just knew that I trusted that. I went with Lisa, who took it to Dawn Steele, who loved it, and I went home with a deal to write the movie.

Now, there's no such thing as a "first draft" in Hollywood. There's a thing called *draft inflation*, where your
first draft is in fact more likely your fifteenth draft. But
it's called a first draft, because the studio doesn't want to
show it to the executives until it's ready.

**So you do however many drafts are necessary for it to
become a first draft.**

And you send it in and get your response. And the
response to the first draft of GHOST was wonderful. I
got calls from everyone in the studio, it seemed, saying
we're going to make this movie, this is great. And I was
delighted, and Dawn Steele said, "Next Christmas we'll
be going to the premiere together." Little did we know
that it would take a year just to find a director, let alone
go into production!

Frank Oz, director of LITTLE SHOP OF HORRORS, was
the original choice, but his vision of the movie involved
a budget the studio was not willing to go for, and Frank
was gone. Then, I heard that the they had another
director lined up: a fellow named Jerry Zucker. And I
said, AIRPLANE? It was a total trauma for me.

When I met with Jerry he wanted to make a lot of
changes, and I found that very painful. But I said to
myself, look, Jerry's going to be directing this movie, I'd
better find a way to make this work. And I called him
and said, "Let's you and I go out to dinner, with the
understanding that we cannot talk about GHOST. Let's
just talk about life." And we did, and discovered each
other as people, and formed the foundation that became
an extraordinary professional relationship and one of the
most wonderful personal relationships I've ever had.

**So you were able to approach the rewriting process in a
better frame of mind.**

Yes, and I wrote nineteen drafts with Jerry. Most of that
rewriting was aimed at getting Jerry invested in the
creative process, to have a personal stake in the movie.

Even when the changes took the story far afield from where I thought it should be, I made those changes, relying on his intelligence to see that we were going in the wrong direction. And in the end, what we ended up with was very close to what I had originally intended. A little more broad-based, perhaps, and certainly the humor factor was expanded—and that was all good, because it went right for the commercial mainstream. The original version of the script was darker, more muted.

What this whole experience taught me is to not abandon my work too quickly. It might have been easy to become frustrated with the changes, and just throw up my hands and turn the movie over. That happens to many writers. Instead, I learned to try to lead the director, through the writing, to a point where I believed we needed to go. Better to compromise and make it work, than to lose it completely by giving up.

When you speak of leading a director, or an audience, in the direction you believe they should go... what direction is that? What do you look for in your work?

I believe a movie should have a multiplicity of ideas. To have certain depths, so it plays on different levels for different people. So a ten year-old can find something in it, and an eighty year-old can find something as well. I like a film to have a depth of purpose.

In GHOST, there are elements of a thriller, a romance, a mystery, and a comedy, and even though people told me I was creating a pastiche, I didn't set out to do that. I just found no problem in writing all of these together in the same movie. And I don't think the audience minded that. If anything, it felt like a full meal, they got a lot for their money. Writing pure genre pieces, and sticking to one element, is not enough, at least not for me.

Both movies ended on a positive note. Was this calculated in order to comply with Hollywood's demand for happy endings?

I don't calculate. Those endings reflect the fact that I am a deeply optimistic person.

Some people (in the audience) have to be brought to their own optimism through different cinematic techniques. Certain people want a light story to engage them in a fairly simple way, that doesn't call into question a lot of the complexities of human experience, and for them I wrote GHOST. It casts a wide net, and gives people a way of seeing life that is very affirming. I believe JACOB'S LADDER also gets you to that point, but it's more for people who are caught by the world, people for whom life is a more difficult experience, and need to be aware of the psychic end, and the metaphysical dimension of their psyches. I wanted to probe that depth, but not without purpose. I really feel that if you don't bring people to the light, you shouldn't take them on the journey. I would never want to leave anyone in darkness.

Story Outline
GHOST

ACT I

A young couple, MOLLY and SAM, and a friend, CARL, are doing some demolition on the way to renovating a unique apartment. Sam finds an Indian head penny, dated 1898, and calls it a good omen.

Sam and Carl make their way through busy New York City streets, arriving at a downtown office building, the ground floor being a prestigious bank. Before going in, Carl admires an expensive car. Sam advises him to finish making payments on the inexpensive one he's got, first.

On a very crowded elevator, the two pretend that one of them has a severely contagious, possibly fatal disease. This is obviously a game they've played before, but they still enjoy the reaction it gets.

The elevator delivers them to a busy corporate setting. Sam has an office and a secretary, and holds a higher ranking position than Carl.

Sam needs Carl to do an emergency transfer of funds. Carl requests the "MAC" code, something Sam is apparently in charge of. Sam provides him with the new code which enables him to make the transfer.

A huge statue is being delivered to the apartment. It has to be craned in. Molly and workmen are risking a long drop, but are unable to get it in the window. Sam arrives, hooks his hands on the ledge, swings out, and kicks the statue. it swings back within reach. We see sculpted pots and other pieces in the apartment. The apartment looks great. Molly wants to get rid of a big armchair of Sam's, but he insists it fits him, and in fact, comes with him. She agrees.

Later, in bed, Sam is uneasy and restless. She questions him: is it about moving in together? He says no, it's just that every time something good happens to him, he's afraid he's going to lose it. She tells him she loves him. He says, "Ditto." They see a news report of a plane crash. He feels a sense of foreboding, wonders if he should cancel an upcoming trip. She tells him he has nothing to worry about, he leads a charmed life.

It's very, very late at night. Molly is throwing a pot on a wheel. Sam enters, and joins her in the most suggestive, sensual pot-throwing demonstration ever seen. The pot becomes a phallic object they both grope with wet, gooey hands.

In the office the next day, Sam discovers that there is too much money in some of the accounts. He mentions it to Carl, who offers to help out. Sam insists on doing it himself, calls it a personal vendetta. Mentions that he has changed the MAC code. Carl inquires as to Sam and Molly's plans for the evening. Sam tells him they are going to see *Hamlet*, and invites Carl. Carl declines.

That night, walking down the street after seeing *Hamlet*, Molly and Sam pass through a seedy area of town. Molly brings up the subject of commitment. Sam has never said, "I love you." He just says, "Ditto," after she says it. They're interrupted by a TOUGH-LOOK-ING THUG, who follows them down the street. Sam wheels on him, but the guy has a gun. There's a struggle. A gunshot. The thug races off down the street, followed by Sam. Sam gives up the chase, returns to Molly—only to see himself lying on the street, blood gushing from a chest wound, Molly weeping over him.

Sam wakes up screaming, as if from a nightmare. But this isn't the real world he's awakened to, everything is very strange. A soft, inviting light invades the room, and Molly appears on the other side of the bed, beckoning him to stay. He's torn between the light and Molly. He turns away from the light.

In a hospital, Sam sees his body covered with a sheet. He's dead. As he tries to absorb this, an OLD MAN starts talking to him. He's another dead man, waiting for his wife to join him. He tells Sam to get used being this way; it's going to last a long while. Together they watch as efforts to revive a patient fail, and as warm sparkling lights from above fill the room, the deceased man's soul departs the body and rises with the light. The old man says he was lucky; sometimes the "other ones" come.

At Sam's funeral, Sam sees another ghost.

At the wake, Sam sees all the people who cared for him.

That night, in the apartment, Sam is with Molly, although, of course, she can't see him. She talks to him as though he's there. She says she can almost feel him. He's frustrated in his efforts to contact her. The cat, however, is somehow able to sense, even see him, and hisses.

The next day. Carl helps Molly sort some of Sam's stuff. They find Sam's address book, and Molly puts it in a shoe box. In leaving the apartment with some trash, Carl has put the shoe box on top of the pile. He apologizes to Molly for his mistake. Carl and Molly leave the apartment, closing the door.

Sam is left behind in the apartment. He can't open the door. He discovers he can go through it. Just as he's about to, the lock turns. The thug who killed him has come to the apartment, and Sam is powerless to do anything but watch as he prowls the place. Molly comes home. Sam is completely frustrated at his inability to warn Molly, or stop the thug. The thug watches as Molly begins undressing, and starts to approach her room. Sam scares the cat, which springs up onto the thug's face. The thug flees. Sam follows.

They board a subway. Sam encounters another ghost, a powerful spirit who chases him from that compartment, hurling him out and breaking glass in his fury.

Sam continues tailing the thug, entering a very bad part of town. From a mailbox, he learns the thug's name: WILLY LOPEZ. He follows Lopez into his apartment, and listens to a phone conversation. Lopez was looking for something, and assures the listener he'll go back for it.

Sam exits Lopez' apartment building, and sees a sign advertising a "Spiritual Advisor. Contact the Dearly Departed for $20." He goes inside.

ACT II

ODA MAE, the spiritual advisor, is a con artist, as is evident to Sam as he watches her supposedly make contact with the spirit of a woman's dead husband. When he voices his skepticism, Oda Mae reacts. She can hear him!

After she kicks everyone out and tries to recover, Sam talks with her. He tells her that a woman is in great danger, and he needs Oda Mae to make a phone call. He'll haunt her until she does.

In Molly's apartment, the phone rings. Oda Mae says she has a message from Sam. Molly hangs up.

Sam is at Oda Mae's apartment, late at night, obnoxiously singing, "I'm Henry the Eighth I Am," over and over. Oda Mae can't sleep, can't get rid of him. She relents: she'll go see Molly in person.

Oda Mae goes to see Molly. Molly won't let her up. Oda Mae starts shouting up at the window, mentioning things only Sam would know. Molly finally comes down.

They talk in a nearby diner. Molly can't let herself believe, starts to leave. Oda Mae says Sam says he loves her. Molly says Sam would never say that. Sam tells her to say, "Ditto." Oda Mae yells at the departing Molly, "Ditto." Molly turns back.

In Molly's apartment, Oda Mae explains to Molly that Sam's soul has hung around because he still has work to do, and hasn't let go of this life yet. He can't, because Molly is in danger. Sam knows who killed him. His name is Willy Lopez, and he was in the apartment, and he knows where he lives...which happens to be in Oda Mae's neighborhood. Oda Mae has heard enough, says she's done her part, and leaves.

Sam listens in as Molly tells Carl about Oda Mae and Sam. Carl tries to talk some sense into her, tell her she's vulnerable right now, doesn't want to admit Sam is gone. She wants to go to the police. He tells her they'll think she's crazy. He offers to check it out himself, if it will make her feel better.

Sam follows along with Carl as he goes to Willy Lopez' address. Carl walks up to Willy's apartment, and goes right in. He knows the guy. Carl is the one who paid Willy to go after Sam! He's been laundering money, and needs the MAC code from Sam's wallet in order to free four million dollars in drug money from some accounts. He stands to gain $80,000 himself.

Molly is at the police station. They are skeptical of her story, to say the least.

Carl is in Molly's apartment, going through Sam's stuff, searching for the MAC code. He tears a page out of an address book.

Back in the police station, Molly is shown Oda Mae's vast criminal record, mostly in confidence games and forgery. The officer is sympathetic; says that these people are experts at learning all about the deceased, in order to get money from the bereaved. Offers to press charges, but Molly declines.

At the bank's office, Carl successfully enters the MAC code. He can now access the drug money, and receives instructions over the phone detailing precisely how that should be done. It all must be handled by four o'clock the next afternoon.

In the apartment, a disconsolate Molly breaks the jar with Sam's lucky Indian head penny, sending it rolling down the stairs. Sam is there, and tries to contact her. He can't. There's a knock at the door. It's Carl. Molly can't hear Sam's shouted warnings as she opens the door. Carl tries to seduce Molly. This so upsets Sam that he is able to somehow knock over a picture, which breaks the mood enough for Molly to catch herself, and back off.

Sam heads for the subway, leaping from car to car, in search of the ghost whose energy was so strong he could break windows and hurl objects. He finds him, and faces him down. The ghost relents.

In a subway station, the ghost tries to teach Sam that moving objects is all in the mind. He has to focus all his emotions, his hate, frustration, rage, and love, at the object.

Still in the subway, but on his own now, Sam practices his newfound skill. In passing a poster for his bank, he reacts with a triumphant shout.

At Oda Mae's place of business, Sam walks in on a seance—and a roomful of spirits. The place is wall-to-wall with ghosts, waiting their turn to contact the living. Orlando, a ghost frustrated with the wait as Oda Mae talks with Sam, leaps into Oda's body, "possessing" her for a short time. When he exits her body, he is exhausted. Oda Mae kicks all the spirits out of her room. But then, Willy Lopez comes in, and Oda Mae is able to escape with Sam's help.

Later, Sam tells Oda Mae that he has a plan that will keep Willy or anyone else from bothering her again. She reluctantly agrees to participate.

Wearing her finest dress and accompanied by Sam, Oda Mae struts into the bank. Coached by Sam, but not without some comedic gaffes, Oda Mae fills out a signature card for a new account, signing the name, Rita Miller. That's the name on the account that now holds four million dollars.

Meanwhile, Carl is at his desk, and gets a call.

Back in the bank, now on the third floor, Oda Mae is now trying to see Lyle Furgeson, a high-ranking bank official. With Sam's help, she is able to convince Ferguson that they'd met before during a party; one in which Sam asserts Furgeson was so soused he wouldn't remember anything. Furgeson finally agrees to meet with Oda Mae.

At Furgeson's desk, Oda Mae, still posing as Rita Miller, startles the official by requesting a withdrawal of four million dollars. She's closing her account.

At the same time, Carl is upstairs, setting the transfer of funds in motion.

Oda Mae successfully completes the transaction, and holds a cashier's check for four million dollars. As she leaves, Molly enters the office area, and spots her. Molly talks to Furgeson, and learns that Oda Mae had used a different name in closing an account. Now more than ever, Molly suspects Oda Mae as a fraud.

Carl tries to access the account—and finds it closed! He panics, racing from machine to machine, but the MAC code only returns an "Account Closed" message on the screen. Carl is beside himself.

Out on the street, Sam is able to convince a VERY reluctant Oda Mae to turn the entire cashier's check over to a couple of nuns collecting for the Catholic church. He says it's the only way she won't be traced. She does it, but not without a titanic inner struggle.

Later that night, in the office, Carl is vainly pounding at the keyboards, trying to find the lost millions. Sam is watching, gloating. He starts to "haunt" Carl; moving chairs, turning computers on and off, and finally punching the keys on a keyboard to type out, "Sam" over and over.

Back in Molly's apartment, Carl is desperate and enraged, barely keeping himself in check as he grills Molly, trying to find out what has happened. Molly no longer believes that Sam's spirit is around, and is sure that Oda Mae is a fraud. She mentions having seen her at the bank, and that she'd used the name Rita Miller. At that moment, Carl knows he's been had. He takes action, talking to Sam's ghost when Molly leaves the room. He says he'll cut Molly's throat if Sam doesn't get him the money tonight.

Act III

Sam races to Oda Mae's place, arriving just in time to alert her and her friends to the fact that Willy Lopez and Carl are coming for the money.

As Willy searches the apartment, Sam starts haunting the place, making objects fly everywhere, terrifying and finally panicking the thug.

Lopez races outside, and in a blind panic runs into the path of a car. He's killed instantly. His soul departs his body, and as Sam watches in horror, demons from Hell come up to get him and drag him down.

Oda Mae and Sam take a taxicab to Molly's apartment.

Oda Mae tries in vain to get Molly to let her in, or even heed her warnings that she is in grave danger.

Finally, Sam convinces Molly by dragging a penny up the door, across empty space, and placing it in her hand. She lets Oda Mae in.

Through Oda Mae, Sam and Molly talk. Oda Mae can take it no longer: she offers to let Sam use her body to communicate one last time with Molly. He does, and as Molly closes her eyes, Oda Mae's touch becomes that of Sam, and in fact Oda Mae becomes Sam, as they share a last dance while the Righteous Brothers wail that "Time goes by so slowly..."

The dance is interrupted by Carl. Sam abruptly exits Oda Mae's body, and is drained, almost too exhausted to move. Oda Mae and Molly escape the apartment, racing outside to a fire escape, and an upper floor in the same state of disarray as the apartment had been in the beginning.

Carl catches Oda Mae, and is about to kill her. Molly jumps him. He throws her aside. He's just about to kill Oda Mae, when a jolt of pure energy saves her. Sam has recovered.

Carl takes Molly hostage, threatening to kill her. But Sam is now a force that can't be stopped. Through the raw energy fueled by his fury, he knocks Carl around like a puppet, hurling him off walls and knocking him off his feet. The battle ends when Carl is killed. His soul departs, talks briefly with Sam, looks back at his own bloody body— and then reacts with stark, screaming horror as the demons from Hell come to drag him away.

Sam goes to Molly and Oda Mae, to see if they're all right. His presence is now so strong, he's visible and audible to both of them. At that moment, the light returns for Sam. Before leaving, he turns to Molly, kisses her, and says, "I love you." She answers, "Ditto." Sam ascends into the light, and we see the many souls waiting to welcome him.

GHOST

INT. MARKET SECURITY BANK AND TRUST - DAY

SAM and ODA MAE approach a fancy part of the bank
housing administrative personnel. They approach a
GUARD who is standing there.

>   SAM
> Tell the guard you're here to
> see Lyle Furgeson.

>   ODA MAE
> Lyle Furgeson, please.

>   GUARD
> Do you have an appointment?

>   ODA MAE
> No, I'm here for the fun of
> it.

>   SAM
> Don't say that! Tell him Rita
> Miller's here.

>   ODA MAE
> Tell him Rita Miller's here.

                    GUARD
          Just one moment, please.

                     SAM
          Don't embellish.

                   ODA MAE
          Yes, sir.

                    GUARD
                (turning around)
          Excuse me?

She waves him on.

                     SAM
                  (whispering)
          Now listen, this guy
          Furgeson's a real jerk.

                   ODA MAE
          Why are you whispering?

                     SAM
                (he doesn't know)
          Just be quiet and listen. I've
          known him five years and he
          still thinks my name's Paul.

We see the Guard leaning over Mr. Furgeson's desk.
FURGESON looks up and sees Oda Mae. He shrugs his
shoulders.

                     SAM
                  (continuing)
          He's a social moron. You don't
          have to worry about anything.
          Tell the guard Furgeson knows
          you. You spent time with him
          and his wife Shirley at the
          Brewsters' Christmas party
          last year.

The Guard comes back.

> GUARD
> What is this regarding?

> ODA MAE
> What? He doesn't remember me?
> We were together at the
> Brewsters' Christmas party.
> With his wife Shirley. They
> had that lovely tree... all
> those presents. Why, I'll
> never forget all those beauti-
> ful...

Sam pokes her. She yelps, surprised, and glances around. The Guard gives her an odd look.

> ODA MAE
> (continuing)
> Oops. Gas.

She forces a smile. He smiles back and then goes over to Mr. Furgeson.

> SAM
> This'll be easy. Furgeson was
> so drunk at that party, he
> could have had a conversation
> with Tina Turner and he
> wouldn't remember.

The Guard whispers in Furgeson's ear. Furgeson appears totally flummoxed. He looks up at Oda Mae, embarrassed, and waves. The Guard motions her to come back. She walks proudly over to his desk. He sticks out his hand.

> FURGESON
> Hello, hello. Of course, of
> course. It's been so long.

                    ODA MAE
A long time.

                    SAM
Ask how Bobby and Snooky are.

                    ODA MAE
How are Bobby and Snooky
doin'?

                    FURGESON
                 (perplexed)
Why, they're just fine, thank
you. Nice of you to ask. And
how is your... family?

                    ODA MAE
Couldn't be better.

                    FURGESON
Well, isn't that wonderful.

                    SAM
Tell him you've been wondering
how they did on the Gibraltar
securities.

                    ODA MAE
So tell me, Fergie, how did
you do on the Gibraltar securities?

                    FURGESON
                 (surprised)
The Gibraltar securities!
Well, it looks like we topped
out, huh?

                    SAM
"We sure did!"

                    ODA MAE
We sure did.

                    FURGESON
                  (impressed)
That was a wonderful tip.

                    SAM
"Good old Randy."

                    ODA MAE
Good old Randy. Got a real
head on his shoulders.

                    SAM
"Her" shoulders.

                    ODA MAE
"Her" shoulders.

                    FURGESON
Sure does. Well... well. So
what brings you here today?

                    SAM
You're closing an account.

                    ODA MAE
I'm closing an account.

                    FURGESON
Well... wonderful. Do you have
your account number?

                    SAM
926-31043.

                    ODA MAE
926-3143.

                    SAM
31-0-43.

She looks up into the air. Furgeson eyes her
strangely.

> ODA MAE
> Make that 31-<u>0</u>-43... Numbers.
> I'm dyslexic.

He punches Rita Miller's number into the computer.
A figure appears on the screen. He stares at it for
a few seconds and then punches it again.

> FURGESON
> (trying to be calm)
> Well, Rita, you'll be with-
> drawing four million dollars
> from us today, is that cor-
> rect?

> ODA MAE
> Four million dollars?!

> SAM
> Say "yes"!

> ODA MAE
> (gasping)
> Yes! Four million. That's
> right. That's right.

> FURGESON
> And how will you want that?

> ODA MAE
> Tens and twenties?

> FURGESON
> Pardon?

> SAM
> <u>A cashier's check!</u> Tell him a
> cashier's check.

> ODA MAE
> A cashier's check.

> FURGESON
> Fine. Of course, you realize
> we're required to get some
> identification from everyone.
> It's just procedural. You
> understand.

> ODA MAE
> Of course.

Oda Mae reaches into her purse and pulls out a
DRIVER'S LICENSE and a SOCIAL SECURITY CARD.
Furgeson gets up and walks away from his desk. He
seems unsteady on his feet. An OFFICER at the next
desk is using a Brillo pad to clean a stain on her
desk. Oda Mae smiles.

> ODA MAE
> You know, if you put that
> Brillo pad in the freezer,
> it'll last twice as long.

The Officer nods appreciatively.

INT. CARD FILE ROOM-DAY

Furgeson lays Oda Mae's ID next to her signature
card. The signatures match up. He nods his head in
approval.

INT. CARL'S OFFICE-DAY

Carl looks up at the clock. It is 3:50. He pushes
down a button on the phone. A SECRETARY answers.

> SECRETARY (VO)
> Yes, Mr. Bruner.

                        CARL
        Get me the First Island Bank
        of Nassau. It's on the
        rolodex.

INT. MARKET SECURITY BANK & TRUST - DAY

Furgeson returns with Rita Miller's signature card
and a cashier's check for $4,000,000. Oda Mae's hand
shakes as she examines it.

                        FURGESON
        I'll just need your signature
        right here.

                        ODA MAE
        Sure.

                        SAM
        Sign Rita Miller.

Sam looks up and gulps. Molly has just entered the
bank and is heading toward them. He jumps up
nervously.

                        SAM
                    (continuing)
        I'll be back in a minute.
        You're on your own. Don't say
        anything foolish.

Oda Mae signs a form closing the account. Of course
the signatures match. Mr. Furgeson examines them
both and smiles. He shakes Oda Mae's hand.

                        FURGESON
        Now you be careful with this.
        It's like carrying cash, you
        know.

                         ODA MAE
                  (positively glowing)
             I sure do.

Sam rushes over to Molly. He is not sure what to
do. He notices a stack of deposit forms on the
counter she is about to pass. He hurries to it and
flicks the entire stack, a hundred sheets, flying
up into the air. Molly, confused, thinks she is
responsible and stoops to pick them up. Sam,
delighted, flicks another stack.

Oda Mae is talking a blue streak when Sam returns
to her.

                         ODA MAE
                      (continuing)
                  Then my mother took all the
                  money from the oil wells and
                  put it in gasoline pumps.
                  Every gas station has 'em you
                  know, sometimes six or more.
                  It adds up.

                           SAM
                  Oda Mae, come on. We gotta get
                  out of here. Say goodbye.

                         ODA MAE
                  (abruptly getting up)
                  Well, I've got to leave. It's
                  been a pleasure doin' business
                  with you. Say "hi" to Shirley
                  and Snooky for me.

                        FURGESON
                  Thank you, Rita. I'll be glad
                  to.

Oda Mae smiles and leaves. There is a new lilt in
her walk. Suddenly Sam looks and sees Molly about
to stand up.

                           253

> SAM
> Hurry up, Oda Mae.

At that second, Oda Mae spots a quarter lying on the ground. She stoops down and picks it up.

> ODA MAE
> (excitedly)
> What a day!

Molly sees her, does a double take, and starts to go after her. Unfortunately, Oda Mae steps onto an elevator before Molly can catch up. The doors close. Molly stops for a moment and then looks back across to the executive area. She sees Lionel Furgeson and hurries over to him.

> MOLLY
> Lionel?

He is surprised to see her and grows instantly solicitous.

> FURGESON
> Molly. How are you?

> MOLLY
> Lionel, a woman who just left,
> a black lady, about my height,
> did you see her?

> FURGESON
> Well, yes. I just took care of
> her.

> MOLLY
> What did she want? Did it have
> anything to do with me? Did
> she ask about Sam?

FURGESON
(not understanding)
Sam? No. Why?

MOLLY
Was her name Oda Mae Brown?

FURGESON
No, Rita Miller. She just
closed an account.

Molly stares at Furgeson. She is not sure what to
think.

FURGESON
(continuing)
Is there a problem?

MOLLY
(hesitating, not sure
what to say)
No. I guess not. Thanks.

She walks away, confused.

_____

Top Secrets:
TOM SCHULMAN

Tom Schulman

DEAD POETS SOCIETY

T OM SCHULMAN'S INTEREST IN FILMS began at Vanderbilt, where he opted to make a film as opposed to writing a term paper for a final grade in an English class. He found himself so enamored of the medium that he enrolled in the University of Southern California Film School, where he spent two semesters. From there, he embarked on a career writing educational films for a company that also allowed him to participate in many aspects of production.

Like most writers looking for a start, Schulman attended some classes and workshops, and eventually settled in with an informal writers' group that developed out of some friendships he had made in a theatre group for actors and directors.

"I did a little of everything with that group, including act," laughs Schulman, a youthful, likable man with a quick wit and self-deprecating good humor. "I had a very inspiring instructor tell me once that in order to write, or direct, you had to know what it was like to get up and deliver lines in front of people." Which Schulman did, in spite of being admittedly "completely terrified" to get up on stage. "But," he goes on, "it was by far the best way to get a true feel for what would work and what would not, particularly in terms of dialogue."

The informal writers' group Schulman participated

in met on a regular basis for the sole purpose of critiquing each other's work. "We would go through something I'd written, or someone else had written, scene by scene and character by character." He remembers those sessions as providing the most valuable kind of feedback a writer can receive, not only because it was completely honest, but was also accompanied by suggestions for ways to correct perceived shortcomings in the script. "It was never just, `Hey, this is great!' or `Gee, this stinks,'" says Schulman. "It was the kind of criticism that made you think, and re-evaluate, and be honest with yourself and your work. And that helped me more than any class I ever took."

Along with a partner, Schulman went on to form a video production company called, "61 Minutes," but the venture turned out to be ill-fated. "We thought that there were people out there with such an overblown sense of self-importance that they would pay us big money to film their lives," laughs Schulman. "We soon learned that there was absolutely no one who wanted to pay us to do that. So, we shot a lot of weddings and bar mitzvahs!"

But during this time Schulman's interest in writing screenplays resulted in a number of spec scripts, some of which were good enough to land him an agent and a number of options. The first such success was a piece that was eventually made, several years later, into a TV movie called SINS OF THE FATHERS. Schulman was understandably elated when the script was optioned. "The first time it happens you think, this is it! Now the money's gonna roll in, the offers are gonna come, and you start looking around for a new car. And then a few weeks later you realize that's not going to happen, and you'd better do another spec script."

He took his own advice and began a horror film, eventually earning enough interest from an independent producer to gain some funding for the writing of the script. However, the movie never got made. "These things—options that don't turn into sales, sales that don't turn into movies—are learning experiences," says Schulman, adding that if nothing else they should be regarded as consoling slaps on the back, and validation of sorts. So, he kept plugging away, and in retrospect can see that he was really searching for the right story to tell.

"It took quite a few screenplays before I reached the point where I both enjoyed writing them, and felt like I had some idea about what I was doing," he says. "I wrote a sci-fi script, some action-adventure scripts, and various other things before DEAD POETS SOCIETY.

It was at his wife's urging ("She told me I just wasn't an action-adventure kind of guy," he laughs) that he finally sat down to write an unlikely piece about a bunch of poetry students at a private all-boys school, and their charismatic teacher. "It felt like such a non-commercial project that I was reluctant," he recalls, "but she convinced me that it was the story that was going to come from my heart, and the one that deserved to be written." So, in 1985, he wrote it.

The astonishing success of DEAD POETS SOCIETY (two years after its release, it was still one of the top video rentals) vaulted Schulman to the enviable status of a "hot property" in Hollywood, especially after his other effort that summer, a rewrite assignment on a quirky little comedy called, HONEY, I SHRUNK THE KIDS dwarfed most other box office entries.

That triumphant summer in 1989 resulted in a "first look" deal with Disney that was signed at the end of 1990, and included in that deal was the stipulation that Schulman would also have the option of producing and directing his work. An enviable position indeed, since screenwriters are unanimous in their conviction that the director wields the final creative power in a film and, if the original "vision" of the script is to remain intact, the writer must also direct.

DEAD POETS SOCIETY is a sterling example of why writers must write spec scripts, instead of hoping to pitch story ideas and have them funded for development. High-concept, it's not. One can only imagine the glazed eyes and sagging faces of development executives being forced to sit through a verbal pitch about a half-dozen boys and their poetry teacher, while the poor writer tries to keep all the names straight and the plotlines succinct. It would have been an impossible chore to pitch DEAD POETS SOCIETY, as Schulman himself admits in our interview to follow.

Still, it is a film filled with "moments": Keating, played by Robin Williams, urging the boys to tear an offensive page out of a textbook, a page containing a mathematical formula that can be used to determine a poem's "greatness"; Todd, with Keating rooting him on like Knute Rockne, finally bursting out of his shell in a lyrical explosion of free-form poetry; and of course, the final, gloriously defiant gesture at the end of the film as Keating leaves the classroom for good.

It is also a very small, *personal* film—the kind many veteran writers advise new writers to focus upon when crafting their early scripts. There is no reliance on special effects, on story "tricks", on comic-book violence or techno-gimmickry. Instead, it is a blending of basic coming-of-age stories that are all catalyzed by the same force: the inciting, inspiring, challenging demeanor of their unorthodox and wholly wonderful new teacher. This is a man who is not simply teaching facts by rote; rather, he is encouraging the boys to *learn*, and to think for themselves. And, in the process, to dare to dream, to set their sights beyond the ordinary, to "Seize the Day".

A powerful message, and a powerful film, combining the elements of tragedy, comedy, romance, and even a bit of mystery and intrigue into a collage of carefully crafted plotlines that come together as a cohesive, moving, memorable story.

Interview with Tom Schulman

DEAD POETS SOCIETY

Did the idea for the script spring from personal experience?

I didn't go to a prep school. Actually, I didn't start out to write about a prep school. At the actor's and director's lab we had a guest speaker from New York named Harold Clurman, a famous Broadway director, and he was unbelievably dynamic and inspiring. After hearing him talk, the next day we would all get together with renewed resolve, saying, "I've *got* to form my own theatre, I've got to get involved, I've got to change the world!" I mean this man could light a fire under you that was incredible.

Then, a few days or weeks later, it would all fall back to normal. But the experience gave me the notion for DEAD POETS SOCIETY: what if a group of students were so inspired that they actually went out and *did* something about it? I think the first draft I wrote may even have involved a group of theatre students, but I threw it out after getting about halfway through. It just wasn't working. So I went back in my memory to my high school days, and remembered a couple of English teachers who had been very dynamic, very exciting. Along with that was the memory of my father always quoting poetry to me, little kernels of wisdom. I put the two together, started taking notes, wrote an outline, and then wrote the script.

Interestingly enough, I had no faith in the story while I was writing it, in terms of marketability or the quality of the work. It seems that happens fairly often; in retrospect, a lot of the things I now consider to be my best work were things that, at the time, I just wasn't juiced up about. And many of the things I thought were great while I was writing them just don't seem to have much punch today. It's a strange phenomenon.

But you went ahead and finished DEAD POETS SOCIETY on spec, and your agent then shopped it around?

No, my agent at the time said, "I think this is the best thing you've ever written, but I don't think we can sell it." So at that point I decided to use that script to find a new agent. It took a while before I found one who said, "Maybe. I really like this, it's different, if nothing else it's a good calling card, and something I can at least get you some work with. But I also think I can sell it."

Well, a year later he still hadn't sold it. Finally a New York producer who had read it about six months previously decided to take an option, and a few months later Disney bought it. Once they bought it, they got right to work and made it.

In reviewing your rather eclectic list of credits, which includes titles like, HONEY, I SHRUNK THE KIDS, THE GLADIATOR, WHAT ABOUT BOB and MEDICINE MAN, it seems accurate to call you a, well, versatile writer.

I love all kinds of movies. And I'm probably just stupid enough to think, "Hey, I'll try one of those!" [Laughter] Maybe I just don't have enough in me in any one area— "Well, that's about all the drama I've got in me, better do a comedy!" [Laughter]

And when you run out of genres, that's the end of the career.

Who knows, maybe so!

Did Disney remain fairly faithful to your original script of DEAD POETS SOCIETY?

Yes. The only major difference being that the Keating character, played by Robin Williams, suffered from a terminal illness in the original version. He doesn't actually die of it, but it is there as the motivating factor, the force that drives him to preach so strongly about seizing the day, and living life to its fullest. [Director] Peter Weir persuaded me that this was an unnecessary element, and pointed out that a dying general leading his men into battle isn't a very courageous man—after all, he has nothing to lose. Peter was absolutely right about that, and it was basically a five page cut. It consisted of one scene where we find out about his illness, and a few lines of dialogue here and there where the kids ask him about it. And that was it, snip, snip, and it's all fixed. Which always makes rewriting a bit easier on the stomach, rather than having to go in and tear the whole thing apart. I think it was a very wise choice, because it eliminated something that might have swallowed the whole movie.

It could well have become a movie about a dying teacher, instead of a man inspiring his students.

Exactly.

To tell the truth, I think there was plenty going on in that film, without that element.

Yes, there was a lot.

And that's something I'd like to address, that is, the layering of plots. Just about every prominent character in DEAD POETS SOCIETY had his own story, had his own beginning, middle and end. How do you structure something like that? Is it something you consciously do?

Yes. In this case, every boy in the movie was driven by a cause, a passion. The Keating character was a sparkplug for the engine, and these boys were the individual pistons. Given the notion that they should live life to the fullest, they each decide to do something different about that. So, their stories just naturally set themselves in motion, and follow a natural progression toward a conclusion. Todd, for example, has difficulty speaking, and is forced to conquer that fear. Knox has a passion for a seemingly unreachable girl, but decides to do something about his feelings. Neil wants to act, and does so in spite of the certain disapproval from his family. Charlie is a rebel without a cause who finds a cause.

Right from the start, I knew this story was not going to be about the teacher, but about the boys, and the effect he had upon them. Most importantly, it would be about the changes within the boys as a result of the Keating influence. That is particularly true about Todd—there is no doubt that he will be a very different person after the events of the movie.

In fact, I felt the story became Todd's story, especially since the pivotal moment—Neil's suicide—was the catalyst for Todd's most dramatic turning point.

The baton had been passed.

When you are structuring all these stories, you must certainly begin with the primary, basic plot: a story about a teacher who breathes new life into a bunch of boys at a stuffy prep school. Once you have your beginning, middle and end, plot points, etc., for that, how do you go about timing the subplots?

Each of the subplots must be timed in roughly the same manner as the main plot, but you must be careful to avoid predictability. In this case, I didn't want each of the boys doing all the same things at each stage of the movie. But generally speaking, they still all have a three-act structure just the same as the main plot, and in fact serve to support the structure of the main plot.

Each boy gets the notion of what he's going to do around page 30; each boy has a real conflict around page 90; with a resolution that takes place ten or twelve pages later. The idea is to make each experience different enough and interesting enough to capture the reader or viewer, and prevent them from saying, "Oh, sure, that was bound to happen, he was due for his Act I break, the other guy just had his and that other guy will be next."

Certainly the real challenge has to come in trying to make each of the stories interdependent, to the point where one couldn't happen without the other.

Right. Each has to drive the other. As far as timing goes, you have to make choices. For instance, I drove Todd's first act break back as far into the story as I could. My sense as I was writing was that he would be the character who was going to change the most, and was also the least verbal and least visible character in the screenplay. Therefore, I thought I could save his first "moment" until almost halfway through the movie.

That would be the classroom scene, where Keating forces Todd to improvise a poem.

Yes. And right or wrong, that happens quite late. It's the kind of thing that might conventionally happen on page 22, instead of page 45, where it did.

In most movies there are perhaps three subplots, and the third usually consists of no more than a couple of scenes here and there that easily resolve. In the case of DEAD POETS SOCIETY, each subplot was a very full story, with some very important consequences. Now, did you consciously assign a priority to these plots?

Because I like to outline before writing, and know what I'm going to write before I begin writing, the experience of outlining shows me which plot will take precedence, and be more significant. I outline using cards, and as I position those cards, I begin to realize who will undergo the biggest conflict, that central conflict upon which the story rides. And sometimes that means I have to be open to the fact that the person I *thought* was going to be the main character isn't; that role belongs to someone else. And yes, I then consciously assign him the most important scenes.

So there is some definite scene "weighing", if not scene counting, that goes on?

Yes, absolutely. Scene counting, too. Also, if a big scene seems to come in too early, that fact is noted with the full realization that the conventional rules of structure are being bent a little.

How do you determine which plot is most important?

I think the character with the most to gain or lose is at least a good candidate for the role of main character, the protagonist, at least in this kind of story. In another kind of story, the character who takes the strongest action will likely be the focus of your main plot-within-the-plot. It logically follows, then, that the person leaning on them the hardest will be the antagonist. I'm always looking for the protagonist and essential background; in this case, Todd, and Welton Academy, a difficult school...

The kind of force that is there to keep him down, to douse his spirit...

Right. His own internal struggle is there, also, so there is always that constant tension, that conflict, that fight, so he's got something to push against.

You can literally feel its weight upon him in every one of his scenes. (Pause) I have a note here on my list of questions that says, "How to pitch a story like this?"

(Laughter) You don't. Don't even try. You pitch it by walking in the door and saying, "It's about a kid in a school and a poetry teacher," and you hand them the script, and you walk out.

On the other hand, HONEY, I SHRUNK THE KIDS is what could fairly be termed a "high-concept" movie.

Now, was that a spec script, or did you pitch an idea...

That was a rewrite assignment, actually, from Disney. The original script was by Ed Naha.

I'd like to touch on the difference in writing a high-concept story as opposed to a character piece. Do you use a different approach?

I don't think there is any difference. Every story has to have a central conflict. That central conflict can *sound* high concept, such as "Kids get shrunk by their father and have to find their way across their yard." Certainly that sounds more snappy than, "A poetry teacher galvanizes a group of students at a stuffy school." However, both are still stories that will require a great deal of work in terms of structure, characterization, and so forth. About the only difference might be that the high-concept picture is less dependent upon the characters than the story, while the other story ceases to exist without those specific characters.

What do you rely on to establish those characters, and differentiate them from one another? For example, in a sitcom the characters are usually quickly identified by their widely varying speech patterns. Dialogue is used to differentiate the characters. But in a dramatic feature, where "real" characters are so important, you can't rely solely on that, can you? Do you actually describe them?

No, no, because in this case the descriptions would be very similar. I mean, boys in a prep school tend to all look alike, unless you're going to go with a fat kid, a skinny kid, a bald kid, the jock, the nerd, those kind of contrasts. That was not what I wanted to do. Each character had to be described by what they were trying to accomplish, and the reason they were trying to accomplish it. That was something that had to evolve as the story evolved—I knew that this was not going to be one of those stories that hooks you by page five. Instead, I had to work on faith, trusting that the reader/viewer would have the feeling that this was going to be about something, and stay with it.

Certainly Keating's energy and command served that purpose nicely. Just out of curiosity, did you picture anyone in particular for that role while writing your script?

Not really, no. Some people visualize stars in the lead roles, and that works for them. You know, they'll write with Harrison Ford in mind, or something like that. I can't really say that I clearly see the face of a person when I create a character. I wish I could, because there's always that nagging feeling that I am not being specific enough. But I know before I write that I have an idea for a person who has a goal, and I put myself in the persona of that character, with that objective as a motivating force.

Sometimes I find that I start a script with a specific person in mind, but by page five I see that he could not be the character any longer. That person would never do the things I am having him do, so I mentally—and quite subconsciously, I think—remold that character into someone different.

For me, it's the goal, the orientation toward an objective, that defines the character. Knowing what that character wants, and trying to be that character thinking of ways to achieve his objective, is the process that leads to the creation of a character for me.

Interesting. What you're saying is that, in spite of DEAD POETS SOCIETY being called a "character movie," the characters actually spring from the story.

Well, of course it's all very symbiotic. But I do think, in the long run, the story is supreme. And I go through this argument with myself all the time: character takes precedence over story, no, story more than character... but the reality is that they are interwoven so tightly it's nearly impossible to separate them, they are wrapped like a strand of DNA or something. (Laughter) God, it should be so good as DNA! They are totally intermeshed, but I still maintain that, in the long run, story is what determines the character.

A very simplistic example would be a story about a man who decides to go overseas and wipe out a bunch of terrorists, and free a bunch of people from prison. Right there you have a pretty good idea about your main character.

How do you work a theme into your story without being heavy-handed? Do you approach your story with theme in mind, or does it just spring forth unbidden?

I go into it thinking about the theme at all times. Theme, character, and plot. I'm always saying to myself as I'm writing, what is this *really* about? What is the real conflict, and what does this all mean? It's a nagging, kind of insecure feeling as I go along, until I really get it, until I know for sure what is behind the story. I'm not comfortable writing a story until that theme has solidified in my mind.

Do you find that the theme takes on more clarity as you progress?

Yes. I find it's specific when I begin, but I don't have a real tangible sense of it. At the end you can really feel it, and taste it, and you say, "I know what this is about!" and you write it down—and it's the same sentence you wrote months before, when you first started. The difference is, before it was just a bunch of words—but now it has an almost visceral impact.

Do you look to each scene to reinforce not only your story, but your theme as well?

Absolutely. But ultimately, the story is the theme, working itself out into an understandable, comprehensible form. If you've got a good story, you've got a theme.

As a final note, I'd like to refer back to your demon-

strated versatility, and ask if you feel that beginning writers, or writers still trying to get their first break, should follow the same course?

In retrospect I guess I was trying to find myself, and each time was trying to bite off something I felt I could chew. I had the idea for DEAD POETS SOCIETY three or four years before I wrote it; I simply didn't feel ready to tackle it. I didn't feel my skills were up to the task. The action genre seemed easier, because it looked easier on the surface. You know, you get a guy, give him a rifle, and at the end the enemy is dead, and that's it! (Laughter) Of course, it's not nearly so simple as it seems. But at the time I was foolish enough to think I could do it, so that's what I tried.

I think you have to write about things you know, with characters motivated by things you can relate to in a personal way. That's not always easy, especially given the prevalence of "high-concept films." It can be very difficult to find something personal in movies like that. But I still think that the more you can personalize the characters in your story, and understand what it's like to be inside those characters, and experience the predicaments they are experiencing, the better your writing is going to be.

Your experience is a good teacher in this, for although your talent was enough to get your work optioned on a regular basis, it wasn't until you wrote the story that came from your heart that you got your "big break."

That's true. From what I've seen, the people who just jump right into the full-blown fantasy feature as their first effort are kind of on the wrong track. To me, it's the simple stories, the stories as close to personal experiences as possible, that lead to the highest caliber of writing.

Story Outline

DEAD POETS SOCIETY

ACT I

HEADMASTER NOLAN welcomes the boys to a new year at Welton Academy, espousing the school's stodgy traditions in a solemn ceremony. Afterward, we meet TODD and NEIL as the parents say good-bye to their children for the semester.

Todd and Neil are introduced as roommates, and we also meet the rest of the boys as they settle into their dorm rooms. It's obvious that they didn't take Nolan's solemn preaching too seriously.

Neil's father comes to the dorm to tell Neil he cannot work on the school annual. When Neil argues with him in front of the other boys, MR. PERRY takes his son out into the hall for a stern tongue-lashing.

Mr. Keating's English class meets for the first time. Keating takes his students out into the hall and urges them to make their lives extraordinary, to "Seize the day." The boys are confused by Keating's unorthodox approach after a stifling day of lectures and assignments, but they like the change of pace.

KNOX goes to dinner at CHET DANBURY's house and meets Chet's girlfriend, CHRIS. It's love at first sight for Knox, and he comes back from dinner mesmerized by the encounter.

In Keating's next class session, the boys read part of an essay that rates a poem's greatness on a sterile, mathematical scale. Keating tells the boys to rip that whole chapter out of their textbooks, a move that is observed by a curious faculty member.

At lunch, the boys find Keating's picture in an old yearbook, and learn that he was a member of the "Dead Poets Society." They question Keating about the organization, they like what he has to say, and Neil leads the decision to hold a meeting that night.

During study hall, the boys peruse a map trying to locate the cave where the meeting is to be held. Todd doesn't want to attend the meeting because he is afraid of reading aloud, which is part of what the Dead Poets do. Neil assures him that he doesn't have to read anything, he can just listen if he wants.

ACT II

After dark, the boys sneak off campus and hold their first meeting, which turns out to be little more than a chance to eat pilfered food, tell ghost stories, and generally screw around. CHARLIE is the only one who has written a poem, but it is written on the centerfold of a girlie magazine. Neil reads a "real" poem by Tennyson.

In class, Keating teaches about the meanings of language through a series of humorous poetry readings. Then he reminds the boys that they constantly have to look at things in a different perspective, illustrating his point by jumping up on his desk and looking around. The boys follow suit.

Keating urges the boys to find their own voice, and tells them to write an original poem to read out loud at the next class. The prospect of this frightens Todd, and Keating knows it.

Neil announces that he's going to audition for a play at a nearby school, even if it means defying his father. Neil also tries to get Todd more enthused about the Dead Poets Society, but Todd is still reticent.

Knox rides his bike to Chris' public high school, and is dejected to see her arm-in-arm with boyfriend Chet.

Keating has the boys line up to kick soccer balls to the tune of classical music, after first reading aloud a line from a poem.

Neil gets the lead part in "A Midsummer Night's

Dream," and forges a letter of permission from his father.

Todd is working on a poem, but doesn't think it is any good.

In Keating's class, the boys read their poems out loud. Knox has a syrupy, yet sincere love poem to Chris; Todd has nothing at all. Keating ropes Todd into a vivid, impromptu vision inspired by a picture of Walt Whitman. Keating and the class applaud Todd's words, and he gains a shred of self-confidence.

In the cave that night, the Dead Poets sit around smoking pipes. Knox is still in a tizzy over Chris, and he decides to call her.

When he does, she invites him over to Chet's house for a party. The other boys don't think he has anything to be excited about, but Knox is satisfied just to know that she was thinking about him.

Keating holds a lesson on conformity in the courtyard. A faculty member watches with interest as Keating has the boys stroll around with each other and observes how they fall in step and end up marching.

Neil finds Todd sitting by himself with his birthday present from his folks, a desk set identical to the one he got last year. Neil gets Todd to perk up and launch the desk set off of a balcony.

At the next Dead Poets meeting, Charlie brings two girls to the cave and takes the name, "Nuwanda."

Knox goes to the party at Chet's house. Knox has a little too much to drink, steals a kiss from the sleeping Chris, and gets pounded by Chet. Chris pulls Chet away, and Chet vows to kill Knox the next time he sees him.

Back at the cave, Nuwanda announces that he has slipped an article into the school newspaper demanding that girls be allowed at Welton. The letter is in the name of the Dead Poets Society, which outrages the other boys and puts them all in danger of expulsion.

Nolan calls a chilling meeting, vowing to ferret out and punish those responsible for the "profane and unauthorized article" that Nuwanda submitted. Nuwanda takes the heat, by way of a pretended phone call from God in which he supports the demand for co-eds.

Nuwanda gets his backside blistered by Nolan's wooden paddle, but refuses to say anything about the

Dead Poets Society and who the members are.

Nolan has a short talk with Keating, and all but accuses Keating of being the reason that Nuwanda pulled his little stunt. He warns Keating to draw the line at preparing the boys for college, and "let the rest take care of itself."

Keating tells Nuwanda that there is a time to be daring and a time to be cautious, and a wise man knows the difference.

Mr. Perry is furious about Neil's deceit and participation in the play, and orders his son to drop out the night before the show goes on. He wants to know if Keating talked him into acting, if Keating is the one distracting him from his "real interests."

Neil asks Keating what to do. Keating tells him to talk to his father, tell him how passionate he feels about acting, about leading his own life. Neil agrees to try.

Knox risks running into Chet when he goes to Chris' high school, follows her into class, and offers her flowers and a love poem.

Neil barely convinces Mr. Keating that his father agreed to let him do the play, and may let him stick with acting.

Chris shows up at Knox's dorm, warning him to leave her alone before Chet injures him beyond repair. But Knox convinces her to go to the play with him, and if she doesn't like him afterward, he'll never bother her again.

Act III

Neil plays his part to a standing ovation.

Knox holds Chris' hand, and she doesn't pull it away.

Neil's Dad shows up for the play, and we realize that Neil had not spoken to him at all. Mr. Perry whisks Neil away, and orders Keating to stay away from his son.

At the Perry household, Neil has a chance to speak his piece, but is too intimidated by his father to say anything. Mr. Perry orders his son to a military academy, so that he won't ruin his life.

Neil commits suicide.

The Dead Poets tell Todd that his roommate is dead. Todd blames Neil's father.

Keating grieves privately in his classroom, over the book of poems he gave to Neil as a gift when the Dead Poets reconvened.

At Neil's memorial service, Nolan vows a full investigation, as requested by Mr. Perry.

The boys are interrogated and await the next step. One of the boys squeals, and urges the others to forget about Keating and save themselves by confessing. Keating is the scapegoat for Neil's death, and there is nothing anybody can do to save him.

One by one, the boys come back from signing the administration's bogus confession. Nuwanda won't sign and is expelled, technically because he struck a fellow student. Todd doesn't want to sign, but under pressure from his parents, he does.

Nolan takes over Keating's English class, and Keating comes out to clean out his desk. As he does, the Dead Poets, led by Todd, salute their former teacher with a final, defiant gesture that may well mean expulsion for all of them.

DEAD POETS SOCIETY

INT. KEATING'S ENGLISH CLASS - DAY

Keating sits in a chair behind the teacher's desk.

> KEATING
> Boys, open your Pritchard
> texts to page 21 of the intro-
> duction. Mr. Perry, kindly
> read aloud the first paragraph
> entitled, "Understanding
> Poetry."

The boys find the page in their texts. Neil reads.

> NEIL
> Understanding Poetry by Dr. J.
> Evans Pritchard, Ph.D. To
> fully understand poetry, we
> must first be fluent with its
> meter, rhyme, and figures of
> speech, then ask two ques-
> tions: 1) how artfully has the
> objective of the poem been
> rendered, and 2) how important
> is that objective? Question 1)

rates the poem's perfection;
question 2) rates its importance; and once these questions have been answered,
determining the poem's greatness becomes a relatively
simple matter. If the poem's
score for perfection is plotted on the horizontal of a
graph and its importance is
plotted on the vertical, then
calculating the total area of
the poem yields the measure of
its greatness. A sonnet by
Byron might score high on the
vertical but only average on
the horizontal. A Shakespearean
sonnet, on the other hand,
would score high both horizon-
tally and vertically, yielding
a massive total area, thereby
revealing the poem to be truly
great.

As Neil reads, Keating goes to the blackboard and
draws a graph. He demonstrates by lines and shading
how the Shakespeare poem would overwhelm the Byron.

               NEIL (CONT'D)
As you proceed through the
poetry in this book, practice
this rating method. As your
ability to evaluate poems in
this manner grows, so will
your enjoyment and understanding of poetry.

Neil stops. Keating pauses a moment to let this
lesson sink in.

KEATING

Excrement! That's what I think
of Dr. J. Evans Pritchard. Now
I want you to rip that page
out of your books. Go on, rip
out the entire page! I want
this garbage on the trash heap
where it belongs!

The boys are tentative. Does Keating mean this?

KEATING

Go ahead, rip it out. Rip it
out!

Charlie Daulton rips out the page.

KEATING

Thank you Mister Daulton. Come
on, make a clean tear. In
fact, rip out the entire
introduction, I want nothing
left of it! Dr. J. Evans
Pritchard, you are disgrace-
ful!

The other boys begin ripping out pages from their
books, having a good time of it. Keating goes into
the anteroom and picks up the trashcan.

INT. MCALLISTER'S CLASSROOM - DAY

Mr. McAllister, the Scottish Latin teacher, exits
his room and walks across the hall to Keating's
classroom. He peeks in the door window and sees boys
ripping pages out of their books. Alarmed,
McAllister opens the door and enters Keating's
room.

INT. KEATING'S CLASSROOM- DAME

> MCALLISTER
> What the hell is going on in
> here!...

> KEATING (O.S.)
> I want to hear more ripping!

Keating enters from the anteroom with the trash can.
McAllister sees him.

> MCALLISTER
> Sorry, I didn't think you were
> in here, Mr. Keating.

> KEATING
> Well, I am.

> MCALLISTER
> So I see. Sorry.

> KEATING
> Anytime.

Baffled and embarrassed, McAllister exits. Keating
strides back to the front of the room.

> KEATING
> This is battle, boys. War! And
> the casualties could be your
> hearts and souls. Now you will
> learn what this school wants
> you to learn. In my class,
> however, if I do my job prop-
> erly, you will also learn a
> great deal more. You will
> learn to think for yourselves.
> You will learn to savor lan-
> guage and words because, no
> matter what anyone tells you
> gentlemen, words and ideas

have the power to change the
world. Now, Mr. Pitts may
argue that nineteenth-century
literature has nothing to do
with business school or medical school. He thinks we
should study our J. Evans
Pritchard, learn our rhyme and
meter, and quietly go about
our business of achieving
other ambitions.

Pitts smilingly shakes his head as if to say "Who me?"

                    KEATING
                (defiant whisper)
Well, I say drivel. One reads
poetry because he is a member
of the human race and the
human race is filled with
passion! Medicine, law, banking—these are necessary to
sustain life—but poetry,
romance, love, beauty! These
are what we stay alive for! I
quote from Whitman: "Oh me, Oh
life of the questions of these
recurring. Of the endless
trains of the faithless, of
cities filled with the foolish... What good amid these O
me, O life? Answer: That you
are here—That life exists and
identity, That the powerful
play goes on, and you may
contribute a verse."

Keating pauses. The class sits, taking this in.

                KEATING (CONT'D)
                (awestruck tone)
"That the powerful play goes
on, and you may contribute a
verse."

Keating waits a long moment.

> KEATING (CONT'D)
> What will <u>your</u> verse be?

CLOSE ON the faces of NEIL, CHARLIE, MEEKS, CAMERON, PITTS, and finally TODD as they contemplate this question.

Top Secrets:
S. S. WILSON
AND
BRENT MADDOCK

S. S. Wilson and Brent Maddock
SHORT CIRCUIT

F
ORGET ABOUT THE SCHWINN "FLEXIBLE FLYER" BICYCLE or the
G.I. Joe Kit—when S. S. (Steve) Wilson was eleven his
eye was on that movie camera kit. At that tender age
he began making films, and found himself particularly interested in the technique of stop-motion animation. Not surprisingly, he ended up at USC Film School as a graduate student,
where he distinguished himself by making the first student
film ever to achieve enough popularity and acclaim to gain
outside distribution. Called RECORDED LIVE, it still airs on
HBO and other cable stations, and is considered the film
school's most successful film ever.

After USC, his first stop was the world of educational
films; not as glamorous a field as feature films, but one in
which many new writers and directors cut their teeth. During
this time, he met aspiring writer/director Brent Maddock.
Both had their sights set on writing feature films, but for a
decade they made their living from educational and industrial films, with occasional, and, as they say, "highly rewarding" forays into animation. The high point of their animated
lives was when legendary cartoonist Chuck Jones told them
they really understood Daffy Duck. "That was the thrill of
our lives," says Maddock.

Both wrote spec scripts separately, with no success.
Then they wrote a script together, with almost no success

("We got a brief option on that one from a lady who never did anything with it," Wilson recalls. "It was all every frustrating.")

They spent a year-and-a-half writing SHORT CIR-CUIT with the intent of making the film themselves and using it as a marketing tool for their talents. The circuitous route it took is typical in the sense that very few projects happen in a totally straightforward manner. Wilson starts the story: "We handed the script out the way we always did, I mean, we were at the point where we didn't even care if we registered things. We figured nobody was going to steal our ideas, since nobody wanted our ideas in any form! So we handed it out to the usual friends, and the odd thing that happened this time was that three people connected all at once. A friend of ours got it to two independent studios, while Brent, in the meantime, was taking a workshop over at U.C.L.A. He took the script down, and had the class read it aloud..."

Maddock picks up the story: "I did this ten week evening course there, and when the class was over we did a reading in class where everyone took a part and read aloud. One of the students, a screenwriter named Arne Olsen, showed it to his friend Gary Foster, a young producer who also happens to be David Foster's son. David Foster is a big-league producer whom Arne knew to be searching for, basically, any script with a robot in it. Gary read it, loved it, had his father read it, they wanted it, and called us in to MGM. And we said, 'Holy shit, MGM!' And we go in, and they start putting the pressure on to sell them the script, and we looked at each other and realized, 'Gee, maybe we should get ourselves an agent here.'"

Wilson continues, "Meanwhile, two other friends have connected, and suddenly there's a bidding war. Everybody is furious at us, calling us all kinds of names for doing a multiple submission, and we said, 'You gotta be kidding, multiple submissions? Nobody ever read anything we submitted before!'

Caught up in the confusion of this unexpected success, they found an agent who made a "terrific" deal for them, and they were on their way. They hit the high points—getting their script made into a major picture—and also one of the low ones—having another writer brought in to do rewrites on their own script. As you'll read in the interview that follows, the result was a picture considerably broader in its comedy than the original creators had in mind, and more prone to stereotyping than they would have liked. Nonetheless, they are grateful that the film was made, and subsequently had another payoff: being hired by Steven Spielberg to rewrite three scripts for his company, Amblin' Productions.

As Dennis Fischer pointed out in his *Hollywood Reporter* review of SHORT CIRCUIT, "the basic formula followed by director John Badham and writers S.S. Wilson and Brent Maddock is that of a Disney wildlife adventure film, only instead of some forest denizen coming out of the woods and finding himself in the clutter and confusion of human civilization, we're given the newly 'living' Number Five, formerly an advanced military weapon equipped with a very powerful laser."

The notion of character arc, the transformation of the character (or in this case, robot), forms the emotional center of the film. Initially the machine follows orders and is a good little tool of the military-industrial complex. Then, as is wont to happen in horror and science fiction films, lightning strikes. The gadget short-circuits, and escapes. Initially it understands and speaks only precise commands, not human-style conversation. When Ally Sheedy reads it an encyclopedia article, it asks for the volume and speed-processes it—and then the rest of the set and all the other books in the house. Now it's smart—in the intellectual sense, but not in terms of feeling or true understanding. By watching television, Number 5 picks up the popular language and begins to sound and act human, with tell-tale influences of, among others, George Raft, John Wayne, Humphrey Bogart, and John Travolta. Having turned human, possibly ultra-human, it's equipped to take on its military former masters, and become the perfect sidekick to Ally Sheedy. In the process it also helps enlighten its creator, played by Steve Guttenberg, who previously hadn't considered the full implications of his war games.

The mechanics of the plot aren't worth spending a lot of time discussing; what makes the picture work is the relationships, especially between the Ally Sheedy character and the little bucket of bolts. As the *Variety* reviewer pointed out, "Sheedy makes an otherwise predictable story seem clever, funny, and fresh. Scripters (Wilson & Maddock) get credit for some terrific dialogue that would have been a lot less disarming if not for the winsome robot and Sheedy's affection for it." Therefore, credit must be given not only to the writers, but also to robotics engineer Eric Allard, creator of No. 5.

SHORT CIRCUIT is not an innovative film; you'll spot many echoes of other films, starting with the original FRANKENSTEIN, all the way up to E.T. But what makes it worth a second and third look are the little twists given to familiar ingredients, and the way that it persuades the audience to care about the fate of an assemblage of cogs and nuts and bolts.

SHORT CIRCUIT

Let's discuss methods and guidelines you use in pacing your scripts. I would imagine that your backgrounds as editors and animation writers must help. What do you do to keep the pace and rhythm moving along through your scripts?

WILSON: I have a two-part answer to that. The first lesson we learned on SHORT CIRCUIT was how long scripts *really* are, versus how long you think they are. When we first turned it in, it was 125 pages, and they loved that. Then the director had it retyped in a standard studio format, and it grew by ten pages. And he turned to us and said, "This thing has to be made twenty pages shorter." We were drastically unhappy, and positive there wasn't anything in there that could possibly be cut—which in fact wasn't true. He leaned on us a lot to do the cutting. He didn't want to waste time shooting something he was just going to throw out editing. It was an important lesson for us. Each time we see a script produced, we're astonished by how much falls out of it. There is almost always more in a script than really should be there, or needs to be there. Almost always.

Of course, you can't always spot the excess. Some of it has to be there because the actors aren't there, and the scene isn't there. The ideal situation, of course, would be for the writer to stand there next to the director, and when the line comes up that isn't needed, he can chuck the line.

We just finished an intensive period of work at Amblin', [Amblin' Productions] with Steven Spielberg, where we did three rewrites back-to-back. A delightful period, because everyone there really knows filmmaking, editing, effects, and everything, you can really get down and have nitty-gritty conversations...and you can argue, too, you can go to Steven and say, "I don't like this idea, and this is why." And if he disagrees with you he will be eloquent in his reply, as opposed to other situations where they might just say, "But this is what you're gonna do," or, "But we need a male Caucasian lead."

Anyway, at Amblin' they are very sensitive about length, and they think 110 pages is already a long script.

MADDOCK: I don't know where this came from, but for the longest time in film schools, classes, wherever, people have talked about films in terms of being 120 pages long. One minute per page. And yet, most feature films aren't two hours long, they're ninety minutes long. Maybe a hundred minutes long. So if you're going to come in with a 120-page screenplay, a lot of your script is going to have to be thrown away. It's better to throw it away yourself in the writing, than to have them do it in the editing.

It's amazing, when you write a screenplay and then go away from it for awhile, have some friends comment on it, and then you come back, you can see so many things that are unnecessary.

How do you determine what is unnecessary, and what isn't?

WILSON: An example would be something that [director] John Badham went after us for in SHORT CIRCUIT. A lot of the speeches by Crosby—and keep in mind that ultimately the entire character fell out—but in rereading our original script I found myself saying, "Good Lord, is this guy ever going to shut up? How many times is he going to make this point about his career, and what he has done, etc."

And yet certainly at the time you were writing and rewriting, you felt it all to be very necessary.

MADDOCK: It all seemed perfectly logical and appropriate. It seemed that every twenty-eight pages he should restate what he's thinking. [Laughter] You just don't realize it when you're writing sometimes, but movies aren't really that long. When you watch a movie, you take it in one big gulp. So if somebody says something on page twenty, you're going to remember it for the rest of the movie, it's not that long a period of time. And things resonate through a film, and if it's said and done right, it will be remembered, and you don't have to keep repeating and repeating it.

WILSON: You only say things once. As we study films, and we're doing that more and more these days, we look at what's really there, and we find that the really good films adhere to that rule.

Okay, so one way to improve pacing is to eliminate the superfluous, and in fact, search for the superfluous even after you think you've made your last cut. What's another way?

WILSON: We outline in excruciating detail, or at least we used to. We have now done it enough times we don't go into quite the detail we used to, but it's still pretty comprehensive.

MADDOCK: For the current script we're writing, I have about a hundred and fifty three-by-five cards up on the wall of my office. I work on cards, Steve works on his word processor, doing essentially the same thing. A hundred and fifty three-by-five cards, and there will be many more up there before we start writing.

WILSON: That's pretty bare bones, a hundred and fifty.

That's scenes, and a few gags, and one-liners. We'll fill it out much more completely. The point is, when you do an outline like that you begin to see the movie. Outlining is a painful process, but when you finally start to write the movie, it's invaluable. Talk about finding pacing problems, when they're up there on the bulletin board, they're absolutely glaring.

Much easier to see.

WILSON: Well yeah, you haven't written them as scenes yet, you haven't tied things together that have to be sort of unthreaded again. It's all loose on the cards up there.

MADDOCK: You can feel the flow of the movie. I sit there at my desk and look at my bulletin board, and I can just flow right through the movie, see what's going on. It really wastes your time, enthusiasm, and energy if you go to scene writing too quickly. Everybody wants to do it, because that's the fun part of writing movies. Physically typing, getting it down on paper. And you finally have something to show, you know, "I'm a real writer, look at this!" And really, the smallest amount of time we spend is doing that. Most of it is spent figuring the damn thing out.

Of course then, once you're ready to go, it's great. It's as though you've done all your rehearsals, and now you can just jam.

WILSON: Oh, it writes like wildfire. They gave us twelve weeks to do our first picture at Amblin', and we spent eight weeks on the outline. And it wrote easily in four weeks. Now, we were a little worried about this, since the only other experience we had was SHORT CIRCUIT, which took us a year-and-a-half to write, working in our spare time.

When you're getting this overall flow and overall pacing of your movie, are you also thinking in terms of the typical three-act structure?

MADDOCK: I believe in that more than Steve does, I think.

For me there's a very definite three-act structure in
SHORT CIRCUIT, for instance. I don't know if we're
paying as much attention to it now as we did then, but I
think you tend to internalize that sort of thing.

WILSON: My mind is much more linear than that. It
doesn't help me much to talk about a three-act structure,
because it breaks down into much more detail than that
to me. Scenes ultimately lead from one to another,
inexorably toward the conclusion.

Which leads inexorably to the next question. When
determining and setting the overall pace of a script as a
whole, it must be necessary to set a similar pace within
each scene. Now, you've got your outline to help with the
"big picture;" what do you use to pace your scenes?

MADDOCK: I don't know, really. I guess we write the
scene, look at it, and throw out everything we don't
need.

WILSON: We don't approach it worried about pace.
Once our structure is in place, and we think our character motivations make sense, and we haven't tripped over
any holes in our outline, then we split the script in two—
I take one half, Brent takes the other—and we just go
right through. Then we exchange the halves, decimate
each other's work, and do it again. And we go at least
three drafts before we let anybody else see anything, and
that's what we call our first draft.

And the reason for so many drafts, I assume, is that
you're each going through and doing what we've discussed—eliminating the superfluous, the repetitious, etc.
What other kinds of mistakes get caught at this point?

MADDOCK: The common mistake of too much direction.
It's deadly for anybody reading a script to turn a page
and see lots and lots of words. People don't want to see a
lot of words.

WILSON: Big blocks of single-spaced text are visually
daunting.

295

MADDOCK: I think everybody knows to break up the scene direction into smaller paragraphs, but we've also developed—or are in the process of developing—a style that implies a lot more than it says. In eight or nine words, we can say what's going on in the scene, and what the feeling should be.

We look at our early screenplays, and they're just deadly, they go on and on and on with detail after detail.

Probably a lot of that comes out of your experience in animation where detailed description is required. Now, in writing this description, especially in a comedy, isn't it necessary to emulate the light tone of the dialogue?

MADDOCK: It's crucial. Verbs are so important. Instead of, "The guy runs across the room," we say, "The guy bounces across the room." That kind of thing. Instead of "He hurries to the door," say, "He scoots to the door." This can tell a lot.

WILSON: If your character is that kind of Bugs Bunny sort of character, he bounces and scoots! And we deliberately go through and search for the right verbs in our description.

Something more effective than, "He goes to the door."

MADDOCK: Right, why would anybody ever "go" in a screenplay? There are so many other verbs!

WILSON: One reason that people write scripts that are long is they haven't developed the sort of truncated style that we've seen more and more. We picked this up from Matthew Robbins [director of BATTERIES NOT IN-CLUDED]. Matthew has a very nice, very spare style. I'll give you an example.

The first thing that an amateur will do, and we did this a lot is write something like this: "She's scared. She steps back, her eyes go wide. Her breath is short." You try to describe being scared, which is not the job of a screenwriter. However, you want to get across that she's scared, but if you simply say, "She's scared," that's flat. So what do you do?

Find a middle ground?

WILSON: Exactly, and I'll use a scene from BATTERIES NOT INCLUDED as an example. It's not in the movie now, but there *was* a scene where a woman comes home to her apartment, and it's been broken into. She reaches for the doorknob, and finds it already open, the door ajar. Now, even telling you that much you pretty much know what the feeling of the scene is, but in fact, where we might have written, "She steps back, her eyes go wide, etc." Matthew would write: "She reaches for the doorknob, and finds the door already open—strange." And that's nice, and it's all there for the director and the actor.

So, saying a lot with a little can certainly help keep the pace moving along. How about the length of scenes in general? Do you find comedy/action type movies have more scenes and shorter scenes than a conventional drama?

WILSON: In SHORT CIRCUIT II that's particularly true. And something else that happens is a movie gets even more fragmented as it's made than it was in your script. It's astonishing to me what becomes possible through film editing. There are solutions to problems you had in your writing that are eminently easier when you're dealing with actual footage. You may find that you've slaved over this transitional moment in a scene, where the lead comes to grips with some idea, and you start laying in more dialogue, because my God, this is a huge idea, he can't just get it all at once...and later on, you're sitting there in the editing room and finding out this whole speech of yours is utterly meaningless, and what he in fact does is simply look out a window, contemplate the rain, and when he turns around and faces the camera again the light is on him and he has it!

In other words, there are some very creative ways to handle exposition like that without stalling out mid-scene.

MADDOCK: Personally, I'm in favor of an on-screen narrator who comes on and tells you everything you need to know at the beginning, and then you can get on with your movie! [Laughter] It worked for Rod Serling!

Actually, we handle exposition by touching on it as quickly and lightly as possible, and then getting away from it even faster. There's a tendency to dump all the exposition into the first or second scene, and that's no good. Just sprinkle it in lightly here and there on a need-to-know basis, and disguise it as much as possible.

WILSON: Your audience has to know certain things about your characters in order to get involved, and that's exposition. You're not going to get away from it. Even a movie such as TERMINATOR, which would seem to be fairly straightforward, is actually laden with exposition. People don't realize it, it's laid in there very nicely.

Here's something I do, and maybe it will help your readers. On my first draft, I write all my dialogue in clichés, and all my exposition is done in the worst possible way. I'm more worried about the order of scenes and the order of motivations, so I never stop to think about dialogue. In those drafts, people come in and say, "You know, you're the President of this company, Ted, and you've been here for five years now" and so on. I go straight through this way, and then I go back and say, "This can go, this doesn't belong here, throw this out," and I didn't spend any time thinking of the best possible dialogue. Now I can figure out a different way to show that this guy's been the president for five years, maybe come off a shot of a wall plaque or something like that.

You have to constantly think of how people who know each other actually talk. You sometimes find yourself longing for some guy who doesn't know anything at all, like in those old science fiction movies, where the janitor always accidentally got on the rocket, and everything had to be explained to him—"What are we doin' now?" "Well Bill, now we're weightless."

If you have a character who's very strange, maybe you do need to think about having someone around who doesn't know him and needs to bring out some exposition. Otherwise, lay it in there judiciously and cleverly, and you won't be putting the brakes on your overall pace.

MADDOCK: And the last thing I'd mention in regards to pacing is to remember the old rule of beginning a scene as late in the action as possible. Even after you've written it, go back and see if you can eliminate the first few lines, or a bit of the description. You'll be surprised at how much was there you don't actually need.

Any final words of advice?

WILSON: I think all writers who have the chance should get involved in any phase of filmmaking they can, whether it be editing, sound, lighting, anything. Whatever can put them in touch with the realities of making a movie, and give them a more realistic view of what works, what doesn't, and why.

MADDOCK: It's important to remember too that yes, your script will be rewritten. It will be rewritten by directors, by actors, by editors and indirectly even by sound men. But in the best of all possible worlds, everyone is trying to make the best film possible, and if you've done the best job you can of laying the initial groundwork, maybe you won't be too embarrassed by it all.

Story Outline
SHORT CIRCUIT

ACT I

A tank rolls through a peaceful meadow, leading a truck full of fake military troops. From out of several bunkers peer small red-eyed robots armed with lasers, who seek out and completely destroy the military vehicles.

The robots announce to a crowd of military, political, and business bigwigs that "the enemy" is neutralized. DR. MARINER demonstrates the destructiveness and adaptability of the robots, until a rainstorm moves the presentation inside.

The busload of dignitaries arrives at Nova laboratories. The VIP's want to see DR. NEWTON CROSBY. BEN says the reclusive Newton is in a john puking over the thought of talking before a crowd.

But Newton is actually relaxing—playing with a robot and some computers. Ben drags him to the demonstration.

At a post-demonstration reception at Nova, the military maniacs make apocalyptic plans for the robots.

Outside a thunderstorm rages, and robot NUMBER FIVE, while hooked up to a generator, gets zapped by lightning. He looks fried, but runs a good self-test. Number Five falls in line with the other robots to be disarmed, and it's obvious that his circuits are a little out of whack after all.

At the reception, Newton explains that he had wanted the robots to be used for peaceful projects.

Number Five is distracted by a female robot and strolls into the back of a departing garbage truck. The robot notices a butterfly on the road, and seems to appreciate the pretty insect.

The Nova brass discover that Number Five is missing and flip their lids. The search is on.

Number Five gets dumped from the truck and lands in the middle of a herd of cattle.

Newton taps into the robot by radio and tries to call it back, then shut down its power supply, but the unit is malfunctioning.

NOVA SECURITY CHIEF SCHROEDER, a Rambo wannabe, launches an assault force to retrieve Number Five, which is sightseeing its way down a peaceful country road.

Newton and Ben try again to communicate with the robot, but it can only say that it needs more input.

Number Five wanders down the road, reading billboards, exploring the world around it, and looking for more input. Then two of Scroeder's flunkies in an armored car find the robot, and a hectic chase ensues. The armored car crashes and Number Five plunges off of a bridge, but parachutes to a safe landing on top of a catering van driven by STEPHANIE.

Stephanie drives home and with a baseball bat goes after her ex-boyfriend FRANK, who was trying to steal one of her dogs. Her house is a refuge for stray animals, wild and domestic, and Frank thought he'd pick up a few extra bucks by selling one of the critters to a research lab. Stephanie manages to get rid of the creep.

Newton and Ben load a bunch of computers into a Nova van and set off in search of Number Five. They bring one of the more military-minded robots along for protection, in case Number Five's weapons are malfunctioning as badly as the rest of him seems to be.

At Stephanie's, Number Five is rummaging through the catering truck, and Stephanie takes her baseball bat out to investigate. She thinks the robot is a space alien come to take her on a voyage to the stars, and invites him into the house.

Inside, Number Five searches for input to help with his malfunction, while Stephanie teaches him about Earth. The robot is delirious with all the new input, but wants more, and nearly destroys Stephanie's kitchen with his antics. He finally finds the ultimate input device (sort of): television. He settles in for the long haul, armed with a remote control.

Newton and Ben bumble their way through the night, in search of Number Five, and Stephanie wakes up the next morning to find the robot still in front of the TV. He mimics the commercials he's heard, and wrestles her for control of the boob tube.

Outside, Stephanie helps Number Five discover the beauty of nature. Number Five meets her dog, gets chased, and takes a nose dive off of the deck. That's when Stephanie discovers he's a Nova robot. She's pissed, despite Number Five complimenting her beauty.

Stephanie is a hard-core peacenik, and she hates Number Five now. She calls Nova and tells them to come get their killing machine, and the laboratory dispatches its troops.

Act II

Newton and Ben find Number Five on their tracking computer and join the pursuit.

Number Five learns that they're coming to take him away, and he freaks out—he doesn't want to be disassembled. He steals Stephanie's truck to make a getaway; she manages to get inside and take off with him. After a harrowing ride through town, they come to a precarious stop at the edge of a seaside cliff.

Stephanie tries to tell the robot that he is just a machine and won't die if he goes back to Nova. But Number Five says he's alive...

Newton and Ben arrive on the scene as Number Five begs for his life. Stephanie tells them to take it easy on her mechanical friend. As Scroeder's overzealous troops approach, Number Five tries to convince Newton and Ben that he is indeed alive.

Scroeder invades with his machine-gun toting troops, who let loose with their weapons. Number Five

303

cries out for Stephanie as he takes hit after hit, and Newton races out to rescue him, then cuts off his power. The security troops load the robot on to a truck to take him away, while Stephanie pleads for them to bring him back to life and leave him alone.

On the way back to the lab, Number Five comes to and turns himself back on, does a little self-programming and repair, and chases Ben and a guard away, then steals their truck.

Newton drives by a while later and picks up his partner and the guard, then they resume their pursuit of Number Five, who throws his homing beacon into the back of a civilian truck heading the opposite direction.

Scroeder's shock troops ambush the civilian truck carrying the homing beacon, and Newton and Ben go back to Nova, excited by the possibility that Number Five might actually be alive.

Alive or not, Scroeder wants to annihilate the little robot. Howard the Nova boss doesn't care either, and orders Newton to stay in the lab.

The media circus arrives at Stephanie's house. Frank the creepy ex-boyfriend sees her on TV and hears about the reward being offered for the robot.

Number Five makes his way back to Stephanie's house. She grudgingly lets him in for the night.

Newton and Ben try to sneak out of lab, but Howard intercepts them. The two call Howard's bluff and escape in one of Nova's vans.

At Stephanie's, Number Five gets down and boogies with his hostess, and decides he's going to live with her from now on.

The next morning, Frank the ex-boyfriend drives towards the house, where Number Five is doing his messy best to make breakfast for Stephanie.

Before they can eat, Frank shows up with a loaded rifle, ready to steal the robot. They chase Frank away, but now Nova will know where they are, so Stephanie and Number Five must run.

They get lost out in the country, with Newton, Ben, and Scroeder all looking for them.

Howard has sworn out arrest warrants on Newton

and Ben, but Newton stays on the lam to meet with Stephanie at an out-of-the-way bar.

When they meet this time, Newton looks a little smitten with the beautiful girl; she's convinced that Number Five is alive. And Scroeder is spying from the bar.

Meanwhile, Number Five is playing baseball with himself out in a field when he's ambushed by the other robots. It's a battle of wits and technology, but Number Five takes the war machines out one by one. Number Five rewires the defeated robots as Nova troops approach.

Back at the bar, Stephanie negotiates a non-aggression pact with Newton, but when Scroeder shows himself, she accuses Newton of setting her up. Then Number Five blasts into the bar and a battle erupts. The robot whisks Stephanie away, and everybody follows in hot pursuit.

ACT III

Scroeder is crazed with frustration after missing them yet again, and orders the other robots in on the chase. But the mechanical killers aren't quite up to the task—they've been reprogrammed to act like Number Five's TV favorites, the Three Stooges.

Their truck stalled out in the boonies, Number Five makes it known that he's a pacifist—he'll scare people, but killing's out of the question.

Ben catches up with Newton, who talks about how much he likes Stephanie. Then Number Five ambushes them, chases Ben away, and kidnaps Newton.

That night, Number Five brings Newton to Stephanie's camp in the hills. The robot needs input and a man-to-man with Newton, who slowly comes to believe that the robot might actually be alive. And, Stephanie begins to warm up to Newton again.

The next morning, Number Five and Newton are still going at it. And Newton is finally convinced that the robot is a living being, complete with a sense of humor. But the euphoria is interrupted by Nova troops driving up the mountain.

Nova troops and government soldiers corner the

three fugitives. Newton tries to negotiate, but Scroeder has a massive amount of troops and weapons at his disposal, and he's itching to use them. He has Newton and Stephanie hauled out of the way, and the pair is heartbroken when they see Number Five get blown away by a helicopter gunship.

The troops haul off the robot's smoldering carcass, and Newton and Stephanie leave in one of Nova's vans.

Newton's been fired, and as they drive down the road, Number Five pops up from a trap door in the floor of the truck—the destroyed robot was a decoy Number Five made from spare parts! Number Five takes the name Johnny, and the three of them head to a new life in Montana, where Johnny can live in peace.

S. S. Wilson and
Brent Maddock's Pick
SHORT CIRCUIT

STEPHANIE'S POV

of strange colored lights moving around inside her
catering truck.

EXT. STEPHANIE'S HOUSE - FRONT YARD - NIGHT

She comes out, trusty baseball bat in hand, moving
cautiously. She can hear someone RUMMAGING inside
the truck.

> STEPHANIE
> Hey! Get out of there!

The strange lights go OFF. The SOUNDS STOP.

> STEPHANIE
> (continuing)
> Come on, dummy. I know you're
> in there. Get out. I'll call
> the cops!

Nothing happens. After a moment, the lights come
back ON, colors shifting and changing. The
RUMMAGING begins again. She bangs on the side of
the truck.

> STEPHANIE
> (continuing)
> What are you, deaf?

Suddenly the truck's large serving window swings open. Behind the counter stands Number Five. He is an unearthly sight, eyes like flashlights, multi-colored rays of light BEAMING from them.

Stephanie scrambles back, terrified.

ANGLE ON STEPHANIE

She stops in the middle of the yard, her mind racing. Then it hits her.

> STEPHANIE
> Oh my God... I <u>knew</u> they'd
> pick me. I just knew it.

She moves cautiously back to the truck. The serving window is still open. Number Five is exploring the truck's contents, three arms picking up object after object.

> STEPHANIE
> (continuing)
> ...Uhh.. hello?

Number Five turns, eye lights glaring in her face. She's thrilled, awe-inspired.

> STEPHANIE
> (continuing)
> Well, I guess... welcome to my
> planet.

Number Five gazes at her briefly, but seems more interested in popping ketchup and mustard packets all over the place.

Stephanie gathers her courage and enters the truck.

INT. CATERING TRUCK - NIGHT

As she comes in, she gets an idea, glances at her
watch, and swiftly scribbles on the menu chalk-
board:

>   STEPHANIE
>   (out loud)
>   First Contact: 10:17 pm.

Number Five backs away to the rear of the truck.
She moves toward him slowly.

Suddenly she realizes she's still clutching her
baseball bat. She instantly launches it sideways
out the window.

>   STEPHANIE
>   (continuing)
>   You know the word "friend"? I
>   hope so... Here I come, nice
>   and extremely friendly.

He pulls his head all the way down. She stops and
gazes at him. He gazes back, cocking his head
curiously. As she thinks of things she points them
out.

>   STEPHANIE
>   (continuing; slowly
>   hitting each word)
>   So... uh, this is... Earth.
>   I'm Stephanie... This is a
>   catering truck. Potato
>   chips... Fritos... Are you
>   getting any of this?

His head rises up a little. She's encouraged.

>   STEPHANIE
>   (continuing)
>   No offense but, is that really
>   (more)

> you, or is that like a space
> suit and you're inside some-
> place, maybe just your brain
> in a little jar or something.

> NUMBER FIVE
> Malfunction.

> STEPHANIE
> (startled)
> Huh? Oooh, you can talk!

> NUMBER FIVE
> Malfunction. Need input.

> STEPHANIE
> Input. That's information,
> right? Hey, I'm full of it!
> Listen, why don't you come on
> in the house. We can talk, get
> to know each other... communi-
> cate.

She starts out. Number Five doesn't move.

> STEPHANIE
> (continuing)
> Come on. It's okay.

She holds out her hand. He stares at it, then holds
out all three of his.

Stephanie beckons with her fingers. He imitates
her. Smiling, she tries a variety of hand gestures.
He imitates them perfectly, but he still doesn't
move. At last she gently takes his foremost hand
in hers.

> STEPHANIE
> (continuing)
> Come on. I'm not going to hurt
> you.

She tugs. He's like an anchor. She can't budge him.

>   STEPHANIE
>   (continuing)
> Uh, come inside... go with
> me...uh, walk this way... uh,
> <u>roll</u> this way. Move out.
> Giddyap? Come forward...

"Forward" is a programmed command word he understands. He lurches toward her.

>   NUMBER FIVE
> Forward.

>   STEPHANIE
> Good! Okay!

But now he's getting too close. She stumbles back.

>   STEPHANIE
>   (continuing)
> Okay, stop. Stop!

>   NUMBER FIVE
> Stop.

He stops, but too late. She topples out the door
and lands on her butt.

EXT. STEPHANIE'S HOUSE- FRONT YARD- NIGHT

She gets up quickly, not wanting to offend the
alien.

>   STEPHANIE
> See? I fell down. Now I'm
> getting up. My butt is bruised
> but, hey, that's okay. Come
> on.

Rushing to the house, she opens the front door.

STEPHANIE
(continuing)
Come on in. Enter. Oh, yeah, I
mean, <u>forward.</u>

Number Five comes out of the truck and rolls toward
her.

Top Secrets:
DAVID ZUCKER

David Zucker

THE NAKED GUN: FROM THE FILES OF POLICE SQUAD!

IN ONE OF KINGSLEY AMIS' NOVELS A CHARACTER thinks about brewing a beer that would be known by the tag line, "It Makes You Drunk." THE NAKED GUN: FILES FROM THE POLICE SQUAD! could be acknowledged with the tag line, "It Makes You Laugh."

NAKED GUN!, like AIRPLANE!, KENTUCKY FRIED MOVIE, and TOP SECRET! before it, is the product of David and Jerry, the Zucker brothers. They began their comedy careers back in Milwaukee, where they were often, according to David, "kicked out of class for doing what we now get paid to do." After a successful student film that featured Jerry running all over a college campus in search of a rest room (termed a "thoughtful, introspective piece" by David), David graduated and decided to find a job, any job, in the business.

All of Zucker's attempts to find work ended in failure. He says he couldn't get a job even at a local TV station in Milwaukee. He traveled to three different cities in search of work, while Jerry finished school. He tried television stations, production houses, commercials firms, instructional and educational producers. No luck. Finally he remembered a classic ploy that self-made executives often boast about when discussing their humble origins: offering one's services for free for a probationary six months. The place at which David made that offer turned him down, too.

The Zucker brothers eventually teamed up with old friend and schoolmate Jim Abrahams. Of course, if you depend on the brothers for the story of the trio's background (or for the story of anything else) you'll get only so far before their mad sense of humor takes over. In an interview with Nina J. Easton in the *Los Angeles Times,* Jerry recalls, "Our fathers were business partners. Our sisters were roommates in college. And our mothers danced at the same topless club."

AIRPLANE!, released in 1980, was the first major step on the journey that would see this team end up among the most successful film-makers working in Hollywood today. Two years later, they did the television series, POLICE SQUAD!, which flopped. Two years after that, their film, TOP SECRET!, opened but was a disappointment at the box office. They also directed RUTHLESS PEOPLE, but the script credit went to Dale Launer (maybe that's why it's one of the few films they've made without an exclamation mark in the title.)

The interview was conducted at their offices, which reflect their general sensibilities: the name plates on the door read "Zucker Brothers Productions" and "Millard E. Flausner, D.D.S, A Professional Corp." Their receptionist was in civvies, but confessed that they often ask her to wear a hygienist's uniform. The reading material was fascinating, too. In addition to a variety of dental tomes, there was "Herman Goering's Workout Book," and "Lesbian Bars of Atlantic City."

But what about NAKED GUN!: what makes this kind of movie tick? It might best be called the kitchen-sink style of comedy. There are verbal puns and visual puns, there's slapstick, there are new jokes, old jokes and very old jokes, there's vulgarity, there are word games, there's—everything. Although the film has a plot, they take every opportunity to digress from it. If you don't like one gag, don't worry, because another one will be along in a nano-second. All right, not a nano-second, but certainly there's a gag every twenty seconds. This movie makes the pace of mere sitcoms feel positively snail-like.

It's hard to tell who most influenced the humor of the writers (including Pat Proft, as well as Zucker and Zucker and Abrahams), but you'll find traces of Laurel and Hardy, W.C. Fields, Abbott and Costello, Hope and Crosby, and the Marx Brothers. Maybe most of all the Marx Brothers.

"Last night I shot an elephant in my pajamas...how he got in my pajamas, I don't know." That's the sort of line the Zuckers would gladly have written if Groucho Marx (or one of his writers) hadn't gotten to it first. Actually, they may yet—(a story about one of the few funny people they probably haven't been influenced by, Oscar Wilde, goes that when one of Oscar's friends made a witty comment, he said, "I wish I'd said that!"; the friend said, "You will, Oscar, you will.") Hmmm, this going off on tangents is infectious...

The brothers and Abrahams spent a lot of time watching television, getting ideas from old TV shows and vintage films. In the case of NAKED GUN, they have admitted to stealing from (among many others) DIRTY HARRY, FAREWELL, MY LOVELY, and DAY OF THE JACKAL. Most of all, they stole from themselves. The film is based on their POLICE SQUAD! television series. That was a parody of all the standard cop shows of the fifties and sixties, and immediately developed a hard-core cult following. Unfortunately, the cult didn't include very many Nielson families and the show was yanked after only six episodes.

It was in POLICE SQUAD that Leslie Nielson, veteran of hundreds of straight roles, first portrayed America's answer to Inspector Clouseau, the moronic Detective Frank Drebin. He was funny then, and by the time the film was made he was funnier still. As critic Michael Wilmington pointed out in the Los Angeles Times, "he's brought out an almost preternatural mellowness in a character who began as a relatively uncomplicated dimwit. Now, when Drebin bangs into a trash can, or crosses his eyes and falls over his foot, or plunges his hand into a tropical fish tank, or sets fire to an apartment while trying to light a match, one can sense an overpowering Angst. Or maybe one only thinks one can."

In addition to Nielson, Ricardo Montalban and George Kennedy also liven up NAKED GUN, sending up the kinds of roles they have walked through a hundred times. There's also an endless line-up of celebrities (including O.J. Simpson,

Reggie Jackson, Priscilla Presley) and look-alikes. Oh, yes, also Charlotte Zucker, better known to the boys as Mom. She plays Ricardo Montalban's secretary. As go the gags, so goes the casting: kitchen-sink time again.

The movie may look like it was thrown together, but anyone trying to emulate this kind of filmic anarchy will soon find it's much harder than it looks. The writers in fact took great care to plot the script. As Zucker details in the interview, their first priority is structure and sequence; only then do the multitude of gags begin to get grafted on to that solid framework. Accordingly, watching the film with the plot in mind, instead of the jokes, will reveal a great deal. Of course, it won't tell you what that elephant was doing in Groucho's pajamas...

Interview with David Zucker

THE NAKED GUN: FROM THE FILES OF POLICE SQUAD!

Were you turned down anywhere because you wouldn't release the script for AIRPLANE! unless you directed it?

Oh, yes. One studio even shopped the script around town, looking for potential directors. But we knew that if we didn't direct this, it would lose at least half of what we wanted it to be, the vision we had. A script is the highest, most perfect form any movie will ever attain, because that is your original vision. The movie-making process is simply an on-going battle to defend the script against all the forces that work to make it bad.

You can lose this battle in so many ways, from the acting and directing, to the editing, right down to the projectionist who shows the movie with a dim bulb. It's a miracle any movie ever comes out well. So we convinced Paramount we were not going to sell them the script unless we had control.

That was a very gutsy move, a gamble you might very well have looked back on with regret.

AIRPLANE! was very special to us. We had worked on writing and rewriting that movie for two years, and we simply didn't trust it in the hands of anyone else. We could have made the up-front money for selling the

script, but it just wasn't worth it to us. Hell, we were
used to living cheaply, we could keep it up for another
year or so if we had to.

**You mentioned that the script is the highest, most perfect
form a movie will ever take. In the kind of madcap,
seemingly undisciplined comedy you have come to be
known for, how do you impose discipline on the script?
How do you rein yourself in, when almost anything
goes?**

The movies appear to be a kind of screen anarchy, but
believe me, the process of getting it up there is much
different. I mean, we're not maniacs, we don't bounce off
the walls when we write. It gets to be a very scientifically
designed process, actually. We spend a lot of time with
cards, marking off the three acts, concentrating not on
the jokes but on the structure and sequence of the story.
It's a very dull first couple of months, but that's how we
spend them.

Once we start on the jokes it becomes a lot easier. And
within our style, we have a certain set of rules—rules
that keep evolving, by the way—things that we know
we can't get away with, things we can try to get away
with and cut out later.

Can you give us an example?

We don't like to break the frame, and tell the audience,
"Well, this is just a movie." We don't like to make those
kinds of jokes, they can get old fast. But occasionally it
can work if the target is good enough. Remember the
little boy in AIRPLANE!, who recognizes the co-pilot as
Kareem Abdul-Jabbar? That pulls us right out of the
movie, but it was such a fun comment on all the athletes
who have recently become actors, we felt it was worth
the risk of breaking our rule.

**The movie is relentlessly funny and extraordinarily busy.
Where do you draw the line? How do you restrain your-
selves from doing too many jokes, too many sight gags,**

just simply overloading and overdoing the comedy?

We write whatever we think is funny, and we keep a handle on the amount of improvisation on the set. We are not the kind of guys who write a script over three weekends; it takes us a good year or so. We write and rewrite and rewrite. At least ten drafts. NAKED GUN was the fewest drafts we've ever done, and it was exactly ten. So, to our way of thinking, by the time we are shooting that script we have already thought of everything funny that could be stuffed into each scene, and there is no need to improvise. That ensures against our including jokes that seem funny when they're thrown in, maybe at the end of a long day of shooting, but that aren't so funny later on. If a gag has made it through our year of rewriting, we figure it must be pretty good, and will probably hold up. So we stick with the script.

Additionally, we plan our shots in such a way that a given joke can be easily excised if it doesn't work, without having an adverse impact on the script. We are very careful to protect ourselves that way. It's a technique that allows us to shoot what seems funny, without locking ourselves in.

We also take our movies out for three previews, while it is still a work print (Ed. note: a work-in-progress, having yet to undergo final editing). NAKED GUN was two hours long when we first previewed it, and we needed to find out what was funny enough to leave in, and what had to go. Only an audience can tell you that. The audience is always right. Remember, humor is a communication process; you're telling a joke. And if people don't get the joke, it's not their fault. Either you told it wrong, or it simply isn't funny.

You spend a long time determining the structure of your story, the act breaks and so on. And yet the plots to movies like AIRPLANE!, or NAKED GUN, are so straightforward and simple, and every point of exposi-

tion so loaded with hilarious and distracting gags, I wonder whether plot takes a rather distant back seat to comedy.

I think so. I mean, let's face it, we are not out to blaze new trails in terms of plot. We're not doing THE STING or THE GODFATHER. A masterly plot is not our trademark, or objective. What we try to do is stick to what is absolutely the most well-worn path of clichés as possible, so people don't have to think about it. There is nothing new in the plot to NAKED GUN. It's the most warmed-over re-hashed James Bond you can find: the beautiful assistant to the bad guy is turned by this amazing sexual dynamo. What is funny is when we plug Leslie Nielsen as Frank Drebin into these situations. There is one thing I should point out, and that is that we still tried to create conflict to keep the story interesting. We treated Ricardo Montalban's character with a hands-off policy in terms of gags; we didn't do the obvious stuff about Corinthian leather, or anything like that. He had to be a real bad guy. And yet we find that people become so accustomed to laughing and finding humor in every scene, that they get to the point where they're grasping for humor, they find it everywhere. The scene with Montalban and Pahpsmir, where the remote-control device is demonstrated, really wasn't intended to be funny, and yet we found audiences literally trying to find something to laugh at.

I'm amazed that improvisation plays such a negligible role in your movies. In thinking back over some of the gags in NAKED GUN I can see where they wouldn't carry nearly the impact in writing that they had on screen. The Leslie Nielsen rendition of the "Star Spangled Banner" springs to mind. It had me laughing so hard I was crying, yet I envision that same scene on paper as, "Drebin butchers the Star Spangled Banner."

But it was written out, "But the ramparts we watched, ba da da da, da da dum." The joke was written, but it's true that the key he was singing in, whatever mysterious key that was, can't be captured on paper.

I will tell you one gag in AIRPLANE! that was improvised. You remember when Leslie Nielson was shaking the woman, and then slaps her? First the stewardess shakes her, then Leslie comes in and belts her, and then slaps her a second time—that second slap was made up. And that clicked as something funny, something that could be expanded upon. So the next shot is of all the passengers lined up with baseball bats, clubs, boxing gloves, whips, waiting for a crack at this poor woman. That was all made up on the spot, we drove our prop man crazy on that one.

Writers often complain that directors take over a project, often to the detriment of the original vision...

They do? Do you know any actual writers who have complained about that? [Laughter]

One or two, yes. But you are in the enviable position of directing your own work. Any thoughts about that?

First, while we stick very closely to the script for reasons I've already stated, I am a lot looser than I used to be. On AIRPLANE! I even insisted at times that the actors say the lines in the same cadence I was hearing in my head when we wrote the lines! I'm not quite that strict now.

Second, I really sympathize with writers who spend a year or so on a project, and then have to turn it over to some director who may very well ruin it. I'd be horrified. While we generally had a good experience on KENTUCKY FRIED MOVIE, since then we've never written anything we haven't directed.

It's nice to be in that position.

It is. We made our stand many years ago. But there are many writers out there who don't want to direct, it's not something that everybody is either qualified to do or interested in doing.

William Goldman mentioned that he would never want to direct, he considers the work too brutally hard.

Right. It just depends on how far you want to go to protect your script. How much importance you attach to the final product. To have something go on the screen, with my name on it, that wasn't everything I wanted to be—that would be distressing.

Did you find that happening to you during your television stint with *Police Squad*?

We wrote and directed the first episode, but the rest were taken over by other directors, and that was frustrating. I was a pain in the ass on the set, because depending on how strong or weak the directors were, I was there to fill the vacuum. I mean, if one of them had a moment's hesitation I was right there chiming in, it was tough. Even with the best directors, I found myself frustrated at times with the way things were going. It may not have been the wrong way to do it, it just wasn't the way I would have done it.

Was that the biggest frustration of doing television comedy?

The biggest frustration was that we were used to handcrafting our work, spending a year to write ninety pages. You know, some time to actually think. In TV you don't have that luxury, you have to come up with a half-hour every week. And I think every TV writer will corroborate the fact that there comes a time, about 10 or 11 at night, when you simply say, "This will have to do. We will now stop trying to think of anything better, and just leave this the way it is." And to me, that is not the way to do the best work.

Did you find any advantage to doing television?

The only advantage I think is that you write something in January and it's on the air in February. The immediacy is kind of exciting. The problem is, once it's on, it's done, it's gone. It's like Woody Allen said: "Masterpieces in the sand." No cassette, no nothing! At least our movies are around forever, I mean KENTUCKY FRIED MOVIE still plays in Germany at film festivals or wherever.

The money in TV is much better than in movies. These guys who work on staff, and then create their own series make a whole lot of money. But I think that anyone who is able to work in TV for that long deserves whatever they can get, it takes an incredible amount of talent and an incredible amount of work.

Police Squad lasted a very short time on television, yet the very same premise, lead character and all, found great success on the big screen. Why is that?

For a number of reasons. First what we tried to do on TV were little half-hour movies, and our movies are simply better suited to a larger screen. There are so many little details going on, all of which are vital to the full impact of the comedy in each scene—and they're simply too small to see on the television screen. Also, when something subtle happens on a big screen, with a large audience, there is a group awareness of something going on. If you hear someone laugh, you start to look for something, like that piece of cheese creeping slowly across the top of the refrigerator. On TV all that stuff passes right by.

Many times when a person watches television they don't really pay close attention. They answer the phone, they get up and get a beer, they talk to someone in the room, whatever. But in our brand of comedy you really have to pay attention, because there is a lot going on. And the best way to ensure that attention is in a darkened room with the seats facing forward, and a stiff admission price!

If you look at what is successful in TV comedy, you'll find that there is nothing subversive, not too much in the way of subtlety. It's all pretty overt, and it has to be.

There is even a laugh track on most shows to help point out the funny parts. In a movie theatre, the audience response does that for you, and much more effectively.

Finally, there is the number factor. By that I mean that for a television show to be a success, you have to appeal to an enormous number of people, far more than you have to pull into a theatre to make a movie a success. It's possible that this style of comedy is simply not suited to television, or at least it wasn't at the time *Police Squad* was on. On the other hand, maybe it would have eventually caught on if the network would have been willing to stay with it longer, but I'm not willing to say that with real conviction. To be honest, it was a relief when it was canceled. We just wouldn't have been able to keep up the comedy.

The fact is, this kind of comedy, undisciplined as it may appear, requires a great deal of discipline and work.

There is a very fine line you walk. You run the risk of getting too cute or too clever. The worst accusation you can level at a comedy is, "It's not as funny as it thinks it is." You have to always retain that element of surprise, while avoiding the easy jokes, the puns and things that people in the audience are already waiting for and expecting.

In speaking with Stephen de Souza about writing action, he mentioned a "Whammo chart" that dictated every ten pages there should be a big piece of action, a whammo event to keep the script moving. Do you have a similar rule when structuring your jokes?

There is a certain rhythm to our comedy, but to be honest a great deal of that happens in the editing room. When we are writing we do keep pacing in mind, of course, and try to provide relief from frenetic actions scenes with quieter calmer scenes. Hills and valleys, as Jeff Katzenberg always says.

The other structural point to remember in comedy is that

your third act had better be huge, one continuous laugh. The baseball game served as the setup for that climactic finish in NAKED GUN. We knew going in that we wanted Drebin to go undercover as the umpire to foil the attempt on the queen's life, and from there the comedy just took off. In fact, we worked back from the third act. In comedy, the jokes are the easy part.

Then what's the hardest part?

Working out the plot, the structure, and that all-important ending. In our minds, the ending counts for fifty percent. And I'm talking about the last *five minutes*. Fifty percent. Because if you fail to tie up the whole thing with that last great joke, or that last great scene, it's like beating the other team for all four quarters until the final minutes, when you lose. Alex Karras once said about playing the Packers, "We'd be beating the Packers up and down the field the whole game, but then we'd look up at the scoreboard at the end of the fourth quarter, and we'd lost!" Good plots have good endings.

Any advice to aspiring writers?

Quit now. And realize that the first step in becoming successful is to disregard that advice.

Story Outline

THE NAKED GUN: FROM THE FILES OF POLICE SQUAD!

ACT I

Beirut—The terrorist leaders of the world meet and plot ways to teach American imperialists a lesson. But Police Squad undercover officer LT. FRANK DREBIN teaches the bad guys a lesson of his own, in a battle the Three Stooges would have been proud of.

Los Angeles—A man in black (NORDBERG) eavesdrops on a boatload of drug dealers, then moves in to make the bust. But the undercover cop is the one who gets busted. Busted up, that is. Broken. Battered. Shattered. Crushed. Cracked. Bent. Burned. Etc., etc., etc.

Lt. Drebin returns to L.A., where he learns, from his colleague, ED, that his wife has left him. The two cops drive to the hospital to visit what is left of Nordberg.

Drebin learns the name of the ship Nordberg was assaulted on. But not before jogging his memory with a few new, accidental injuries.

Drebin briefs a group of reporters on Police Squad's plan to protect QUEEN ELIZABETH during her upcoming visit.

Ed and Drebin drive down to the harbor to investigate Nordberg's case. A dock worker says Nordberg was a dirty cop.

In a ritzy downtown office building, Drebin questions the wealthy VINCENT LUDWIG (one of Nordberg's assailants) about the happenings on his pier. Ludwig is barely cooperative, Drebin is a raving klutz. So is Ludwig's assistant, JANE, who shows Drebin through the pier's files. Later, Ludwig coaxes Jane to get on Drebin's good side.

Drebin returns to the police station, and discovers that Nordberg's clothing was dusted with heroin. Frank is given 24 hours to prove Nordberg innocent—the Queen will arrive in a day, and Police Squad can't risk the embarrassment of having a dirty cop on the force.

Act II

Ludwig talks business with a MR. PAHPSMIR, and demonstrates his ability to control people through hypnosis. The two men plot the assassination of the Queen.

Pahpsmir sends a hypnotized assassin Nordberg's way, but Drebin intercepts the killer. The chase is on. And all over the place. It's a humdinger of a pursuit, with lots of bullets, squealing tires, explosions, and fireworks: the Fourth of July kind.

Frank goes home that night to find his door unsecured. He investigates, and after a nice gymnastics workout he finds Jane in the kitchen, boiling a roast for supper. The two enjoy a romantic dinner by firelight, and Drebin pumps the woman for information. Then he pumps her just for fun.

Fun on the town the next day—Jane and Drebin have fallen for each other.

That night, Drebin breaks into Ludwig's office, looking for clues. He finds what he needs, then destroys the evidence (accidentally, of course). He also destroys the entire office, and finds himself out on the building's ledge, hanging by a limb.

Ed and Drebin try to explain the previous night's exploits to the Mayor. She pulls Drebin off the Queen's security detail.

At home, Jane tells Drebin that Ludwig wants to meet with him.

Drebin goes to his meeting (at a meat packing plant), where a bad guy takes a crack at him. But the cop wins the battle.

Drebin drives from the stockyards to the Queen's

reception, where Jane is dining with Ludwig, who is surprised to see the klutzy cop still alive. Drebin accuses Jane of consorting with Ludwig, and dumps her.

The Queen meets her admirers, and gets a friendly flying tackle from Drebin.

Drebin's been thrown off of Police Squad, and is cleaning out (somebody's) desk when Jane shows up, proclaiming her innocence in Ludwig's plot. She tells Drebin that a baseball player will kill the Queen during the big game.

Act III

At the game, Drebin swaps clothes with an opera singer to get close to the players, so he can search for the killer. But first he kills the national anthem.

Next, it's time for Drebin to play umpire. As the players come up to bat (and slide into bases and field balls and scratch their crotches), umpire Drebin searches them for weapons.

But he can't find the killer. He has to delay the game at all costs...and he does a nice job of it. But is he in time? The hypnotized right fielder/assassin moves in to kill the Queen...Jane alerts Drebin, who tackles the killer (and empties the dugouts)...it's a marvelous display of American culture for the Queen, as the baseball players brawl, Ludwig drags Jane away, and the killer slips free to try and do his dirty deed. But Drebin takes him out (with a little help). Ed joins in the pursuit of Jane and Ludwig (who finally gets cornered and goes over the edge.

But what's this? A delayed hypnotic order sends Jane to kill Drebin. Good ol' Drebin pulls her out of it with a melodramatic marriage proposal that leaves 70,000 people in tears.

All's well that ends well. The Mayor promotes Drebin to Captain, and Nordberg is going to live. *If* he can keep away from Drebin...

THE NAKED GUN: FROM THE FILES OF POLICE SQUAD!

INT. FRANK'S APARTMENT

FRANK does the traditional rolling on the floor behind the couch, then makes his way across the floor using flips. His moves resemble an Olympic floor exercise. He checks out the room. Dives, and rolls into his bedroom. No one there. He does back-flips out of the bedroom. Through the living-room. Stopping at the kitchen door. He hears a SOUND from inside the door. He bursts through it.

INT. KITCHEN

Revealed is JANE. She's cooking. Stirring something on the stove. She's only wearing one of Frank's shirts. Looking seductive and gorgeous.

> JANE
> You're late.

> FRANK
> (putting his gun away)
> It depends on what I'm late
> for.

                    JANE
          You said we should have dinner
          sometime. Tonight became...
          sometime.

     She pokes a hunk of meat in a pot. Shows it to Frank.

                    JANE (cont.)
          I'm boiling a roast.
               (suggestive)
          How hot and wet do you like
          it?

                    FRANK
          Very hot. Awfully wet. You
          seem to know your way around a
          kitchen.

                    JANE
          I'm just as handy in other
          rooms of the house.

                    FRANK
          That shirt looks familiar.

                    JANE
          It should, it's yours. I
          didn't want to get stained or
          wrinkled. At least... not yet.

                    FRANK
          Mind if I slip into something
          more comfortable?

                    JANE
          I'm great at undoing things.

                    FRANK
          Consider them... undone.

     He exits.

INT. LIVING ROOM

Jane has set a table in front of the fireplace. The
lights are trimmed. It's romantic. Frank enters.
He's just straightening his tie. He's wearing
another dark suit and dark tie.

                    FRANK
          There. That's better.

                    JANE
          I hope you brought your appe-
          tite.

                    FRANK
          I've brought everything.

                    JANE
          Well, then... dig in.

They sit. And begin to eat.

                    FRANK
               (tasting the beef)
          Interesting. Almost as inter-
          esting as those photographs I
          saw today.

                    JANE
               (nervous)
          I was young. I needed the
          work.

                    FRANK
          They were taken at Ludwig's
          docks. A ship came in. A
          Panamanian ship. It wasn't on
          Ludwig's records.

                    JANE
          Probably an oversight. How's
          your...meat?

FRANK
You be the judge of that.

He places a piece of meat in her mouth. She seductively sucks on his finger.

JANE
Mmmmm.

FRANK
I've got nine more.

He takes out a photo of the "I Luv You."

FRANK (cont.)
Have you seen this ship?

JANE
I don't know. I don't think it's one of ours, but we deal with so many ships... Has Officer Nordberg been able to... uh, tell you anything yet?

FRANK
No, unfortunately there was an attempt on his life and he's back in a coma.

JANE
Oh, that's terrible. The world is such a violent place.

FRANK
If it wasn't, then I'd be out of a job—I'd be back on the circuit, riding motocross. But I'd give it all up tomorrow to live in a world without crime.

                        JANE
            That's beautiful.

She kisses him.

                        FRANK
            This is all happening too
            fast.

She kisses him again.

                        FRANK (cont.)
            I've been hurt before.

                        JANE
            I'm sorry.

Her game is over. She's falling for this guy.

Frank shakes his head, sadly.

                        FRANK
            It's the same old story. Boy
            finds girl. Boy loses girl.
            Girl finds boy. Boy forgets
            the girl. Boy remembers girl.
            Girl dies in a tragic blimp
            accident over the Orange Bowl
            on New Year's Day.

                        JANE
            Goodyear?

                        FRANK
            No. The worst.

                        JANE
            Oh, you poor dear.

She gives him a hug. Tears well up in her eyes.

                    FRANK
          Now, now. I didn't mean to
          upset you.

                    JANE
                (in tears)
          No... no, it's not that. Oh,
          why did you have to be so
          wonderful? Frank, there's
          something I ought to tell you.

He puts his finger over her lips.

                    FRANK
          There's no need to say
          anything.Whatever your past
          is...it doesn't matter any-
          more. Maybe...Maybe we're just
          two lonely souls that have
          found each other.

                    JANE
              (gazing at him,
                 lovingly)
          Hey, funny face.

ON JANE

She unbuttons one button, her shirt falls seductively to the floor.

ON FRANK

He unbuttons one top button. His suit peels off his
shoulders seductively and falls to the ground. He
stares at her in wonderment.

                    JANE
          I want you to know, I practice
          safe sex.

                    FRANK
          So do I.
INT. BEDROOM

Romantic MUSIC up.

They're rolling around on the bed, in romantic
embrace. They are each wearing huge body condoms.
They fit skin-tight, their arms fitting through
special sleeves as though they're going to be
handling plutonium. The faces are distorted, pulled
tight as behind a stocking.

MUSIC swells as they roll around the bed in ecstasy.
We hear lots of SQUEAKING sounds.

——————————————————————————————————

A FEW LAST WORDS...

THERE YOU HAVE IT. THE TOP SCREENWRITERS working in Hollywood have given you a behind-the-scenes look at how they came up with their successful film scripts. You've had Stephen de Souza's insights into opening and structuring action films (including his "whammo chart"), Nick Kazan's approach to handling an extremely complex story, William Kelley's elegant structure for a simple story, the perseverance of Bruce Joel Rubin through nineteen drafts of GHOST...and much more.

If you are simply someone who enjoys going to the movies, these insights should help you watch them with a fresh eye. You'll start noticing more about how the films you see are structured, how their characters develop, and how visual images are used to help create the tone of a film, as well as to impart information. We hope this will add to your enjoyment of the world's most vibrant art form.

If you are also an aspiring writer, the information in this book should help you develop your craft. By reading the interviews and studying the structural outlines and the sample pages, you'll be able to see how professional writers have applied the principles that all the scriptwriting books talk about. Whether you're looking at our *Successful Screenwriting* (*Writers Digest Press*) or any of the others, the lessons of those books will take on greater clarity now that you've read this collection.

The interviews in this book first appeared in *The Hollywood Scriptwriter*, a monthly newsletter that Jurgen Wolff founded and that's now published by Kerry Cox (for a sample, send $2 to 1626 N. Wilcox, Suite 385—Dept. TS, Hollywood, CA 90028). The *Scriptwriter* interviews the best writers in the business, and it has been fascinating to see what these writers have in common. Perhaps you will have deduced the same traits in common from reading this book:

—They believe in their vision and are committed to bringing it to the screen. They're not out to duplicate anyone else's success or follow trends;

—They know that success in screenwriting is not about writing one hit script, it's about developing one's craft script after script;

—They know that screenwriting can bring huge rewards, but also requires dedication and self-discipline;

—They want to help new writers as other writers helped them when they were starting out. These are some of the busiest writers in the business, yet they all were generous with their time and expertise.

We are aware that this book may make it seem Hollywood still primarily is the preserve of white males. That's not as true as it used to be, and we are working on further "Top Secrets" volumes that will be dedicated specifically to the contributions that women writers and writers of color are making to the film world.

Furthermore, if screenwriting is your goal and passion, we hope you will find your own name on the list of top writers interviewed in a future edition.
